The Politics of Identity

To Rebecca Greenhalgh
and Euan Kenny

The Politics of Identity

Liberal Political Theory and the Dilemmas
of Difference

MICHAEL KENNY

polity

First published in 2004 by Polity Press

Polity Press
65 Bridge Street
Cambridge CB2 1UR, UK

Polity Press
350 Main Street
Malden, MA 02148, USA

A catalogue record for this book is available from the British Library.

Library of Congress Cataloging-in-Publication Data

Kenny, Michael.
　The politics of identity : liberal political theory and the dilemmas of difference / Michael Kenny.
　　p. cm.
Includes bibliographical references and index.
　ISBN 0-7456-1904-5 (hb : alk. paper) – ISBN 0-7456-1905-3 (pb : alk. paper)
　1. Liberalism.　2. Multiculturalism.　3. Pluralism (Social sciences)
4. Group identity – Political aspects.　I. Title.

　JC574.K45 2004
　320.51 – dc22

2003019978

Typeset in 10 on 11 pt Sabon
by SNP Best-set Typesetter Ltd., Hong Kong
Printed and bound in Great Britain by MPG Books, Bodmin, Cornwall

For further information on Polity, visit our website: www.polity.co.uk

Contents

Acknowledgements   vi
Preface   vii

1 The Character and Origins of the Politics of Identity   1
2 The Politics of Identity in Liberal Political Theory   22
3 Citizenship, Public Reason and Collective Identity   43
4 Civil Society and the Morality of Association   63
5 The Public Faces of Identity Politics   89
6 Identities in Motion: the Political Ethics of Social Movements   109
7 Liberalism and the Politics of Difference   128
8 Liberalism and the Politics of Recognition   148
9 Conclusions   169

Notes   181
References and Bibliography   186
Index   204

Acknowledgements

The completion of this book has been aided by the generosity of three different institutions. In 2002 I was the beneficiary of a Research Leave Award granted by the UK's Arts and Humanities Research Board. I was granted a semester's sabbatical leave by my home institution, the University of Sheffield, in the same year. And some of my early thinking about this topic was undertaken during my tenure as a Charter Research Fellow at Wolfson College at the University of Oxford.

I am also indebted to a number of colleagues who have provided me with advice and support at different stages of this project. James Meadowcroft, Nick Stevenson and Leif Wenar deserve special mention for their willingness to discuss ideas relating to the book in some of Sheffield's finest, and worst, pubs and restaurants. During my time in Oxford, Michael Freeden provided welcome doses of hospitality and critical insight. Tony Payne has offered advice and encouragement at various stages of the life of this book. Andrew Gamble, Duncan Kelly and Rajiv Prabhakar all read an earlier draft of it, offering various suggestions and criticisms for which I am very grateful. More generally, over the last few years, I have benefited from conversations on topics covered in this volume with Anthony Arblaster, Matthew Festenstein, Bob Stern, Andrew Vincent and Maureen Whitebrook.

I owe gratitude to David Held and the editorial staff at Polity Press for their patience and support; Rebecca Harkin for her enthusiasm at an early stage of the book's development; and, latterly, Rachel Kerr and Andrea Drugan, who have seen the book through to completion.

Above all, however, I want to thank my son, Euan, for the joy that he has brought his parents, and for all that he has already taught me about the subtleties and pleasures of a new identity; and Becky, who has been an unfailing source of love, support and good advice throughout the life of this project. This book is dedicated to them both.

Preface

The idea of a politics based upon group identity, as opposed to interest, reform or ideology, has entered the public consciousness of a number of democratic states over the last two decades. It has become the subject and source of contrasting hopes and fears for political actors and thinkers alike. Within Anglophone political theory, this idea is associated with some contentious philosophical disputes on such topics as the merits of allocating rights to minority groups; whether 'difference' is now the regulative principle through which selfhood and morality are operative in (post)modern society; the implications of moral disagreement and social pluralization for the possibility of political co-operation; the purported incommensurability of political values; and the moral and social challenges confronting civil society and democratic citizenship. The idea of a politics of identity has become salient because it is related to many different developments and topical political concerns, and elicits powerful reactions from its friends and enemies alike.

Within the world of academic political theory, the implications of identity politics have been framed predominantly in relation to two particular normative arguments advanced by a group of Anglo-American political philosophers. Some of the major liberal thinkers of the last two decades have questioned whether liberal democracy is compatible with claims and actions rooted in the discourse of unique group identity. Some go further still, seeing in the rise of identity politics, and its intellectual popularization, a major threat to democratic society. A related second argument is that a form of politics that encourages individuals to see themselves as having ties and commitments to encompassing groups is unlikely to allow them to be, or to reason as, citizens. The practices and rights that underpin democratic citizenship are, it is suggested, imperilled by identity claims. The main voices contesting these positions are those of pluralists who have mounted ambitious critical assaults upon the intellectual foundations of liberal philosophy. From within this diverse camp (which includes multiculturalists, advocates of a politics of 'difference', and defenders of the ideal of group recognition) there emanates the assertion that identity politics signals the demise and limitations of the liberal polity and some of its constitutive political and moral norms.

This book has its roots in the author's curiosity about the prevalence of these contending views and a growing scepticism about their analytic and normative value as liberal political arguments. Why is it that the social and political phenomena placed under the heading 'identity politics' have been so swiftly and completely appropriated by these rival frameworks? Is it right, as some analytic philosophers maintain, to interpret identity politics as 'something' that liberals must simply oppose? And is it wise to explain away the claims and import of the many different movements, groups, communities, networks and organizations cited as instances of the politics of identity in relation to the interpretations that moral philosophers offer? My sense of unease with both of these competing positions has been informed by a growing awareness that it is not only in relation to this particular theme that an overarching rivalry takes centre stage between one form of liberalism that believes it has truth, progress and reason on its side and another that is militantly pluralistic and multicultural. This dichotomous divide has come to structure the terms of debate on an increasing range of political and moral controversies (Mendus, 1993). And it is not only prevalent within the seminar rooms, journals and conferences that constitute the *habitus* of political philosophers (Katznelson, 1996). It figures prominently within public debate more generally. The reaction of many opinion-formers and commentators to the events of 11 September 2001 provided a particularly potent and, to my mind, worrying instance of the power and limitations of this polarity.[1] Neither of these alternatives, I will argue, provides sufficiently robust or rounded moral responses to the dilemmas associated with identity politics. Like other students of political thought, moreover, I am troubled by the relationship between these rather impoverished invocations of liberalism and the richness, diversity and subtlety of insight that characterized the historical development of the traditions of European and American liberal political thought.[2]

The principal aims of this book are to introduce readers to the various arguments about identity politics that these rival liberal philosophies have generated; and to provide critical reflections upon their adequacy as *specifically* liberal responses to these issues. This second aim relates to an ongoing debate about the character of contemporary liberal political theorizing more generally. For many political philosophers, liberalism signals a set of supposedly non-disputable moral precepts – usually defined as some combination of the values of equality, liberty and, sometimes, social justice – that are wielded as benchmarks against which contentious normative claims are evaluated. This, however, is merely one way of utilizing and understanding liberal political theory. This approach can lead its more unwary adherents to neglect the contingency and complexity of the political, to simplify multidimensional, complex political problems, and to take as given, rather than exploring, the normative presuppositions of liberal philosophy (Newey, 2001).

Like other contemporary analysts of political ideas, I deploy a very different approach to liberal political theory to that sketched above. I follow those who see liberalism as a historically evolutionary, culturally contingent, and internally diverse 'family' of partisan political ideas.[3] On this view, liberalism is a contestable, fluid and complex ideational terrain, rather than a set of unassailable moral precepts or methodological prescriptions.[4] I introduce and critically evaluate both rationalistic and particularistic forms of contemporary liberal philosophy. In contrast, I suggest the merits of liberal approaches to politicized identity that seek to interweave universalist and particularistic ethical commitments and combine the values of autonomy and diversity. Among the latter are arguments, for instance John Rawls's political liberalism, that revive some of the most profound moral and political insights of the European and American traditions of liberal thinking. While I do argue that liberals should favour certain positions over others, I do so from the presupposition that a variety of political and moral arguments can legitimately claim a liberal heritage.

This book arises, then, from a sense of scepticism about some currently fashionable philosophical claims upon liberal political theory, and a particular interest in evaluating the worth and implications of the ways in which political theorists have interpreted the politics of identity. It is organized so as to highlight that arguments about central concepts within liberal democratic thought – notably citizenship, associations, and civil society – have shaped the ways in which many liberals respond to identity politics. In chapters 2, 3, 4 and 5, I show how various critical conceptions of the character of identity politics have emerged from some of the main contemporary liberal theories of democratic society. These arguments overlap in their tendency to present the politics of identity as alien and threatening to a liberal political order. I also consider, in chapters 7 and 8, how the introduction of apparently novel conceptual concerns – with 'recognition' and 'difference' in particular – has been central to the efforts of liberalism's pluralist critics to reconstruct the foundations of liberal political thought. All of these chapters are organized according to a thematic logic, a focus that enables emphasis upon the diversity of liberal arguments pertinent to some of the central concepts invoked in relation to the politics of identity.

As well as providing a guide to these arguments for the reader, I present a critical evaluation of the effects of a debate polarized around the choices offered by a liberalism founded upon the 'comprehensive' values of autonomy or individuality, on the one hand, and efforts to justify a multiculturalist recasting of liberalism on such grounds as the moral worth of cultural inheritance, the regulative norm of difference,

and the importance of recognition, on the other. I point out some important distinctions and disagreements among the last camp, but I also draw
attention to a common philosophical trait that is germane to these different pluralist arguments – the tendency to assert the merits of a particularistic philosophical outlook as a rival to purportedly defunct forms
of universalist liberal reasoning. All too often, the political theorizing of
such phenomena as identity politics appears to require an all-or-nothing
choice between the Manichean alternatives of Enlightenment hubris and
multiculturalist particularism.

These are by no means the only normative choices that liberals should
regard as pertinent in relation to the claims, dilemmas and moral implications of the politics of identity. This is so for several reasons. First,
neither of these contending perspectives has a monopoly upon critical
reason. There are some important insights regarding the character of
liberal democracy, and the dangers and promise of identity politics,
within both sets of arguments; but there are some important flaws and
blindspots as well. Second, liberalism is an internally diverse ideological
family and is home to many arguments that suggest rather different
approaches to contemporary problems. Some important liberal thinkers
have developed political theories in which universalist ideas are imbri-
cated with particularistic insight. In contemporary debates, arguments
that adopt this structure are especially apposite for the task of unpicking the moral dilemmas associated with identity politics, not least
because these merit more context-sensitive analyses than liberal philosophy tends to offer. Within contemporary political theory, such a stance
is, to some degree, reflected in the paradigm of political liberalism, a perspective that pluralist critics have too swiftly dismissed. From within this
paradigm there emerge important arguments about the importance of
the social bases of self-respect and the value of civility that are of particular relevance to identity politics.

A third reason for exploring an argumentative terrain beyond either
of these two positions concerns the politics of identity itself. The claims,
dilemmas and actions associated with this paradigm are, I believe, impossible to capture within any singular, or narrowly conceived, politico-
ethical theory. This is so for various reasons: because of an abiding
ambiguity in the ways in which individuals relate to the collective identities to which they belong; since identity politics in part represents one
facet of a broader behavioural and rhetorical repertoire that groups can
accentuate or downplay; and because some associations and groups that
arise in relation to various unchosen identities – for instance, those based
on disability, race or gender – are the sources of moral value and social
capital, and may thus be conducive to the democratic good.[5]

To understand how liberal philosophers have responded to the dilemmas posed by identity politics, a consideration of the national background and preoccupations of particular authors is invaluable. Some

important fears and anxieties about these social phenomena are framed within particular normative constructions of them – as, for instance, the enemies of democracy or as vehicles of social emancipation and personal expression. These are wielded to promote and reinforce certain normative arguments and to de-legitimate those of opponents. In considering the political significance of identity politics, therefore, it is worth considering how and why political theorists came to focus upon this 'problem' and to consider the wider political context pertinent to the normative representations of these phenomena. Given the importance of social particularity and uniqueness to the rhetoric of identity politics, the paucity of interpretative attention given to the national contexts in which this paradigm has emerged is striking. I have therefore opted to draw attention to two particular national settings – the United States and Britain. I do not follow this rule rigidly or universally. So I consider, for instance, the important ideas of the Canadian scholar Charles Taylor, because he and other figures have had a major influence upon the ways in which Anglo-American liberal philosophers have approached questions of social identity and culture in the last decade. But some degree of national specificity allows us to consider how differences of national political culture and ideological tradition have shaped ideas about the nature and importance of identity politics.

There are also particular historical reasons for juxtaposing the United States and Britain. For many British intellectuals, identity politics has, until recently, been seen as a peculiarly American phenomenon and, consequently, as an alien presence on their own political scene. Moreover, it makes sense to consider the importance of a specifically Anglo-American intellectual space within which a number of important ideological developments and political conversations have taken place within the recent and longer-term past. Despite some differences, there persists a commonality of intellectual discourse across these national communities, an attribute that has, for instance, underpinned the emergence of a distinctive Anglo-American analytical approach to political philosophy (Barry, 1999).

In terms of the politics of identity itself, there are some pertinent generic differences between those Anglophone contexts – Australia, New Zealand and Canada above all – where the question of the rights and claims of indigenous peoples take centre stage, and Anglo-American concerns with such developments as recent waves of immigration from Africa, Asia and Latin America; the salience of religious groups in civil society; the cultural and moral impact of forces such as the women's and gay rights movements; and a common debate about the purported decline of the civic culture and the rise of 'anti-politics'. At various points in the argument I allude both to the commonality of intellectual concern among Anglo-American philosophers and to some national differences in the ways in which identity politics is theorized by them.

As should by now be clear, the main focus of this study is upon liberal political theorizing in particular, and normative arguments about the social forces and forms pertinent to the politics of identity more generally. It does not purport to offer an in-depth examination of the movements, groups and communities placed under this heading, nor is it an exhaustive survey of the different analytical and historical interpretations of them. It does consider some of the political and moral dilemmas that these forces raise, and it introduces research findings about some of their activities and impact. But readers interested in empirical or historical material about ethnic minorities, major social movements, or new kinds of network in civil society are advised to consult the literatures devoted to each of these topics. There is now a plethora of such studies and a good deal of historical and social theoretical interpretation of these groupings. This book aims to provide an in-depth examination of the ways in which Anglo-American liberal theorists have chosen to represent and interpret the politics of identity. It also aims to justify the merits of a different kind of liberal approach to some of the major questions typically pursued by political philosophers about the politics of identity.

The book has a framework, and takes several argumentative turns, that may appear somewhat heterodox to those who approach political theorizing as a sub-set of moral philosophy. At various points in the argument, notably chapter 6, I follow the relatively unusual strategy of considering whether liberal theory might benefit from a re-engagement with social theorizing so that some of the empirical and conceptual complexities of group identity might be better understood. What may appear like an unusual move can in fact be seen as a return to the character of earlier phases of liberal theory.

In another respect as well, I depart from the practice of current philosophizing in my treatment of identity politics. Among Anglo-American liberal philosophers, the dilemmas and developments associated with the politics of identity are frequently corralled into 'set-piece' debates over such issues as the legitimacy of allocating rights to groups; the validity of exempting groups from universally applicable laws; and whether individuals are responsible for the costs that their cultural practices impose upon them (Barry, 2001a; Kelly, 2002). These are seen by many as the quintessentially 'hard cases' posed by identity-based political claims – problems with which any serious political theorist interested in cultural diversity would need to engage. While these issues are undoubtedly important in both moral and political terms, they do not represent the *only* valid normative starting-points or contentious questions that political theorists can legitimately pose in this field. By contrast, I consider the relationship between liberal arguments and social identity from a different vantage-point, examining the character and merits of the ways in which liberal philosophers have framed the dilemmas generated by the politics of identity, rather than attempting to inject into a cluttered intellectual market a further, purportedly non-contentious, account of the moral significance of identity politics.

The legalistic focus of many Anglophone political philosophers has to some degree diverted attention for liberals from the centrality of some of the questions raised by the emergence of a politics of identity. Is democratic citizenship compatible with arguments and mobilizations that invoke social identity? More specifically, can a fundamentalist Christian, a devout Muslim, or a politically aware lesbian also be a good citizen? And is it possible to offer public reasons that are acceptable to one's fellow citizens if one develops political arguments from the vantage-point of such identities?[6] Does the politics of identity introduce a virus into the associational cultures of modern civil society that ultimately threatens this relationship? Or are there moral and social values to be discovered in the many movements, networks and groups that practise identity politics? In considering these questions, I evaluate the disparate arguments of a range of contemporary liberal theorists, including Kantians, liberal egalitarians, liberal republicans, 'difference' theorists, advocates of a politics of recognition, and proponents of political liberalism. Differing aspects of the politics of identity are illuminated by these different positions, but it is the last of these – Rawls's political liberalism – that, I suggest, offers the most promising synthesis of contending liberal moral principles in relation to the challenges that this political paradigm offers. For this and other reasons, I question the widely held belief that current forms of pluralism necessitate the abandonment or wholesale reconstruction of liberal political theory. I also caution against the widely expressed 'common sense' that the politics of identity signals nothing but trouble for a democracy.

The polarized response of Anglophone liberalism has to some degree exerted a constricting effect upon the political arguments available to liberals, and has resulted in a more unidimensional appraisal of identity politics than is helpful. The liberal political tradition in fact offers a variety of ways of reconciling the values of individuality, citizenship and diversity. Indeed, it is in relation to accounts of the values underpinning democratic citizenship, I will argue, as opposed to such criteria as the value of difference or cultural authenticity, that liberals should consider the inequalities and harms effected through imposed identity.

The squeezing of the spectrum of plausible and useful liberal arguments into the rival poles represented by Kantian universalism and ethical particularism is something that is itself in need of explanation. One reason for this narrowing of liberal doctrines is the self-enclosed character of academic political theorizing which has resulted in the neglect of important social and psychological considerations.[7] Another is the hegemony of a philosophical commitment to what Raymond Geuss labels 'pure normativity': 'in most run-of-the-mill cases normativity gives us a clear decision that seems plausible only because the analysis that must precede the normativity judgement renders a complex situation artificially simple and perspicuous' (2002: 332). And, in historical terms, the inattention to liberalism as an evolving body of thought has engendered a forgetfulness about some of the important political and social influences that have shaped its development.

1

The Character and Origins of the Politics of Identity

Our contemporary condition is marked by the emergence of new forms of identity politics around the globe. These new forms complicate and increase centuries-old tensions between the universalistic principles ushered in by the American and French Revolutions and the particularities of nationality, ethnicity, religion, gender, 'race', and language. (Benhabib, 2002: vii)

Introduction

The idea that a new kind of politics, one founded upon the peculiarities of social identity, has emerged in democratic life is an increasingly familiar one. It is associated with a host of movements, groups and cultural communities that are committed to the practice of identity-based politics. Though these groupings occupy an ambivalent, and sometimes uncomfortable, role within democratic politics and society, to the surprise of many commentators, their influence, appeal and impact appear to be growing. For proponents of some of the leading traditions of modern politics, such developments elicit puzzlement and downright hostility.

Some commentators see the politics of identity as indicative of a qualitative alteration to the character and culture of democratic states (Wolfe and Klausen, 2000; Elshtain, 1995). According to them, the principal motivational axes and dynamics of modern political life have undergone a fundamental transformation in the last thirty years. Identity politics reflects a shift away from political alignments driven by individual interest or ideological debate towards a culture in which citizens cluster under the banner of an encompassing group, with its own collective personality and distinctive culture. Such an understanding underpins various pessimistic accounts of contemporary political life in which a purported 'golden age' in the life of the democratic state is contrasted against the new barbarism signalled by the rise of identity (Schlesinger, 1998). But engagement with the politics of identity, I will suggest, need not lead to the contention that liberal democracy is in terminal decline.

A quite different, long-established understanding of the salience of group identities in social and political life invokes the tradition of American exceptionalism (Lipset, 1996). Identity politics, on this view, is integral to the *differentia specifica* of American political culture, and reflects the relative weakness of the federal state, as well as the unusual significance of ethnic and religious groupings in its civil society. While there is some merit to the claim that the US differs in many important ways from other Anglophone states in these respects, the basis for this exceptionalist account has been eroded substantially in the last three decades (for reasons that are discussed below).

The normative merit of a politics founded upon 'identity' or 'difference' has lately become a major topic of debate and the target of extended critique in Anglophone political theory. Much of this, within the US especially, revolves around critical examinations of the challenges and threats that identity politics poses for 'settled' accounts of liberal democracy. As we shall see, this perspective has sustained various influential critical accounts of the moral dysfunction of this new kind of group pluralism. Arrayed against this critical consensus is a rival position. This coheres around the desire to assert the merits and political significance of group pluralism, and highlights the importance of minority cultures in particular (Kymlicka, 1995; 1998; Carens, 2000; Young, 1990; Parekh, 2000; Williams, 1998), drawing upon various liberal and non-liberal sources. In chapter 2 I sketch the contours of these opposed positions. Taken together, they are responsible for some of the most influential normative-political constructions of the politics of identity.[1] Several general intellectual genealogies for these perspectives have been traced back within the lineages of Western thought, and broad traditions such as romanticism, moral pluralism and philosophical monism invoked as the precursors of contemporary arguments. Yet, interestingly, some more recent political contexts and influences have been less fully explored. In this chapter I place emphasis, therefore, upon the importance of the crisis and reformation of socialist and social democratic thought in the last thirty years. The debates that arose from the demise of the New Left in both the US and Britain form an especially important backdrop to contemporary philosophical arguments.[2]

Understanding the politics of identity

The closely related terms 'identity politics' and the 'politics of identity' are widely used to refer to a number of transformations in group behaviour and political argument.[3] Within Anglophone political theory, these terms are typically deployed to highlight the appearance, since the 1960s, of new kinds of social mobilization based upon various collective identities that were previously hidden, suppressed or neglected – both by the dominant culture of liberal society and by the agenda of the political left. The women's and gay liberation movements are often regarded as paradigmatic instances of this kind of identity-orientated mobilization. These and other movements argued forcefully for the merits of a distinctive, common identity that shaped the interests and outlook of individuals who possessed these particular social 'markings'. The politics of identity is said to have given

> individuals . . . a connection to political projects based on elements that are very basic to their self-conceptions. Members of these groups see themselves as having in common certain important characteristics that set them apart from the larger population – a commonality that is based on difference. (Hoover, 2001: 201)

This interpretation of identity politics – as a collective description of those social forces which have tried to politicize cleavages once regarded as arbitrary and non-political – is a popular one, not least among sympathetic intellectuals. Emulating the example of these movements, other groups, it is suggested, followed suit and adopted a similar kind of particularistic rhetoric and sense of mission. In their wake, identity politics has become a fixture on the political landscape, disrupting and undermining familiar ideologies and political alignments (Hoover, 2001; Purvis and Hunt, 1999). This 'new politics' is inherently subversive of established ideas about the appropriate boundary between questions that are political and those that are not.

Yet, different national contexts and concerns tend to shape the perception of the social forces driving this politics (Ivison, 2002; Kymlicka and Opalski, 2001). Among Australian and Canadian theorists, for instance, these are presumed to be movements leading the struggles of indigenous peoples over land rights (Kymlicka, 1995). In the US, the idea of the politics of identity is applied in relation to long-established tensions between religious groups and the state, the moral and political struggles associated with the separatist desires of groups such as the Amish, and in response to the salience of race and ethnicity within political life (Edsall and Edsall, 1991; Kymlicka and Norman, 2000). In Britain and Western Europe more generally, the politics of identity is widely regarded as the product of political conflicts associated with the clash between the cultural practices of the majority and various immigrant and religious minorities.

As the range of collective subjects to which the term applies has expanded, the question of what exactly it is that they have, or do, in common has become more salient and problematic. One widely accepted answer to this question concerns the unchosen character of the identities central to many of these groups (Galeotti, 2002).[4] These mobilizations arise against a backdrop of social 'markers' that individuals have not consciously chosen – as black, gay, Latino or Amish, for example – though religious affiliation occupies an ambiguous position in this regard (as we shall see in chapter 2). But the interpretation of the contemporary politics of identity as the drive to politicize 'ascriptive' identity is plausible only up to a point.[5] Some unselected collective identities have for a long time provided the basis for extended and potent political struggles – most obviously in the case of nationalist movements – a fact that appears to undermine the novelty of the paradigm of identity politics.[6] In moral terms, as we shall see (in chapter 2), the duality between identities that are chosen and those that are ascriptive is too stark to capture the complex ethical dilemmas that identity politics poses for liberalism – for instance, in important, ongoing debates over whether individuals should bear the costs of unorthodox cultural practices (Cohen, 1999; Barry, 2001a; Caney, 2002; Kelly, 2002: 71–4). These normative complexities aside, it is clear that the desire to politicize 'markings' that are not straightforwardly chosen – on such bases as race, gender, class, disability and sexuality – is a necessary, if not sufficient, feature of the emergence of identity politics.

A different answer to the question of what exactly it is that these groups have, or do, in common can be found in interpretations that see in them an underlying political or ideological message. This is often expressed through the idea that these forces are united in the challenge they offer to established conceptions of what is political and what is not, and to familiar political traditions. For some interpreters, they are engaged in heroic struggles to demand recognition of their worth in the face of disparagement and discrimination, or to make salient questions and relationships that have been hitherto de-politicized (Williams, 1998; Young, 1990; Taylor, 1994). Interpreted in this way, identity politics contains an emancipatory logic that is carried forward in the guise of many different, particular battles against injustice, and issues forth in the common ambition to challenge the boundaries and conventional content of politics.

Such an argument is simultaneously appealing and problematic. How novel exactly is this challenge? In modern democratic politics, these are by no means the first forces to seek to unsettle established notions governing what should be central to politics, or indeed to politicize relationships and questions that liberalism has wanted to remove from the political realm (Calhoun, 1994; Melucci, 1989). These were among the central motivations of a myriad of political traditions, including socialism, communism, fascism and nationalism. Viewed historically, contemporary groupings might be seen as the latest in a long line of forces that have sought to contest established ideas about politics and to bring into public view relationships and inequities rooted in civil society.

For some of their critics, what distinguishes these groups, and the pluralism they have spawned, is a more precise political impulse – their hostility to liberalism (Macedo, 1990). As we shall see, some liberals are inveterately opposed to groups that practise identity politics because they appear to violate the norms of democratic interchange and equality (Waldron, 1992). While it is certainly the case that some of these groups and communities are resistant and hostile to liberal values, as a generic characterization of identity politics this view has some obvious descriptive limitations. The idea that all, or even most, of these groups regard themselves as fundamentally opposed to liberal culture and beliefs is inaccurate. Many are critical of certain liberal values. But this Manichean ideological reading of these groups underplays the different kinds of accommodation with liberal values and mainstream cultural practices that they have established, as well as the propensity of groups and movements to forge various relationships with state institutions, policy communities and political actors over time (Dalton, 1994; Dalton et al., 1990).

A related attempt to explain the social significance of identity politics arises from the idea that they are quintessentially opposed to the cultures and values of modernity. Some social and political theorists seek to defend a moral distinction between the worth of groupings that attack, and those that defend, arbitrary and irrational forms of tradition. These thinkers applaud, in particular, those left-libertarian movements, campaigns, issue networks, affinity groups and self-help organizations that are socially iconoclastic, calling established traditions and customs into question (Giddens, 1994; Beck, 1999). These forces are typically contrasted against movements and communities that practise tradition-bound, or conservative, forms of identity politics in which the collective identity of a group is fixed and reified. The difficulty with such an argument is that apparently 'modern' collective subjects, such as the women's movement, have a propensity to incarnate alternative traditions rather than transcend tradition altogether.[7] Aligning identity politics with tradition-bound communities and social movements is therefore self-defeating. The rhetoric of group uniqueness that some groups employ often makes these communities disposed to the idea that they possess a singular culture with a unique set of repressed or neglected traditions.

The idea that many of the minority communities formed by immigrants, religious groups and ethnic minorities are simply anti-modern and pro-tradition is equally weak. While this describes the preservationist impulses pursued by some groupings, such a characterization neglects the ways in which individuals within them negotiate the interface between liberal norms and cultural traditions. More generally, it makes sense to regard the turn to encompassing community as deeply bound up with the processes of social individuation (Bauman, 2001; Beck, 1999). Some of these collective assertions of identity seem to have appropriated the hallmarks of individualist thinking, rather than rejected this paradigm entirely. This is particularly apparent in the tendency to talk of identity groupings as the possessors of unique collective personalities (Vincent, 1989).

And in terms of liberalism, specifically, some of its leading theorists have persuasively argued against the possibility of defending a moral distinction between cultures that are more tradition-bound than others. In the work of Isaiah Berlin, for example, there is a clear justification for the merits of attending to non- and anti-liberal sentiments and arguments in order to understand liberalism's blind spots. His pluralistic moral convictions placed him in the camp of those liberal philosophers who do not believe that the liberal conception of the good is the only one that is worthwhile (Gray, 2000a; 1995b). The relationship of groups to both the modern and the traditional is, for all these reasons, inherently ambiguous.

These various attempts to establish the meaning of the politics of identity in relation to grand political and social narratives are perhaps less useful than the enemies and friends of these different social forces realize.[8] They tell us too little about the different moral and social processes that shape the existence and impact of these groupings, and they fail to address the range of dilemmas that these generate for established political traditions. This latter feature is more clearly addressed in interpretations that stress the impact of this new cultural politics upon the political agenda, and specifically its capacity to generate new moral controversies. Some of the most contentious issues in democratic political life in the last two decades arise from these sources and cut across established political alignments and affiliations. Examples include issues, such as abortion, that are the source of apparently irreconcilable moral conviction and are associated with identity groupings – in this case, feminist campaigners and religious groups (Ferree et al., 2002; Lovenduski and Outshoorn, 1986). Various contentious questions relate to the growing militancy of identity-based social groups and a conservative backlash against their self-assertion, as in the case of debates about gays in the military (Hunter, 1991). Others have long been staples of democratic life but have acquired a new degree of contentiousness in political contexts where identity claims are prevalent, as in the case of debates about the basis for both maternity and paternity rights (Lovenduski and Randall, 1993; Young, 1986).

There is, then, no obvious consensus about what defines and distinguishes the politics of identity. Does this term describe a particular series of sub-national groups seeking entry to the political sphere or an anti-democratic and anti-liberal virus within group life? Political philosophers have, on the whole, been uninterested in the origins of these phenomena, and more concerned to fix their normative significance in relation to supposedly uncontentious accounts of the practices and norms of liberal democracy. The main question that preoccupies them about the politics of identity is whether it signals the emergence of an enemy at the gates of liberal democracy. They wonder too whether a new kind of pluralist logic has emerged in democratic civil society, in which group diversity replaces the norm of interest-based association. In focusing upon these questions, they neglect the possibility that the political claims advanced by these different groupings, and their politico-ethical impact, may require a more variegated set of analytical and normative responses. Rather than holding to any one of these interpretations alone, therefore, it is more useful to retain a pluralistic sense that there are different axes along which these forces should be interpreted. Each of these supplies grounds for suggesting that 'identity politics' does represent a qualitatively different paradigm to a group politics mediated by the pursuit of interests, and various political scientists have developed convincing conceptual and empirical arguments to this effect (Offe, 1998; Inglehart, 1997; Bickford, 1999). Below, I suggest three such dimensions that are pertinent to this approach to identity politics, at least in its British and American manifestations. Each of them offers important clues about the distinctiveness and significance of the practice of identity politics. It is along these three different dimensions that the idea of the politics of identity makes sense and its multifaceted ethical character begins to take shape.

New political subjects

I have already alluded to the problem of deploying identity politics as a descriptive category in relation to a particular sub-set of social groups. But some consideration of the particular kinds of collectivity that are drawn to, and engage in, the politics of identity is clearly important. This is especially so given the complex and contingent histories of the communities and movements associated with it. In the United States, for instance, the politics of racial identification possesses a singularity and sensitivity that is not reflected in the treatment of, for instance, the disabled. Analyses that rely upon an unreflective listing approach (which lumps together ethnic minorities, women's groups, churches, national minorities, etc.) when delineating the new subjects of politicized identity tend to neglect the specificity of each group's history and ideological singularity.

The propensity to see identity politics solely in terms of the emergence of new kinds of groups has sometimes encouraged sympathetic analysts to restrict themselves to consideration of those collectivities that they find most amenable or exciting, and to avoid others as a consequence.[9] But the politics of identity is practised by a range of groupings and communities, some with a markedly conservative and anti-democratic mentality. Indeed, many of the groups associated with this mode of politics are fundamentally opposed to one another. This theme has emerged more clearly in the wake of some important attempts to consider the ethical tensions between groupings that are positioned relatively closely to liberal norms – liberal and socialist feminists, for instance – and communities that are overtly hostile to liberal culture. This issue has been at the heart of the philosophical dispute occasioned by Susan Moller Okin's essay 'Is Multiculturalism Bad for Women?' (1999). Other tensions, for instance between gay rights and some religious activists, are equally pervasive. Identity politics is practised by groups that are as likely to be mutually hostile as allied in a grand anti-liberal coalition.

The normative conclusions drawn about the politics of identity depend greatly, therefore, upon which groupings are regarded as its chief exemplars and perpetrators. Nancy Rosenblum argues that political theorists tend to focus on a disproportionately narrow range of social groups when theorizing civil society (1998a). What, she asks, of those clubs, associations and communities that play a role within the social culture of democratic states but sit awkwardly with the preferences of (mainly liberal) political theorists? If the politics of identity is understood as a mode of group politics that makes important claims upon its members, and is seen as being committed to bringing challenging, uncomfortable issues to public view, a much wider array of social groupings than is conventionally considered appears pertinent to it.

New model pluralism

A second integral interpretative dimension of identity politics concerns the kind of pluralism it represents. The demands for 'recognition' made by a swathe of social groupings in the last thirty years often takes the form of claims for special kinds of legal protection and state support. The proliferation of such demands appears to signal the rise of a new ethos within the associational life of democracies. Discussing these developments in the American context, Sheldon Wolin argues that this 'cultural politics' is characterized by the idea that the preservation of group differences is a condition of the inclusion that its proponents demand: 'a reserve clause, as it were, in the social contract', while they simultaneously demand full membership of the community (1993: 465). The very terms upon which liberals have envisaged the adjudication between different moral beliefs may well be inapplicable in a political paradigm where group uniqueness makes a sense of 'difference' an inescapable condition:

> if anything, new forms of cultural diversity have now produced conflicts and disagreement so deep and troubling that even our standard liberal solutions, modelled on religious liberty and tolerance, no longer seem adequate or stable. To borrow a distinction from David Hume, many current disagreements are not merely conflicts of interest but conflicts of principle. (Bohman, 1995: 253)

Perhaps most troubling of all about such an idea is that the resort to the democratic adjudication of the conflicts emerging from these differences may make matters worse, not better. According to some theorists, the very logic of democratic deliberation itself is under attack from the divisions generated by identity-based differences.

The politics of group recognition is in certain respects a significant departure from the model of interest-based pluralism advanced since the Second World War by various political scientists and liberal theorists, even though the differences between these models are easy to overstate (Dahl, 1963; 1967). Wolin points to the shared values to which many interest groups and associations subscribed in this earlier period – 'patriotism, religion, family, private property, and the Founding Fathers'. These he contrasts with the new politics of difference, associated with groups founded upon ethnic, gender and linguistic cleavages, that relies upon 'provocation, flaunts fixed differences, and tirelessly exposes past injustices so distant in time as to strain common understandings of justice, responsibility, and remedy'. He speaks for many in emphasizing the distinct character of these pluralist waves, seeing in the first a politics of diversity and in the second a politics of 'difference' (1993: 465). Integral to the latter is the de-centring of the category of the citizen, a development that many democrats find especially troubling. It is through the dethroning of the idea that the impartial, public-spirited citizen is the normative agent of a democratic community that the new politics of cultural difference exerts its subversive impact. Whether such a move damages the prospects and possibility of democratic citizenship has therefore become a considerable ethical dilemma for political theorists and legislators alike. So too has the question of whether the growing legitimacy of human-rights norms infringe upon, or indeed enable, demands for group rights (Miller, 2002a). But it is in relation to the norms and principles of democratic citizenship within individual democracies that, as David Miller persuasively argues, the question of group rights associated with the politics of identity assumes primary ethical significance – both because many demands for group rights invoke the norms of egalitarian citizenship and since others imply the revocation of these norms (2002a).

The suggestion that there has been a qualitative shift in the character of citizens' relationship to the state because of the power of identity groups is based, in part, upon the idea that these collectivities claim the attributes conventionally associated with a single personality. They are often envisaged as a social personage, a plural subject driven by a singular collective will and coherent value-set. If each of these identity groups is seen as the bearer of an irreducibly different 'personality', then for their members the difference in respect of which they are unique is irremovable and constitutive of their own sense of purpose and identity (Waldron, 1992). Observing the rise of the notion of groups as unique personalities, Wolin wonders whether the compromise and bargaining associated with pluralist diversity is now possible (1993). Beneath the rhetoric of collective identity, and the deep obligations that individuals should feel to, say, their ethnic community, lurks the idea that each of these groupings has an irreducible individuality and that each must struggle to achieve its self-realization, whatever the social and political costs.

This idea of an inherent conflict between the new model pluralism and liberal citizenship is pervasive within Anglophone political philosophy (Kymlicka and Norman, 2000; Kymlicka, 1998; Miller, 1995a). But it by no means exhausts the possible, and plausible, ethical characterization of this politics. Some theorists argue that groups practising identity politics make demands that imply the extension and realization of some of the central norms of liberal politics – democratic inclusion, non-discrimination and equality of respect above all (Miller, 2002a; 2002b). Wolin puts this potential synergy in a historical context:

> The policies and laws that were put in place to equalize opportunities to work, vote, and learn were, in large measure, the result of large protest movements that had attracted the support of many citizens who were not themselves victims of discrimination and often were its beneficiaries. (1993: 472)

These particular, historically embedded forms of social protest and cultural resistance have been instrumental in educating public understanding about how patterns of injustice and exclusion work in various social settings and in relation to particular kinds of groups (Smith, 1997).

New political controversies

An additional, important dimension of meaning associated with the politics of identity involves the processes whereby issues that were once hidden from public view emerge as matters of political concern. This trend takes various forms, depending upon such factors as the political culture of a given state, the openness of its party system to newcomers, the range and nature of its actors' ideological alignments, and the character of its policy-making community (Dalton et al., 1990). One aspect of this trend is the visibility within various democratic communities of touchstone issues that arise from moral and political conflicts generated by entrenched, deeply felt cultural affiliations and differences. Some political observers stress the increased frequency with which flashpoint questions of this kind appear on the agendas of democratic polities, and point to the challenge they offer to prevailing ideological patterns and party managers (Inglehart, 1977; 1997). These questions may provide the sources of new kinds of social antagonism and political energy, often generating greater interest and commitment, as well as new divisions, among the populace at large.

In the United States, such controversies include creationism in schools, the ethics of affirmative action, the presence and status of gays in the military, and debates concerning the content of school and university syllabuses appropriate to a multicultural and national community. And in Britain recent examples include the Salman Rushdie affair, debates over the question of faith schools, controversies arising from local authority funding of anti-racist or gay rights groups, and the question of how homosexuality ought to be represented within schools. None of these issues are in themselves entirely novel. All have precursors and roots in earlier periods. But it is the 'touchstone' quality of these controversies that is arguably what is most politically distinctive about them. This is identifiable through their salience in public life, often fuelled by incessant media coverage, the increasing propensity for individual citizens to experience these questions as central to their own political and cultural self-understandings, and the generation of new sets of 'friends' and 'enemies' upon the political landscape in their wake. Some commentators go further still, with the contentious claim that, given the erosion of interest that many citizens show towards mainstream politics and the pervasive cynicism towards public officials and authorities, the rise of this new paradigm is part of a qualitative shift in democracies towards a kind of 'life politics' as opposed to one rooted in interests or ideology (Giddens, 1994: 90; Beck, 1999).

Beyond American exceptionalism

Although it is misleading to reduce these social phenomena to any single moral formula, the many manifestations of identity politics are linked by the idea that some particular aspect of a person's identity is not reducible to such standard categories as interest, welfare or class, but is experienced as of independent political significance. Such a judgement, however, brings us into direct opposition with the long-established view that the challenge associated with powerful, encompassing groups in civil society is a uniquely American matter.

Such an idea has been widely echoed in political commentaries on both sides of the Atlantic. As an analytical claim, the notion that these trends are singularly American has, however, fallen into abeyance of late, and much contemporary theory emphasizes the generic character of the dilemmas posed by the politics of identity and the normative responses these should elicit from democrats. The idea that identity politics is now an observable international trend reflects some important similarities between developments in different national contexts. And yet the shift away from a concern with national specificity in theorizing social identity and cultural diversity is in some respects debilitating (Carens, 2000). The character and significance of the dilemmas thrown up by identity politics are framed in different ways according to national context. To illustrate this, I offer a brief outline of the political and intellectual debates through which the notion of a politics of 'identity' emerged in both the US and Britain. I highlight, in particular, some organic, and rather neglected, connections between these earlier debates and the ways in which current theorists conceive the political challenges associated with collective identity.

In the British case, rather than being an incidental or idle observation, the idea that identity politics is an American phenomenon has been an important one. It has supported the recent argument that intense disputes generated by religious or moral belief, and the salience of race and ethnicity in political life, are alien to the normal functioning of domestic political life. The corollary of this fairly common understanding is a tendency to consider controversial questions associated with racial inequality and injustice, and tensions between minority cultural practices and majority norms, as disruptive of, or unconventional supplements to, the political *status quo*.

The assumption that group identities play a singular role in the political life of the United States and constitute one aspect of its exceptional character enjoys a lengthy pedigree (Lipset, 1996). Two different aspects of the American state's purportedly unique historical development are usually invoked in such arguments. These concern its status as a nation-state forged in relation to successive waves of immigration, as well as the centrality of chattel slavery to its economy and culture until the second half of the twentieth century. Race continues to be a major source of political tension and alignment in US political life (Edsall and Edsall, 1991). A further feature of its social development that commentators have stressed, ever since Alexis de Tocqueville's *Democracy in America*, is the range of sects and churches in its civil society.[10] The salience of the relationship between church and state has, as a result, emerged as a central theme in American constitutional debate.

European-based commentators have often reiterated these apparently distinctive features of American social life and considered their effects upon its purportedly unique political culture. They have also made much of the contrast between the breadth and autonomy of associational life in the US and the limited room for manoeuvre of groups dealing with corporatist arrangements and overbearing state forms in Western Europe. As the historian Eric Hobsbawm puts it, identity politics developed in the US

> because it has always been a society unusually interested in monitoring its social and psychological temperature, blood-pressure and other symptoms, and mainly because the most obvious form of identity politics – but not the only one – namely ethnicity, has always been central to American politics since it became a country of mass migration from all parts of Europe. (1996: 39)

The assumptions sustaining such a contrast have, however, been substantially eroded in the last twenty years. In part, this is because the idea of civil society and the virtues of associational activity have been rediscovered since the 1980s by political writers and thinkers across Europe

(Keane, 1988a; 1998b). Equally importantly, since the late 1960s a wave of social movements has exercised a considerable impact upon the political cultures of various West European states. While some of these have waned in influence, they have spawned subsequent generations of grassroots campaigns and protests on an array of political and moral questions (Tarrow, 1994). Among this first wave of movements were several that arose in relation to hidden or disparaged group identities, as in the case of the women's and gay liberation movements. These have proved to be precursors for the proclamation of the unique cultural character of a host of other groups. Thus, the study of extra-parliamentary politics in Britain, for example, consisted until the 1980s of the analysis of interest groups, and sometimes the labour movement. Latterly, there has been a marked upsurge of scholarly interest in ethnic groups, minority cultures, and other kinds of protest movements (McKay, 1996). During the 1980s, a diverse array of organizations and extra-parliamentary political campaigns paved the way for the revival of a tradition of indigenous, independent social protest. Some of these campaigns – notably those against road-building programmes and the export of live animals in the 1990s – enjoyed widespread public sympathy and favourable media coverage (McKay, 1998). As extra-parliamentary protest has become established as a significant political force alongside conventional politics, movements and groups orientated towards social identity have become more publicly visible and vocal. Over the last fifteen years these mobilizations have played an important role in bringing various contentious issues into public life, including such questions as the regulation of hate speech and the merits of minoritarian traditional practices, for instance fox-hunting. Where these forms of protest were once seen as distinctively American, they have increasingly become staple features of British politics.

Perhaps most dramatic of all the changes that have, on the British scene, unleashed a *Zeitgeist* in which the discourse of identity is more commonplace has been a growing awareness of the political impact of ethnic diversity (Saggar, 2000). In the years following formal decolonization in the 1940s and 1950s, the two main political parties sought to manage and restrict successive waves of immigration from the Commonwealth. They did little, however, in the way of preparing for the cultural implications of multicultural and multiracial life. The mindset of the colonial power continued to pervade state institutions and the culture at large. The resultant tensions that have come to the surface of political life over the last few decades have found different kinds of social outlet and have been the source of important moments of subaltern protest, for instance the rise of the mass peace movement of the 1950s and 1980s and the anti-racist mobilization of the 1970s (Gilroy, 2001). There have simultaneously emerged networks and parties on the far right committed to biological and cultural forms of racist ideology (Thurlow, 2000). In recent years, one of the most visible conflicts generated by ethnic differences has arisen in the context of tensions in some British cities between working-class whites and Muslims. Controversies relating to the practices of some minority communities, such as arranged marriage and female circumcision, are increasingly salient in national and local political life (Blunkett, 2002). Rather significantly, the role of the US in these various political debates has changed quite considerably. From being an exception of little relevance to the politics of race in the UK, the American example is invoked as exemplar and dire warning in some recent high-profile commentaries (Freedland, 1999; Gray, 1998). Comparisons with the US have become staple ingredients in debates about British politics more generally. While apocalyptic or adulatory appropriations of the American experience still tend to prevail, some commentary places emphasis upon the singularity of the British context in order to make sense of the particular forms and impact of the politics of identity within it. The histories of various ethnic groupings, and minorities within them, have been explored and emphasized in recent studies (Modood, 1998).

While the trajectories and experiences of many of the groups spawned in relation to collective identity are complicated and particular, all three of the interpretative dimensions of the politics of identity discussed above are pertinent to British civil society since the 1960s. Commentators observe the depth and breadth of its group life, as well as the dissemination of the political logic of group individuality among, for instance, radical gay activists, groups of feminists, ecological radicals, disability campaigners, and some Islamic communities. In national political life, government ministers find themselves engaged by the public and the media on a wider range of social and cultural issues than has hitherto been the norm within parliamentary politics. A net result of these developments is that issues, relationships and cultures once confidently regarded as beyond the pale of politics have moved to the forefront of public debate. Some of these engage the energies and passions of supportive and opposed citizens. While in many ways the political rhetoric of social identity remains weaker and less pervasive in Britain than in the US, it is striking how rapidly in the last decade a connection between culture, group identity and political outlook has emerged in mainstream political discourse.

Despite their recent appearance within conventional political debates, many of the concerns and hopes about cultural diversity in general, and the politics of race especially, were first aired in the 1960s. There is an organic connection, in both the US and the UK, between the emergence of some of the leading identity-based social movements and the ideas disseminated by New Left intellectuals in particular. In the American context, this connection is widely recognized; but in the UK it is rarely observed.[11] Yet, several generations of New Left intellectuals have played an important role in promoting the idea that social identity is an important and legitimate basis for political argument rather than an alien presence (Hall, 1988; Rustin, 1985; Rowbotham et al., 1980). Among the early New Left movement that arose in the late 1950s and early 1960s an interest in the plurality and particularity of the sources of social identity combined with increasing scepticism about the merits of traditionally conceived labour movement politics (the death of the 'labor metaphysic', in the words of C. Wright Mills) (Kenny, 1995). Some figures in this milieu sought inspiration in an indigenous tradition of socialist pluralism developed by such figures as Harold Laski and G. D. H. Cole (Hirst, 1994). Among the younger intellectuals in this movement, an impatience with orthodox reformist politics was also apparent. Such insights were developed further in the wake of the explosion of dissent that characterized the late 1960s, and which led to a potent student movement, a high-profile campaign against the Vietnam War and a diverse counter-cultural scene (Young, 1977).

But the New Left was also a home for Marxist, socialist and social democratic thinkers who tended to regard the turn towards group identity with suspicion. Despite these warnings, and the marked hostility that the celebration of the so-called new social movements of the 1970s and 1980s elicited in some quarters, some important fusions of socialist and feminist ideas held the imaginations of many radicals for a while (Rowbotham et al., 1980). Following the downturn experienced by the Labour Party in the 1980s, some began to argue that the left needed to break from some of its core traditions and embrace the various dynamic currents of activism and movement emerging in civil society (Smith, 1991; Hall, 1988). As a consequence, debates about the political character and social import of, for example, the women's, anti-racist and gay movements figured prominently in some of the fractious theoretical and political disputes that divided left intellectuals trying to come to grips with the ascendancy of the political phenomenon of Thatcherism in that decade.[12] More recently, some New Left figures have continued to argue for a leftist brand of multiculturalism, and have been criticized as a result by the heirs of earlier generations of social democrats and socialists (Barry, 2001b; Hutton, 2001). The notion that different social identities deserve respect and are of significance for their members has, however, percolated throughout the British Labour Party and into the trade union movement over the last two decades. Such ideas were given a radical programmatic edge in the 1980s by various Labour-controlled local authorities that tried to implement rainbow-coalition policies in the teeth of fierce media hostility (Hall, 1988). In the Labour Party nationally, efforts to found an autonomous space for black and Asian members were defeated in the 1980s, but the notion of developing procedures to generate more women MPs remains a live issue.

Unlike in the US, in Britain the idea of harnessing the disparate agendas of various left-libertarian social movements to the traditional goals of social democracy and socialism proved a popular response to the rise of identity politics until the 1990s. As socialist ideology has temporarily fallen into abeyance, and the Labour Party has developed a more centrist, technocratic orientation in government since 1997, the idea of a left opposition that draws upon movements and currents in civil society has receded. Tensions continue among social democratic intellectuals, however, dividing those advocating multiculturalist policies from proponents of egalitarian liberalism (Barry, 2002). This conflict was publicly aired in response to the government-sponsored report produced by the Runnymede Trust into the future of multicultural Britain (chaired by the political theorist Bikhu Parekh) that appeared in 2000.[13] According to the social democratic writer Will Hutton:

> The Report's authors were so full of grievance about Britain that they failed to recognise the danger in inviting a largely tolerant culture to rank some intolerable practices and attitudes among Britain's ethnic communities – notably towards women – as equal in moral standing to their own . . . Thus arranged marriage, violence towards women, the wearing of chadors and so on are not examples of diversity and multiculturalism but intolerable infringements of basic human rights. If the left goes wobbly on this, it might as well give up. (2001: 4)

Identity politics in the US

The notion that the politics of identity arises from the particular pathology of American political life has only recently begun to fade. Alan Wolfe and Ytte Klausen, for example, pose a stark contrast between the European social model and the cultural politics that prevails in the US (1992). They warn the European left of the dangers of abandoning the social aspirations embedded in the welfare state in favour of the blandishments of identity: 'What for other countries are peripheral if not downright trivial issues – prayer in schools, condoms for teenagers, drinking, Armageddon, the theory of evolution, date rape, and the pledge of allegiance – in this country constitute moments of intense, almost furious, concern' (1992: 241). The consequences of this propensity to turn culture into a political battlefield have been pernicious in the extreme: 'The smart politician is the one who mouths cultural platitudes for general consumption while supporting the self-interest of those immediately concerned with specific public policies' (1992: 241). What should be the central political and economic questions of a liberal capitalist order have been displaced by issues of 'religious belief, taste, and cultural preference' (1992: 242). As a result, they warn, the civic unity and social solidarity that underpinned the formation of welfare states in Europe has been rendered impossible in the US: 'We shine light on the shadowy regions of the soul even as we darken the stage on which our common destiny is enacted' (1992: 242).

These authors draw upon the influential reading of the 'culture wars' of the 1990s offered by James Hunter (1991). The latter's historical account of Americans' propensity for cultural politics is grounded in a deep-rooted sense of national exceptionalism. On this view, the intensely fought religious conflicts produced by successive waves of immigration from Europe in the nineteenth century have been transformed into an antagonistic struggle over culture. In Wolfe and Klausen's paraphrase: 'Culture in America is war by other means' (1992: 242). With the demise of religion as a primary source of political division, Hunter observes the coalescence of a distinctive political outlook shared by the fundamentalist wings of different congregations in conjunction with secular conservative forces. This consists of a deep-seated opposition to the currents of moral liberalization associated with the 1960s. He also charts the formation of a fundamentalist worldview that bound together these cultural conservatives on a host of issues, ranging from the question of prayers in public schools to gays in the military.

One of the principal features of these new, divisive conflicts, Hunter argues, is that they are driven by perspectives that are incompatible. These controversies are generated by two fundamentally antagonistic conceptions of national history and purpose, and underlying models of self and community. These result in 'different conceptions of moral authority . . . different ideas and beliefs about truth, the good, obligation to one another, the nature of community, and so on' (1991: 49). Even apparently minor issues have the potential to mushroom into political bombshells, inducing extensive, often hysterical, media commentary and widespread political mobilization. In antagonistic combination, these perspectives have given birth to clashing moral visions and contrary tendencies throughout America's cultural life (1991: 43). Although theological sectarianism has ceased to be the force it once was, Hunter allots a major role to religion, both as the source of much of the moralism emanating from both sides of this divide, and because, since 1945, conflicts between liberal and conservative exponents within particular religions and denominations supplanted intra-religious conflict (1991: 97–102). The realignment of the public culture which has been the result of this new cultural polarization is embedded in a 'shifting configuration of religious and political associations and organizations' (1991: 107), each propounding a rival vision of public life and social authority. Hunter's analysis has been especially influential in pinpointing the deleterious impact of the politicization of culture in the public sphere. A highly polarized discourse structures debates on a range of moral and cultural issues. Cultural politics and a concern with identity are, according to this view, the contemporary manifestations of deeply rooted, historical developments that are unique to American society.

Exceptionalism also informs a very different account of the rise of the politics of identity that has come to the fore in a number of retrospective accounts of the demise of the political radicalism of the 1960s. Divisions that emerged among left intellectuals of that era have helped shape the expectations and fears aroused by identity-based political argument.

Several leading commentators have located the emergence and break-up of the New Left during these years as the crucible of this narrative. Richard Rorty's account of the history of the American left, *Achieving our Country* (1998), is a leading light in this historiography.[14] Rorty charts the displacement of the progressivist agenda pursued by the non-communist left in the early years of the twentieth century in favour of a tripartite concern with psyche, self and cultural insurrection that emerged from the counter-culture of the late 1960s. He is especially critical of the adoption of a political outlook in which the project of protecting marginal or vulnerable identities is deemed antithetical to a sense of American national identity and the possibility of a progressive rendering of it. This focus upon the New Left is central to various other influential historical accounts (in particular Gitlin, 1995; and Lind, 1996). Several of these offer a narrative similar to Rorty's, arguing that the New Left movement that swept across American universities and cities in the mid- to late 1960s gave birth to a succession of splinter movements – black power, the women's movement and gay rights, among others. In Oedipal fashion, these turned upon their political forefathers, especially the traditions of socialist and social democratic radicalism that prevailed before the Second World War.

The American New Left was, indeed, home to a bewildering range of initiatives, experiments and ideas. Encompassing a range of political traditions, styles of protest and intellectual influences, it was from its inception the site of deep, often rancorous disputes. The cultural and ideological reverberations of the projects and debates it spawned were considerable, and echoed well beyond its constituent membership. At its height, when it became a focal point in the struggle against the Vietnam War, this current provided an important point of political orientation for many groups, disaffected students and political leftists. The desire to retell the story of how this radical coalition fell apart under the weight of the many different hopes and expectations of its participants, and the quest to allocate blame for its demise, are central themes of this historiography. So too is a contentious and partisan account of the birth of the politics of identity.

One of the most important morals of this historiography is the assertion that the New Left was the parent to the various splinter groups that took their own identity and experiences of oppression to be constitutive concerns. As a consequence, the language of exclusive group particularity was given radical credibility. New Left intellectuals indulged, rather than opposed, these developments, some of which spawned sub-cultures in which violence, ethnic purity and moralistic fervour prevailed (Gitlin, 1995). As the movement gave way to the logic of the splinter group, with notorious results in the case of the Black Panthers and Weathermen, its critics argue, it cut itself adrift from its formative goal of establishing a coalition of various groups united by the goal of social change. According to Todd Gitlin (1995), the abandonment of this project was the result of an increasingly rejectionist rhetoric towards American culture as a whole. In the eyes of Rorty (1998), this anti-American posture meant the defeat of the progressive project of building an alternative version of American society. Symbolized in the declaration of war upon 'Amerika', the New Left remodelled its language and aspirations on the militant politics of difference.

One of the keynote voices in this revisionist historiography belongs to Paul Berman, who has provided a controversial and entertaining account of the emergence of the lesbian and gay movement out of the Stonewall riots (1996). He charts the rise of a sense of group particularity among political radicals in this period, a consequence of the disappointment felt by many at the gap between the emancipatory rhetoric of the New Left and their own particular plight. The vision of a common political and social struggle disappeared from the horizon, Berman complains, once the specificity of group oppression and cultural distinction supplanted the idea of a shared moral and political purpose. Activists were increasingly encouraged to lay claim to 'historic grievances' to earn the right to be heard. But the language of grievance proved a divisive and corrosive basis from which to conduct collective action (1996: 156). Within different activist communities the idea emerged that those united by a common history of oppression – as blacks, or gays, or women – constituted a community. Once individuals regarded themselves as its members, a natural progression was to invent and promote a common culture that sustained a robust difference between the rejected mainstream and the uniquely constituted group. Little room was left for the wider political vision and reforming ambitions once dear to the New Left. Instead there emerged the idea of a 'democracy of communities' (1996: 157), a precursor of the model of the rainbow coalition proclaimed by later radicals and difference-centred political theorists. Berman shows how these identity groupings became increasingly insular and conservative in their relationship with their members. To criticize a group's practice or behaviour was to be seen as rejecting and insulting 'the dignity and the rights of an entire population' (1996: 159). The cultural politics each pursued betrayed a self-confirming logic of difference. Rather than persuading mainstream America of the injustices perpetuated against gays, for instance, the new cultural politics centred upon the public performance of rituals, practices and public displays designed to demarcate the community from the wider society. Berman highlights a trait common to many identity-based communities – the propensity for sectarian division:

> In any movement based on building up a cultural identity, sooner or later someone will step forward to declare his own identity to be truer and more authentic than everyone else's, and will announce a grave impending threat to the collective identity, and on that basis will take into his hands the right to make decisions for all, and to unmask traitors, and to carry out the executions. (1996: 161)

Each of these movements developed a particular momentum and outlook of its own. Yet the identity of each depended crucially upon an Oedipal relationship with the vehicle of social emancipation from which it was born. The self-referential rhetoric of political resentment, sectarian suspicion and moralistic guilt-tripping grew paradoxically out of a movement that began from the premise that all of its parts had a common stake in the achievement of social justice and emancipation.

One of the main claims of this historiography, one that is fiercely contested by other leftist historians (Lott, 1999), is that the turn towards a cultural politics that was insular and exclusionary has had a number of damaging ethical and political effects for subsequent generations of social democrats and liberals in the US. Some claim that sections of the white working class, feeling excluded by the coalition of minorities that the Democrats sought to construct, were as a result driven towards the Republican Party from the 1970s onwards (Gitlin, 1995). Others suggest that the embrace of identity, and the turn towards the motifs of cultural deconstruction and the therapeutic restitution of the self, resulted in the fateful disengagement of the intellectual left from mainstream politics (Rorty, 1998: 75–107).

Conclusions

In both of these national contexts, the social forces and intellectual figures gathered under the banners of the New Left have played an important role in shaping understandings of what is supposedly at stake in the emergent politics of identity. There are some important and under-examined connections between these earlier debates and the more recent upsurge of interest in social pluralism and cultural diversity within the ranks of political philosophers. In both countries, there are continuities of personnel between these earlier positions and contemporary political theory – Charles Taylor, Michael Walzer, Stuart Hall, Cornel West and Richard Rorty being important examples. And in both, attempts to juxtapose and reorientate social liberal and social democratic ideas in the wake of 'difference' have shaped the rancorous quality of contemporary philosophical debates (Katznelson, 1996). The tendency to regard such groups as inherently antithetical to the project of creating a just and egalitarian republic, and as the source of a pervasive particularism that takes Enlightenment rationalism as its target, constitutes the starting-point from which much current reflection upon the relationship between liberalism and the politics of identity begins. Throughout this book I will suggest that the influence of this dichotomous pattern of debate remains pervasive. Some important characterizations of the politics of identity arose in these contexts from the implosion of socialist thought and politics and the break-up of the New Left coalition.

One further influence of these debates upon contemporary arguments is the shared assumption they have bequeathed about the novelty of 'cultural politics'. In historical terms, this presumption is questionable if we consider earlier movements and communities that also fit the three criteria outlined in this chapter. Current instances of the politics of identity might be better understood as connected to established cycles of social protest and communal development (Calhoun, 1994; D'Anieri et al., 1990). And discussion of their implications was as central to nineteenth-century social and political thought as it is now, though different groups tended to be prominent then (Tilly, 1985). The precursors of today's social movements arose in this earlier period in the guise of forces that also sought to bring important social relationships and experiences into the political world – for instance, in the shape of the labour and suffragette movements. Identity politics in many ways constitutes a recurrent, perhaps cyclical, phenomenon that has its roots in the establishment of a distinctively modern polity and social order.

2

The Politics of Identity in Liberal Political Theory

Introduction

Many liberals are uncomfortable with the idea that claims and arguments based upon unique group identities are a legitimate presence in democratic life. In this chapter I consider why some theorists are convinced that liberalism and the politics of identity need to be conceptualized as fundamentally antithetical. One problem with this notion is that it overlooks the pertinence of some core liberal values to social struggles conducted in the name of group identity (Habermas, 1993; Miller, 2002a). Equally, some of the dilemmas that these forces generate can be interpreted as current versions of problems that have long been familiar to liberalism. One such example is the marked contrast between the often shallow and resentful ways in which citizens regard their public roles and mutual obligations, on the one hand, and the depth and meaning some find in group belonging, on the other. The question of how this tension should be managed at the level of the individual citizen and the wider challenge of inculcating citizenship in diverse and unequal societies are familiar themes in the history of liberal political thought.

The idea that liberalism and the politics of identity are fundamentally incompatible is rooted in the image of an ongoing, inescapable conflict between a liberalism that is 'the armed wing of the Enlightenment' (Young, 2002: 173) and a culturally sensitive alternative position that is embedded in a strongly particularist philosophical disposition. This dualistic contrast, however, squeezes from view liberal projects that interweave universalist and particularist ideas in other ways. The notion of an overarching clash between the liberal 'West' and the non-liberal 'Rest' collapses all sorts of intellectual and moral distinctions beneath its weight and generates rather one-dimensional liberal responses to political phenomena. There are various reasons, I will suggest, for adopting a less

dichotomous attitude towards the place in liberal democracies of movements and groups that seek to politicize aspects of group identity.

Liberalism and the politics of collective identity

Commentators have traced the influence of a number of political and
cultural traditions upon the ideas sustaining the politics of identity –
among these, romanticism and conservatism (Baumeister, 2000; Benhabib, 2002; Parekh, 2000). Each informs contemporary assertions of
social distinction and the proclamation of the unique personality of
identity-based groupings. There is much to be learned, for example, from
comparing current arguments with those collected by Isaiah Berlin under
the heading of the 'Counter-Enlightenment'. The romantic heritage, in
particular, informs contemporary conceptions of the importance of
group identity and culture (Berlin, 1999). Romantic emphases upon the
unique character of certain kinds of belonging and the particularity of
each individual's potential are clearly visible in the politics of identity.
So too is the desire to fix the distinctive character of a person, group or
nation in relation to a purported essence, typically defined in terms of
core attributes or cultural characteristics (Benhabib, 2002). Herder's
conception of the moral singularity of discrete cultures is an especially
important source for many current ideas about the importance and
worth of cultural diversity (Barnard, 2003; Taylor, 1991a). The legacy
of such ideas continues in the form of characterizations of multiculturalism that present groups as cultural islands, each isolated from, and
largely incomprehensible to, one another.

In the eyes of many liberals, the romantic tradition provides the key
to the interpretation of identity politics. Continuing its critique of
Enlightenment thought, current advocates of group pluralism, they
suggest, repeat the fallacies of anti-rationalism, and set themselves
against modernity's ethical promise to emancipate the individual from
custom and hierarchy. The displacement of older kinds of group pluralism in the name of identity, critics argue, represents a damaging development for democratic societies. The clubs, societies and associations
that liberals regard as healthy and functional to civil society arise from
uncoerced choices. Identity-based groupings, by contrast, promote a sectarian and determinist logic whereby one arbitrary, unchosen part of a
person's overall identity is rendered a defining feature of their beliefs and
destiny (Gitlin, 1995). Identity politics appears to violate the liberal idea
that individuals should be the authors of their own lives, and that
autonomous persons are capable of achieving some kind of critical
detachment and reflection upon the communities and cultures they
inhabit. Giving prominence to such identities as race, gender or sexuality within political theory, therefore, 'fails to respect sufficiently the value
of individual self-determination' (Laden, 2001: 4). Liberalism, on this

view, is inherently antithetical to the politics of identity, and the latter is a fundamentally alien presence to a liberal polity (Schlesinger, 1998).

This characterization rests, above all, upon two recurrent argumentative claims. There is, liberals often suggest, a fundamental incompatibility between the moral requirements of citizenship in a democracy and the obligations demanded of individual members of overly encompassing communities (Macedo, 1990; 1995). A second, related objection is that the values of liberalism are not culturally biased, as theorists of 'difference' or identity maintain (Barry, 2001a). Liberalism is a moral and political philosophy distinguished by its readiness to found a legitimate, constitutional state upon impartial principles of right (Dworkin, 1978). The politics of identity, by contrast, threatens to undermine the conditions of a constitutional republic, ensuring an increasingly divided body politic and eroding the foundational values of democratic interchange (Elshtain, 1995).

The first of these arguments, regarding the subjectivity appropriate to democratic citizenship, is considered further in this chapter. This liberal philosophical claim has been challenged by a multiculturalist form of liberalism that has revised and adapted the communitarian account of the self that made much headway among political theorists in the 1980s. This liberal alternative has raised some challenging questions about the character and requirements of autonomy in pluralist societies and the importance of culture to the self (Raz, 1986). Below, I discuss the leading positions in these debates and point to the merits of an alternative liberal account of the liberal self within contemporary political thought, one that is not tied to a strong conception of either autonomy or community. This account is compatible, I argue, with a robust egalitarian response to the harms associated with some imposed identities.

The second objection has a bearing upon long-standing tensions between the power of groups and the needs of citizenship. If the many different kinds of mobilization that arise from, and appeal to, collective identity are regarded as instances of romantic irrationalism, then it makes sense to argue, as some liberals have done, that the turn to group identity sets democratic cultures on the road towards cultural Balkanization (Schlesinger, 1998). 'If citizens possess only a finite stock of political loyalty, they will have less of it for the demands of national citizenship' (Wolfe and Klausen, 1992: 234). Whether this is the only plausible way for liberals to conceive the relationship between contemporary group life and the imperatives of citizenship is considered further in chapter 3.

Rethinking the liberal self

In direct response to the liberal claim that individuality is endangered by politicized identity, there has emerged in the last decade a moral argument that presents autonomy as central to a multicultural reformation of liberalism (Kymlicka, 1995; Raz, 1986). This seeks to persuade liberals to take more seriously the struggles of minority cultures against the liberal state. Multiculturalist liberalism gains power and momentum from the tendency for cultural difference to emerge, as Seyla Benhabib puts it, as a 'ubiquitous synonym for identity' (2002: 1). It is within the language of cultural difference and specificity that many of the distinctions, experiences and moral differences in democratic life are now encoded. The propensity to couch group distinction in the language of cultural difference represents an important development in democratic life. One consequence of this culturalist turn has been the growth of demands from subaltern minorities that their cultures deserve protection and promotion by the state. Legal authorities and political institutions are increasingly called to rule upon the cultural practices of minority groups, just as political actors find cultural references and symbols ever more powerful tools as they attempt to capture and hold the increasingly evanescent loyalty of citizens.

Against this backdrop, liberal multiculturalism gains impetus from its critique of the deontological assertion that the state can be neutral with respect to the cultures and ethnic backgrounds of its people (Parekh, 2000; Kymlicka, 1995). This neutralist claim is the product of a philosophical brand of liberalism that seeks to present its political arrangements and cultural preferences as beyond the fray of competing political perspectives and contentious moral doctrines (Gray, 1995a). Yet, in historical terms, liberalism has developed and deployed a variety of cultural norms and nationalist projects (Kymlicka, 1995). It has also, in the late nineteenth and early twentieth centuries, provided a powerful legitimization of the colonial policies pursued by European states, propounding the notion of liberal democracy as a higher form of social order and a civilizational standard against which other cultures were found wanting (Mehta, 1998). Once the cultural preferences and particularities of liberalism are unmasked, multiculturalists suggest, the assimilationist and nation-building projects that liberal states have undertaken come into view. These critics draw our sympathy towards those minority cultures that resist the informal, as well as explicit, attempts by the liberal state to ensure compliance to liberal culture, principally through the hegemony of its apparently universal and impartial norms (Young, 2001; Young, 2002). They stress the importance, therefore, of the resistance conducted in the name of a variety of group identities and national minorities. The latter are constituted through unique, differentiated cultures, each of which, *pace* Herder, represents a source of intrinsic value for its members (Baumeister, 2000: 10–11). The politics of identity is read by multiculturalists through their critique of the monocultural logic at the heart of liberal political ideas and rejection of the universalist rationalism that has sustained the liberal democratic ideal. Its principal dynamic is one of resistance to the normalizing and assimilationist ambitions of the hegemonic culture that prevails in the liberal democratic state (Deveaux, 2000b).

Kymlicka's multiculturalism

This position has been developed with skill and passion in a number of important contributions to contemporary political theory in the last fifteen years. The ideas of the Canadian theorist Will Kymlicka have been especially influential among these (1989; 1995; 1998; 2002). His arguments invoke an important distinction between multi-nation states (where cultural diversity arises from the incorporation of previously self-governing, territorially concentrated cultures into a larger state), and polyethnic ones (where cultural diversity arises from individual and familial immigration) (1995: 6). In the first kind of polity, national minorities bear the brunt of the state's efforts to build a coherent culture of nationhood, and they lead an increasingly vocal resistance to such efforts. In the second situation, it is ethnic minorities that are the principal obstacles to the homogenizing ethno-cultural policies of the state. Importantly, Kymlicka offers a more precise delineation of the subjects of the multicultural democracy that he advocates than is typical of many multiculturalists. Observing the implausibility of the notion that all social groupings possess a distinctive culture, he argues that only those that generate a 'societal culture' – defined as 'those practices and institutions that cover the full range of human activities, encompassing both public and private life' (1995: 75) – are subjects that the state ought to regard as worthy recipients of cultural rights (1995: 18). This stance leads him to exclude from ethical concern 'the sorts of lifestyle enclave, social movements and voluntary associations which others include within the ambit of multiculturalism' (1995: 19). At other points in his writing, however, he accepts that the arguments he makes in respect of ethno-national cultures may also be applicable to women or gays (Kymlicka and Norman, 2000).

The distinction between those few groups that possess a societal culture and those that do not is indicative of a characteristic feature of liberal multiculturalism. Kymlicka stresses the value of societal cultures because these are presumed to offer 'meaningful' ways of life across a range of activities that span the social, educational, religious, recreational and economic domains of life. These cultures matter because they can provide a sufficiently stable and diverse context of choice for the exercise and cultivation of individual autonomy (1989). Stability is at times invoked in his argument as a condition of choice because such a culture must offer a reasonably broad array of life-plans from which the individual may choose, and a scheme of ordinal ranking for the prevailing values within it. But emphasis upon stability conflicts with those properties required of any culture that succeeds in reproducing itself over time

– the capacity to adapt to social, economic and political change, and to be sufficiently responsive to those other cultures with which it co-exists (Stevens, 2001: 201). Kymlicka's hesitancy about the status of those social groupings that fall outside the ambit of his ethno-nationalist model, and particularly those arising in relation to other ascriptive identities, is rooted in his commitment to the idea that groups matter in so far as they generate a coherent, independent and stable cultural matrix. He rightly observes that many gay communities, for example, do not possess an entirely independent and coherent culture of this kind. But he does not consider whether the same may be true of national, as well as sub-national, groupings (Kukathas, 1992). His model presumes that the cultures generated by ethnic and national minorities can be delineated separately from others, 'and that the boundaries between these groups and the contours of their cultures are specifiable and relatively easy to depict' (Benhabib, 2002: 4). As Kymlicka himself notes, these are difficult conditions to apply in the case of many salient ethnic identities whose cultural practices are the results of a mélange of different influences and traditions.

The example of African-Americans represents more, therefore, than an exceptional case for this position. It in fact throws into relief a deeper conceptual ambiguity. Multiculturalists typically assume that there are such things as whole cultures, and, in Kymlicka's case, the more established and stable these are, the greater their moral worth for individual members. But Kymlicka and others fail to distinguish between the reified presentation of cultures, by intellectuals, elites and political actors, in which coherence, stability and depth are inevitably emphasized, and the contingent, socially constructed and plural character of any actual cultural formation. The notions that cultures align with fixed populations and that a non-contentious version of a culture in a modern setting can be offered are both questionable (Benhabib, 2002). Cultures are continually modified social constructions. They are inherently fluid and prone to intermingling with elements from beyond themselves. Hybridity, as much current cultural theory suggests, is the condition of existence, not an exceptional state, for cultures in modernity (Gilroy, 2001; Bhabha, 1994). Normative multiculturalism often draws upon anthropological conceptions of culture that emphasize the interactivity of various elements in a culture and the totality formed by its many different signifying practices and traditions. A culture is conceived as a system, on this view, and as independent from and prior to the 'intentions of those through whose actions and doings it emerges and is reproduced' (Benhabib, 2002: 3). In modern contexts, however, there are good reasons to favour more sociologically derived conceptions of the cultural. In these, more relational and pragmatic ideas about cultures and their subjects are prevalent, and a corresponding emphasis upon the variable meanings that agents derive from cultural resources is central.

Not only should liberals be wary of multiculturalist ideas about what cultures are, but they might also question their assumption about the selves that are shaped by these cultures. In some accounts, the relation between individuals and cultures is conceived in quasi-communitarian vein. Cultural formations are regarded as the determinants of the ends and identities of their members. A tension arises here between two different ideas that Kymlicka wants to advance: that individuals are to some degree constituted by their cultural influences (hence the status of culture as a primary good); and that they are beings who can choose between cultural options. This latter process appears to be constrained, and perhaps invalidated, by this first condition.

Like all other social products, cultures are subject to historical change and evolution. This condition of existence presents a major obstacle to multiculturalist efforts to generate coherent ethical goods from whole cultures. Why, for instance, should we accept that the contemporary, contingent form of a culture is the version that ought to be recognized, rather than one that has passed or that may be about to emerge? To remain meaningful sources of personal value, or 'contexts of choice' in Kymlicka's terms, it seems likely that cultures have to adapt and evolve with regard to various social dilemmas and rival cultures. Acceptance of their inherent mutability undermines the notion of integrity, and indeed authenticity, upon which multiculturalist arguments often rely.

In the public debates that have been aired in many democratic states, moreover, multiculturalism has become tagged with various unfortunate associations. Critics have observed that, in conventional parlance, the term is used to signal the problems generated for the mainstream by those who are 'different' (Alibhai-Brown, 1999). Such a view constructs immigrants and ethnic minorities as inherently disruptive elements, rather than beings whose lives are affected by various arbitrary inequities, and who possess the capacity to forge unique selves. As a political and intellectual framework, multiculturalism posits the clash of cultural systems as the principal dynamic through which groups interact and inequalities emerge. This generates the recurrent, and misleading, image of a set of non-liberal cultural islands surrounded by the high waters of mainstream liberal culture (Modood, 2001). Such an understanding threatens to reify minority cultures when these are, in fact, complex and contingently formed mosaics.

The attempt to interpret identity-based politics through the lens of the minority nation is, therefore, sociologically flawed and morally troubling. It results in the normative claim that one's sense of ethno-national identity is inherently more important to one's moral personality than other social traits. But, is being a Catholic in Northern Ireland, for example, inherently more ethically significant for one's individuality than being, say, an unemployed, gay man living in Belfast? The sensible answer is that all of these 'identities' are potentially important, depending upon what is going on around this person, and on what their own goals happen to be. But such a sense of political contingency and respect for the agency of particular persons is extrinsic to many multiculturalist accounts.

It is at the level of metaphysics that the clash between liberal individualism, on the one hand, and the arguments of multiculturalism and difference theory, on the other, have been most fully aired. But these disputes also have echoes within political debates animating the public spheres of contemporary democracies. The divisions between broadly liberal public commentators and writers that have opened up on such questions as the *fatwah* issued against the writer Salman Rushdie, or the implications of the terroristic actions of 11 September 2001, mirror these polarizing intellectual impulses. Within the Anglo-American context, this duality takes shape between self-styled upholders of the liberal heritage of free speech, autonomy and social progress and those arguing that liberalism is merely one among other cultures, and needs to jettison its hegemonic ambitions. Public disputes have also broken out over the stance Western liberals should take to illiberal practices like arranged marriages or female circumcision, and more generally about the status of non-Western immigrant cultures in the West (Carens and Williams, 1996; Modood, 1998; Parekh, 2000). Given the importance of liberal ideals and values to the national traditions and self-understandings of both the United States and Britain, these disagreements are of considerable political, as well as moral, significance. In the broadest philosophical terms, the clash between a Kantian-influenced liberal philosophy, on the one hand, and a multicultural alternative, on the other, has been central in shaping the normative debates that have captured the attention of Anglo-American political theorists. In the following sections I suggest that the polarized quality of these disputes has diverted attention from other important liberal ideas. In particular, a strand of liberalism persuasively emphasizes the moral importance of harms associated with ascriptive identity. In so doing, it takes a lead from neither of the schools of thought outlined above. Giving emphasis to this perspective is an important part of the process of generating a more complicated map of current liberal arguments, and a deeper sense of the continuing fertility of aspects of this political and intellectual tradition in relation to some of the demands made by contemporary social groupings.

Liberalism and the self

Various contemporary liberal thinkers retain the value of individuality as a constitutive ideal but interpret it as constrained and shaped by the particularities of culture, group and nation (Strong, 1990; Macedo, 1990: 219–26; Benhabib, 1992). There is a growing sense among many Anglophone liberal theorists that liberalism ought not to be founded upon the ideal of the unencumbered self attacked by communitarians

(Sandel, 1984), but relates to complex, culturally and socially constrained agents (Gill, 1986; Appiah, 1996). Citizens on this broad view 'select, interpret, and evaluate stories, histories, and customs in attempts to make the best out of the various cultures given to them' (Gutmann, 1993: 185). The social agency of individuals arises from the cultural and hermeneutic traditions into which they are born, and through which they come to express their unique intentions. Such an approach yields the image of the self as a constrained identity-builder (Appiah, 1996: 96; Wallman, 1983; Taylor, 1985). This broad approach is by no means incompatible with a recognition of the moral importance of social identity and group membership. While cultural traditions and identities arising from ascriptive markings undoubtedly shape the options and self-understandings that individuals possess in fluid and socially pluralist contexts, the capacity of individuals to forge meaningful life-plans, and stitch together satisfying identities from available cultural materials, continues to be morally and socially significant.

As a political tradition, liberalism is indeed distinctive for its sensitivity to the precarious character of the construction of personal identity. This typically involves the deployment and adaptation of narratives about oneself and the groups to which one belongs (Somers, 1994; Whitebrook 2001). The notion of narrative has been revived of late because it invokes the fluidity and contingency through which both agency and self-understanding develop, and suggests the importance for individuals of ideas, myths and shared understandings. To understand these processes, however, liberals should avoid the 'strong' multiculturalist idea that individuals merely parrot the 'scripts' given them by their communal cultures (Appiah, 1996: 98; Baumeister, 2000). A totality of factors – cultural, economic and social – affects the abilities and freedom that individuals have to devise new scripts or rework familiar ones. In the course of these self-constructions, the cultural materials offered by imposed identity play an important and ambiguous role. They can provide sustaining and redemptive stories and sources of solidarity, as their interpreters often suggest. But they can also fix and limit the horizons of individuals, offering mirror images of the essentialist and restricted ideas of the dominant culture.

This emphasis upon the contingent and constrained aspect of agency is not, as some claim, alien to liberal thought. As Meira Levinson observes, such an approach has been enunciated by various philosophers reluctant to ground liberalism on the comprehensive moral doctrine of autonomy (1999: 91). It offers an especially fertile perspective for thinkers keen to engage with the social and moral significance of the affiliations and influences that shape individuality in contemporary civil society. On this view, agents are still the bearers of the capacities to evaluate the beliefs and commitments that they, and others, hold. Moreover, in morally and socially diverse societies, reflection upon one's own beliefs is likely to be enabled by the proliferation of options, ideas and influences (Raz, 1986). Multiculturalists remain unhappy with the impact of even this diluted sense of individuality upon, for instance, faith communities, seeing it as inherently hostile to such identities (Macedo, 1995). But liberal approaches to individuality can encompass the idea of the faithful as beings who are capable of 'second-order judgements' about those values and precepts with which they identify (Levinson, 1999: 91). Individuals content to live according to established traditions or moral codes ought not to be regarded as entirely passive social agents. They can be seen as exercising the agency that a democratic order requires, in terms of the identification they have with a community (Mason, 2000: 58).[1] Even in the most demanding of faith communities, individuals face decisions about the degree and character of their involvement. Agency is also pertinent to pluralist societies because there is nearly always a balancing to be effected between one particular communal affiliation and the pull of other collective ties. It is almost impossible for an individual's life-plan and day-to-day decision-making to be entirely determined by a single community.

This sense of the social agency of individuals, beyond the ideals of autonomy and community, is an important feature of contemporary liberal thought. John Crittenden offers an extended elaboration of such a position, suggesting that individual identity is constituted by the interplay of individual autonomy and constitutive relationships (1992). He labels this the ideal of the compound self, and introduces to his version of it the somewhat forgotten liberal notion of self-development. Drawing upon various socio-psychological models of the formation of personal identity, Crittenden posits a self that arises in fractured, highly pluralistic societies, but surmounts the discordance of multiple loyalties and fragmentation by showing itself capable of learning the merits of social involvement and co-operation. This kind of position is merely one of several developed within the ambit of Anglophone liberal theory that align neither with the model of the unencumbered self nor with that of the closed community. In considering the relationship between liberal political theory and identity politics, it is worth recalling the diversity of metaphysical ideas contained within this tradition. Few leading exemplars of Anglo-American liberalism can be fitted neatly, and without distortion, into the categories of individualism or communitarianism that still figure within philosophical debate.

Equality and culture

A parallel debate has broken out over the character and implications of the principle of equality within liberal thought. Liberals have approached the question of the potential compatibility of political arguments rooted in the specificities of group difference and equality from opposed directions. For some, equality means that individuals should be treated equally, irrespective of their colour, creed or social background (Dworkin, 1978). Brian Barry argues that the demands made by subaltern groups and movements are legitimate in so far as they conform to egalitarian norms such as non-discrimination, the normative corollary of the principles of equal treatment and opportunity (2001a). Multicultur- alists, by contrast, strive to show the cultural and normative bias of egalitarian ideas. They highlight the postulation of commonly shared moral attributes underpinning liberal egalitarian thinking and the poten- tial for unfair discrimination against those who are culturally 'different'.[2] Abstract ideas about equality are necessarily subject to cultural and social mediation when applied in the real world (Parekh, 2000; Bader, 1997: 792). For some pluralists, the centrality of the value of equality is simply overstated by liberalism. More typically, however, multicultural- ists propose a reinterpretation of the implications of this central liberal value, seeing it, for instance, as a principle that requires contextualiza- tion and particularistic reinterpretation. They echo Richard Rorty's sug- gestion that we view groups and communities founded upon collective identity as forces that seek to bring a certain concreteness to the abstract sketches of 'the good old egalitarian utopia' (1999: 235). The diverse demands of such groupings do not provide the basis for abandoning equality, but illustrate the necessity of sensitivity to the social specifici- ties and contingencies that mediate the elaboration and application of universal norms. Egalitarians need to consider the possibility that there are forms of suffering and humiliation about which their liberal fore- bears, and they themselves, may be only dimly aware (Rorty, 1999: 236).

Is the idea of reinterpreting equality in the context of social particu- larity compatible with liberalism? Many liberals accept that egalitarian principles do seem to require some understanding of the particular needs and forms of exclusion experienced by social groups (Phillips, 1999). The idea that these justify special provision for certain groupings so that their members can be treated as equals is, however, far more contentious (Levine, 1998; Barry, 2001a: 19–62; 2002). These different approaches to equality have become apparent in debates over questions such as whether cultural minorities should be exempt from universally applica- ble norms – as, for instance, in the case of communities in liberal soci- eties wishing to pursue customs such as arranged marriage or polygamy. Liberal egalitarians are relatively comfortable when a group's moral claim takes the form of making sure that a public good or social service is extended to its members, if this helps overcome discrimination on the basis of an abitrary characteristic or private behaviour – as in the case of the provision of ramps to public buildings for the disabled. But con- troversy arises over whether affirmative action, for example, can also be justified in order to equalize the access of the members of disadvantaged groups to public goods, such as university places or jobs. For an egali- tarian theorist such as Barry, the principle of equality does not stretch to compensating individuals whose culturally informed practices and preferences put them at a disadvantage in relation to legitimate laws and democratic values (2002).

These questions are the subjects of continuing debate among liberal philosophers (Miller, 2002b). In these different cases, philosophical contestation falls back upon increasingly refined discussion of the implications of the principle of equality of opportunity (Miller, 2002b: 45–9); whether equality means the provision of goods and opportunities to all, irrespective of social specificity, or the equalization of basic opportunities and resources available to all; and about what constitutes an unfair, as opposed to an unlucky, burden. While various philosophical 'solutions' to these differences have been advanced, it seems likely that the concept of equality within liberalism will continue to yield contrasting, plausible responses. A tension is endemic to egalitarian thought, in that a principle such as equality of respect implies that every person should be treated as if they were the same, yet, if we are willing to grant respect to each person's uniqueness as a person, it seems that we are also required to treat others, as much as is morally feasible, on their own terms (Ignatieff, 1994: 17). Feminist theorists have been influential in bringing these tensions to the surface of philosophical debate. Demands for maternity rights raise exactly this kind of dilemma (Phillips, 1997). Should these be justified as a reflection of women's 'differences'? Or do they constitute a levelling of the playing field with male counterparts (Coole, 2001; Phillips, 1999)? Egalitarian feminism has shifted, sometimes uneasily, between universalist emphasis upon removing the arbitrary nature of some gendered differences and arguments that evoke women's particular needs and interests. Not surprisingly, its adherents are familiar with the ambiguities and tensions that arise from the project of balancing arguments that arise from social particularity with the universalist horizons of modern political thought. For many, the principle of equality, when applied to the social relationships established around gender, requires some sensitivity to differences of experience, biology and culture (Phillips, 1997).

Behind these controversies lies the continuing influence of the tension between ethical universalism and social particularity in contemporary political philosophy (Vincent, 2002). Liberal thinkers need to be sensitive to the contexts and cultural differences that mediate the application of egalitarian norms, as well as the different social domains, and their abiding purposes, where these are to be applied.[3] More generally, growing public awareness of the needs and particular experiences of various social groupings has been instrumental in allowing policy- and law-makers to justify special provisions and exemptions for groups on egalitarian grounds. For many liberals, the claims of identity groups are legitimate in so far as they invoke the constitutive norms of democratic citizenship – equality, self-respect and civility. By contrast, multiculturalists argue for a recasting of familiar liberal understandings of equality, seeking to acculturate and particularize this value to the point where its liberal implications are compromised.

But the liberal arguments alluded to here sit at various points on a spectrum between this multiculturalist revisionism and a liberal egalitarianism that seeks to avoid rule exemptions and special provision entirely. Adherents of this latter position are sceptical about the idea that any specific class of harms ought to be considered in relation to such arbitrary facets of personal identity as race or sexuality.[4] In so far as individuals are affected by discrimination and equal opportunity is denied, these persons ought to be protected, and restitution given, on the grounds that equality of treatment applies to all, regardless of social difference. Multiculturalists, on the other hand, draw attention to the importance of cultural processes such as stereotyping and assimilation, and highlight these as the sources of systemic patterns of injustice. The most promising liberal ground lies between these positions. It is occupied by, among others, egalitarian theorists who take seriously the notion that inequalities and harms, such as humiliation, can be effected on the basis of unchosen group identities. These thinkers worry that various imposed identities – whether these be based on race, sexuality and gender, or disability – produce important social harms, depending upon the particularities of individual experience and context (Kiss, 1999; Galeotti, 2002). When such identity 'markings' become socially salient, addressing particular instances of unfairness may well require consideration of the experience, history and situation of a larger group. This makes identifying the character of an injustice perpetuated to individual persons an important, if complicated, task. Certainly, the idea that someone necessarily experiences a moral injury because she belongs to an ascriptive grouping is difficult for liberals to accept. The harms perpetuated to members of such groups naturally vary because of different individuals' circumstances, and due to their membership of other cross-cutting groups (Smits, 2000). What may be a highly significant identity marker in one setting – being gay in a socially conservative village, for example – is not necessarily so in another. Equally, given the contingency and fluidity of the social processes in which personal identity is forged, other cross-cutting classifications are bound to emerge as significant for that person in some respect. These may reinforce or offset the discrimination they suffer. It is foundational to liberalism that no person's life-chances should be determined by, for instance, their ethnic designation alone.

And yet, the idea of injustices arising from some unchosen identities is one that various contemporary liberals urge us to take seriously, though not out of a concern with cultural authenticity or inheritance. Starting from a concern for the successful development of individual capability, and its preconditions, and a commitment to the principle of self-worth, this strand of liberal thinking points to the importance of arbitrarily assigned group memberships. Elizabeth Galeotti suggests that we carefully consider what a democratic state ought to do about cultural practices, such as racism or homophobia, that inhibit individuals' sense of self-respect (Galeotti, 2002). This is by no means an uncontentious stance to urge upon a liberal state. Such practices as racism undoubtedly violate some of the norms dear to liberal and republican thought, and might well be regarded as legitimate objects of state intervention as a result. But they also have a bearing on other foundational liberal values – freedom of speech and conscience most obviously. These different imperatives are not always easy to reconcile. In a recent controversy, the American Civil Liberties Union has argued that those concerned with the liberties of American citizens should join them in defending the right of the Ku Klux Klan to continue its traditional cultural practice of cross-burning because of the overriding value of freedom of speech. A rather different critical response to this issue arises, however, if we consider the social implications of such a public practice for the sense of worth of local citizens who are also African-Americans. Opponents of this practice can offer plausible public reasons about its impact upon the self-respect and sense of inclusion of members of this affected group.

The idea that various kinds of harm associated with the arbitrary imposition of certain identities are of moral concern is by no means universally accepted by liberals, and remains the subject of philosophical contention. Untangling the cultural and moral implications of social processes that result in some citizens finding themselves defined, and their life-plans profoundly affected, by an arbitrary feature of their identity is a complex and important endeavour. Yet there are legitimate liberal reasons for treating harms and disadvantages associated with ascriptive identity as unfair burdens that compromise egalitarian principles. Indeed, the idea that group membership is associated with inequality is by no means new for liberalism: one of the most unyielding ascriptive categories in modern societies is social class. Liberals, since the nineteenth century, have worried about how best to remedy the inequities attendant upon membership of the working class and other sub-groups, including the unemployed, the elderly and the poorly paid. What is more novel, however, is the clamour for group-specific provision – exemptions from laws, public support, or financial aid, for instance – on the same egalitarian grounds. While it is now conventional to treat class as entirely separate in kind from race, gender or disability, the established egalitarian concern of social liberals for the former can be extended to justify some kind of special provision in relation to the latter. As Miller argues, it is certainly possible to argue for certain kinds of group-specific remedy using some of the values associated with democratic citizenship – for instance, the promotion of a sense of inclusion in the polity (2002a). What does seem to generate an unavoidable difficulty for liberalism is the claim that a group's culture, rather than the well-being and opportunities of its individual members, deserves respect upon egalitarian grounds, or that some of the integral values and laws associated with a democracy should invariably be relaxed when these infringe upon non-liberal groups.

There remains, however, considerable scope for liberal concern and the public remedy of identity-based disadvantages on grounds other than cultural integrity. Various liberal theorists persuasively argue that tangible disadvantages arise from some types of ascriptive identity. Others maintain that a just state ought to consider providing restitution for the damage wrought to the self-worth and capacity for self-development of individual members of such communities. One of the main normative difficulties of such a stance, for liberal philosophers, is the notion that identity groupings necessarily arise in relation to identities that are the results of chance, as opposed to choice (Mendus, 2002).

Ascriptive and voluntary identities

Considering ascriptive identities as potential or actual blockages to the self-development of individuals is by no means ethically straightforward. One problem arises from the difficulty of establishing any firm ground from which to distinguish identities that are chosen and those that are ascriptive and arbitrary. This complicates the task of assigning ethical standing to identity groupings, not least because some of these take the form of voluntary associations – with relatively low exit costs for members, and an openness to a broad section of society, such as the National Association for the Advancement of Colored People (NAACP) – while others resemble tightly knit, insular communities (Gutmann, 2003). And, in philosophical terms, it is almost impossible to isolate the moment when choice is exercised in relation to a group membership. An individual's apparently voluntary choice to join a group often turns out, on closer inspection, to have been influenced by other group-based factors – the values of which we are socialized into by our family, neighbourhood and ethnic community, for example. The line between freely joining a group with a strong collective identity, or as a result of some hidden or background cause, factor or influence, is impossible to determine exactly. The example of a trade union is a useful one in this regard. Unions are typically regarded within liberal thought as interest-based associations that individuals can freely join and leave (except where illiberal, closed-shop practices prevail). But the decision to join such a group is in many instances shaped by a range of factors – peer pressure, socialization, and cultural background, for example. Similar influences play a major role in determining whether an individual remains within a union, whatever formal rights of exit exist.

In philosophical terms, it is important to consider whether this sociological ambiguity bears upon the argument advanced by some liberal egalitarians that individuals should be compensated for harms that arise from an arbitrary identity such as ethnicity. There are two reasons to suggest that it does, and that liberals concerned about the values of equality and individuality can pay attention to the problem of imposed identity (though they may still disagree about what exactly the state is morally required to do in response). The first is that we do not need an absolute distinction between these kinds of group identity to allot greater ethical significance to some over others. We might, for instance, replace the binary distinction between identities that are chosen and those that are given with the idea of a continuum along which different degrees of choice and ascription are present. While trade unions are further along this scale than, say, ethnic groups, there are still respects in which the more obviously ascriptive character of ethnicity can be reflected in the moral responses of liberals. The second reason that ascription is morally important is that this category signals the singularity of practices and lifestyles that are rooted within the history, social relations and experiences of a grouping, as opposed to those that are undertaken for pleasure, self-interest or experiment. This is broadly the distinction that has informed some of the jurisprudential reasoning of the Supreme Court in the US in cases where the cultural or religious backgrounds of group members generate practices that violate the law or majority tastes. Although this is by no means an uncontentious distinction, it remains of considerable moral and social worth.

A further illustration of both the importance and the difficulty of this distinction arises in the guise of religion.[5] If religious belief in modern pluralist societies is regarded as freely chosen, then it would appear that faith cannot be an object of legitimate public concern for a liberal state because it does not generate arbitrary disadvantages. Yet many writers include religious groups under the heading of identity politics, and talk as if this were an ascriptive identity. Is this a justified stance? Liberal theorists and constitutional interpreters have long debated whether religion is tantamount to voluntary association (Kukathas, 1992). A particularly powerful liberal contribution to these debates suggests that the notion of 'free choice' in matters of religion is itself a product of a partisan, comprehensive moral doctrine rooted in the values of secularism (Galston, 1991; Nussbaum, 2000b: 167–240). Against such an idea stands the view of many religious practitioners that religion is a matter of faith, not of free choice (Canavan, 1995). Adopting the framework of choice in the case of religion would appear to represent the unreasonable imposition of one contentious moral doctrine on to others, a procedure outlawed in various attempts to construct a 'political' justification for liberalism (a position considered in greater detail in chapter 3). On this basis, Martha Nussbaum suggests that it is fairer to regard religious conceptions of the good as rich and vital sources of personal and political identity (2000a; 2000b). Excluding these from the public domain, or treating religious belief as akin to a pastime, a consumer preference or an 'expensive taste' (Cohen, 1999), rather than in the same terms as nationality or ethnicity, is therefore unjust.

The key to this argument is the sense of intrinsic value that can be ascribed to a sincerely held religious belief, a position that resonates with liberals' respect for the reasonable goods that individuals hold dear. This sense of value arises from an idea that is generic to religious practice:

that the belief it signals matters fundamentally to the believer. John Horton outlines this as follows:

> To be a Muslim or a Jew (or of course a Christian) is to understand one's identity as intimately bound up with membership of that group. It is to partake of a common history and to stand in a particular relationship with that group which is integral to one's sense of who one is. Inevitably the extent of this will vary, but even those who wish to make a complete break with their cultural community cannot but be cognizant of that with which they are breaking. (1993: 2)

The possibility of distinguishing kinds of group membership that relate in a relatively deep way to their members' sense of self-identity is important to the idea of picking out identities that are not simply matters of choice from the many kinds of belonging and membership that citizens forge. Horton's description brings to the fore one further distinguishing element of ascriptive identity. Those who belong to such groups identify deeply with them. And they typically experience membership of such a group culture as morally significant. This last point is also important. Various ascriptive classifications are not ethically important. It is only when group membership generates a collective interest and unique sense of self-understanding in response to experiences of unjust treatment or subordination that ascription becomes morally salient.

Liberal political ethics and the harms of collective identity

This moral response to the harms generated by some imposed identities ought to be separated out from the romantically derived idea about the intrinsic worth of (certain kinds of) cultural inheritance (Taylor, 1994). The latter position points towards a politics of belonging or recognition (an idea discussed in chapter 8). The former implies the extension of established egalitarian principles to individuals so that they can properly enjoy equality of opportunity and respect in the public domain. This position does not turn upon claims about the authenticity of a group's culture. It points to the possibility that certain kinds of injury can arise through the arbitrary imposition of particular identities upon persons. Various forms of maltreatment based upon the experience of a stereotypical and caricatured identity can violate an individual's capacity to form an independent moral personality that is the basis of their individuality.

This position complements several recent philosophical attempts to highlight the centrality to liberal society of the avoidance of social relations founded upon humiliation (Margalit, 1996; Levy, 2000). Avishai Margalit sees in the proclivity for self-assertion among identity-based movements an immanent resistance to humiliation. Any state that wishes to meet the standard of basic decency is required to arrange its agencies and institutions so that they do not perpetuate harmful or cruel representations of minorities. Margalit delineates three different elements in social practices that humiliate: (1) those that treat human beings as if they were not human – as beasts, machines or subhumans; (2) those that lead to a loss of basic control; and (3) those that imply a rejection of a human being from the 'Family of Man' (1996: 144). Steven Lukes's discussion of this position sharpens it in a way that helps flesh out a liberal egalitarian response to unchosen identity (1997). He suggests greater consideration be given to processes and practices liable to generate 'ascriptive humiliation' – forms of maltreatment that result in domination. Ascription is utilized by Lukes to amplify and broaden the familiar liberal concern with discrimination. This kind of humiliation can arise from acts of both commission and omission. Emphasis upon the mitigation of forms of cruelty and humiliation is a familiar strain within the liberal heritage, rather than a contemporary invention (Shklar, 1985).

Identity politics, on this view, offers an important medium for the expression of resistance to instances of humiliation experienced by individuals as members of groups that are disparaged or marginalized. Some theorists, accordingly, focus upon the cultural processes and norms whereby groupings such as Muslims or African-Americans are stereotyped and differentiated in ways that inhibit members from playing a full role in the public life of the community (West, 1994). This can result in quite palpable harms to the confidence and self-worth of their members. It can also generate among those parts of the population deemed 'normal' a marked reluctance to share public space and goods with others (Galeotti, 2002). Harms may well arise from practices, attitudes and behavioural patterns that appear to lie beyond the reach of the law: when male directors disadvantage their female counterparts; when white soccer fans make clear their intolerance of blacks and Asians; and when heterosexual workers freeze out a gay colleague. These practices represent considerable dilemmas for liberal law- and policy-makers keen to promote the norms of non-discrimination and equality of respect. Are public authorities entitled to take direct and/or indirect measures in relation to such problems?

One response to these dilemmas has been to develop the case for the allocation of rights and protections to disadvantaged groups. Another is to demand the cultivation of a sense of recognition of the equal worth of minority groups (an argument I discuss in chapter 8). The alternative liberal position sketched here draws attention to the strong public interest that exists in disrupting exclusionary and aggressive practices that impinge upon minorities. This stance is consonant with a range of liberal theories, for instance Miller's invocation of egalitarian citizenship (2002a) or Amartya Sen's account of the moral importance of the capabilities of citizens (1992). If it can be demonstrated that the capacity of a person to contribute to the civic life of a democratic community, and to form and pursue her own moral ends, is jeopardized by such practices, there may well be grounds for considering the merits of public intervention to offset likely moral harms. An important ethical function of identity politics, in this context, is to highlight that obstacles to the self-development of individuals, and to the formation and exercise of their agency, emerge in complex cultural and psychic forms, as well as through more familiar kinds of socio-economic inequality. Nussbaum defends such a response to some manifestations of the politics of identity, arguing that these arise in opposition to

> the harm of a truncated identity, a diminishing of one's capacities for self-development and self-understanding . . . It is not simply the removal of barriers to self-expression or the exercise of the will that is at issue when we refer to liberation movements as 'identity' movements, but it is the harmful or coercive conditions placed on will-formation and self-formation in the first place that it seeks to address . . . To marginalize a group for which individuals have primary identifications, or to otherwise limit the ability of such groups to enjoy a social space shaped by its needs is to risk harm to those individuals' subjectivity. (2000b: 205–6)

The notion that injuries to the self can arise from social practices that marginalize and stereotype is by no means alien to the liberal tradition. John Stuart Mill was acutely aware of the moral and social impact upon persons of their membership of larger social groupings. In liberal democratic states, there have been various attempts to refine legal codes to reflect growing awareness of the different kinds of harm and interference – psychological as well as physical – that individuals experience. There are good liberal grounds to believe that the unreasonable disparagement of persons, because of an ascriptive element of their identity, constitutes, in Weberian language, a status injury that may be of public concern (Fraser, 1997). Of course, the identification of such a potential injury does not of itself justify state intervention and legal remedy. One important facet of harms generated on the basis of ascription is the variability of their impact and incidence. The assumption that being gay or black necessarily harms the self-worth of all who fit this category has a patronizing dimension, because it neglects consideration of the agency that persons exercise in respect of imposed identity. Blanket categorizations of the effects of stereotyping or exclusion are insufficient to the task of remedying manifestations of disadvantage. Equally, not all proclamations of purported harm require or imply legal remedy. Some of these are motivated by the desire to be heard and noticed within the public culture of a democracy. The subjective consciousness and beliefs of a grouping may be a factor taken into consideration by the state in relation to such claims, but anger itself cannot constitute a sufficient condition for restitutive action.

Conclusions

The social identities that identity politics highlights are not, however, simply the causes of oppression and subordination. They can provide sources of fellowship and cultural self-assertion in ways that may help individual members relate more confidently to the wider society. This moral bivalence lies at the heart of the politics of identity. It gives rise to the claim that a particular social distinction should be set aside so that all are treated as equals, as well as the claim that particular identities deserve more respect. Both of these impulses, I would suggest, are integral to the political ethics of identity politics. In modern societies, some members of ethnic minority groups do not want to feel compelled to heed the voices of their communities when participating as citizens, nor do they want to proclaim and advertise the merits of their culture (Waldron, 2000: 169). They may also resent their ascriptive designation on the grounds of the diversity and uniqueness that they ascribe to their own personal identity, demanding to be treated as multidimensional beings whose complicated character cannot be grasped through the uniform categories of race, gender or sexuality. As Kwame Anthony Appiah argues, in a culture where racial differences are the sources of anxiety and discrepancies of power, African-Americans struggle to have the full richness of their personhood recognized by others (1996: 88). At the same time, however, it is important to heed the solidarity and self-confidence that can arise from the decision to identify with a group formed around one's inherited or imposed identity:

> Within such groups individuals discover a group solidarity that is not accessible to them in political parties. Marginalized members of democratic populations who share a common experience of discrimination or oppression often find particularist political projects centring on their individual group's identity compelling ones, over and against traditional ideological identification. (Hoover, 2001: 208)

Neither of these impulses is inherently contrary to liberal precepts. Rorty, accordingly, presents the impulse to have one's uniqueness respected as integral to the development of Western liberalism (1991: 206). This demand leads to the dual ethics of 'love' and 'justice'. The first of these ideals describes the intuitive openness towards others that emerges within liberal democratic cultures:

> They make these candidates for admission visible by showing how to explain their odd behavior in terms of a coherent, if unfamiliar, set of beliefs and desires – as opposed to explaining this behavior with terms like stupidity, madness, baseness or sin. (1999: 236)

He simultaneously observes liberalism's egalitarian aspiration, typically expressed through the principles of justice. This serves to 'make sure that

once these people are admitted as citizens, once they have been shep-
herded into the light by the connoisseurs of diversity, they are treated
just like all the rest of us' (1999: 236).

Throughout this chapter I have suggested that, contrary to first
appearances, the relationship between liberalism and the politics of identity is not straightforwardly one of antithesis. Liberal political thought
generates different kinds of response to the challenges of identity politics, some of which are more rejectionist than others. Liberal theorists
are right to urge vigilance against communities that wish to violate the
human or civic rights of their members, or that promote aggressively
anti-democratic political claims. But they should also acknowledge that
some identity-based groupings enjoy a more ambiguous relationship with
core liberal values and, indeed, with democracy. Neither forms of liberal
thought that posit autonomy as the hallmark of good character nor
ethno-nationalist models of multiculturalism are well equipped to engage
with the bivalent moral character of the politics of identity. One damaging effect of the prevailing division between these opposed normative
tendencies is to remove from view the philosophical ground that lies
between, and beyond, them. The different respects in which liberalism
and groups practising the politics of identity are intertwined and mutually dependent have, as a result, been underplayed in contemporary
political theory.

3

Citizenship, Public Reason and Collective Identity

Introduction

The fear that the democratic order is threatened by the 'culture wars' unleashed by the politics of identity has become a familiar theme in public debate. Among political theorists, this theme is expressed in relation to two particular concerns. The first is that the commonality and unity of purpose that citizenship requires may be imperilled if citizens are overly aware of group differences. The second concerns the relationship between the political and non-political spheres of life. Identity politics appears to violate some of the defining norms of a liberal democratic polity by seeking to bring private, partisan and emotive concerns into the heart of the political. Out of a concern for the integrity of democratic citizenship, therefore, identity politics has been condemned by some liberal theorists.

In this chapter I consider the merits and implications of these arguments and probe the relationship between identity politics and liberal understandings of citizenship. If it is the case that 'people do not define themselves just as citizens of a nation but, either through choice or necessity, often identify with some smaller sub-group' (Phillips, 1993: 117), are the prospects of democratic citizenship fatally diminished? Can one be a good citizen as well as a devoted member of a religious congregation? Is it feasible to be a politically aware gay man and a constructive and committed citizen? Is there a link between the apparent decline of the ethos of civic duty – being a responsible neighbour, voting in local elections, or keeping abreast of public affairs – and the politics of identity? And does the sometimes angry, and often self-enclosing, rhetoric of politicized identity permit the kinds of public deliberation and social civility that democracy needs?

The return of civic virtue

Contemporary liberals are the inheritors of a rich repertoire of ideas about the implications and value of citizenship. Many agree that citizenship means the equal provision of rights and duties to individuals as members of the political community. But some doubt whether the acquisition of this status is sufficient for the realization of civic unity (Kymlicka and Norman, 2000: 5–7; Dagger, 1997). Despite the claim of various liberal philosophers that citizenship as a status is detachable from the question of the character of citizens, many of liberalism's critics – socialists, nationalists and feminists especially – and some of its adherents, have observed that the idea of the rights-bearing citizen carries some inescapable normative implications (Slawner and Denham, 1998). This procedural understanding has been attacked too for being insufficiently substantive by communitarian and republican critics, who blame the demise of civic culture and social solidarity upon the equation of citizenship with rights (Dagger, 1997; Sandel, 1984). Increasingly, liberals have come to recognize that liberal democracies require an unusually high degree of co-operation and solidarity among their citizens, and that the generation of this stock of mutual sympathy cannot be taken for granted.

Democratic theorists of different kinds tend to agree that citizenship requires a robust common culture and a relatively motivated and public-spirited citizenry. This insight has been central to a marked revival of concern among Anglophone political theorists about the need for, and apparent demise of, civic virtue (Macedo, 1990; Kymlicka and Norman, 2000; Slawner and Denham, 1998). Widespread political anxieties about the purported decline of the nation-state, as well as the impact of multiculturalism, are crucial backdrops to the renewal of republican-style arguments in Anglo-American political thought (Dagger, 1997; Sunstein, 1998). Among political theorists, familiar philosophical conceptions of liberty have recently been challenged by the elaboration of a republican approach in which this value is taken to mean non-domination (Petit, 1999). At the same time, historians of political thought have brought into view a half-forgotten republican lineage (Skinner, 1998; Pocock, 1975). Some scholars claim that liberalism itself once possessed republican variants that have latterly been abandoned (Dagger, 1997; Sunstein, 1998). Adam Smith, for example, combined accounts of the freedoms located in civil society, and the importance of commercial activity, with a concern for the question of how to ensure a sufficiently virtuous citizenry if a republic was not to succumb to the perils of stagnation, corruption and decay.

The return to civic virtue by political theorists is both a product of these intellectual developments and, as suggested above, a response to current political anxieties (Kymlicka, 2002). The worry that the civic culture of liberal democracy is in marked decline has moved to the fore-front of the concerns of liberal political theorists. Apathy, indifference, cynicism and self-interest among the citizens of Western democracies appear pervasive and irreversible. Academic theorists and politicians have, over the last decade, worried about how to renew democracy in the face of such processes. Among liberal philosophers, the idea of a healthy civic life appears both as an independently valuable feature of a democracy and as a prerequisite for the renewal and stability of the liberal order. This civic turn in liberal thought has engendered some un-familiar kinds of argument. According to Stephen Macedo:

> Liberal political institutions and public policies should be concerned to promote not simply freedom, order and prosperity, but the preconditions of active citizenship: the capacities and dispositions conducive to thought-ful participation in the activities of modern politics and civil society. A commitment to individual freedom as a paramount virtue is no warrant for neglecting the civic dimension of our lives. (1990: 10)

Theorists concerned to elaborate the principles of a just state are, then, increasingly drawn towards the problematic of citizenship (Kymlicka and Norman, 2000). Several questions have assumed significance in this scholarship. What can provide the equivalent in a modern political order to the 'civic friendship' that Aristotle modelled as an extension of the daily interactions of Athenian citizens? What does it mean to promote civic virtues in polities when citizens live with strangers whom they do not know, and will never meet? Do our obligations to those who share an identity outweigh those we should feel to other citizens? And what does it take to be, or become, a citizen of a polity such as the United States or Britain – a familiarity with the host language, its institutions, or its traditional ways of life? Social democrats add a different question. In societies in which the logic of the commodity and the model of 'market man' invade ever more domains of social and public life, what can provide individuals with the motivation and desire to act as citizens?

Much of the theorizing prompted by such questions takes the 'fact' of civic decline as a starting-point. Many contemporary accounts of citizenship implicitly posit a golden age against which present realities are found wanting. For some American scholars, as Nancy Rosenblum observes, the implied contrast is with the flowering of groups in the mid-nineteenth century: 'The hey-day of associations in America was the rush into clubs in the mid-nineteenth century . . . This is the "civic culture" social scientists look to for the social capital that overcomes free riding and the tragedy of the commons' (1998a: 100). For other pluralists, it is the idyll of small-town democracy that informs contemporary disap-pointment. Within the British context, the decades after the foundation of the welfare state offer a popular reference against which present real-ities are measured. The 1940s are viewed in some social democratic commentary as a golden age of social solidarity and civic sacrifice in comparison to the age of identity and consumerism (Wolfe and Klausen, 2000).

Against such backdrops, the politics of identity appears as an alien and dangerously novel force. The proliferation of group-specific claims and identity-based political arguments is widely viewed as a contributing cause of the decline of democratic life. Liberal commentators worry that the public at large is more aware of those factors that divide it – ethnicity, religion or gender – than its common interests. If citizens engage in politics with the primary aim of promoting and protecting the way of life of their group, they become instrumental in their approach to politics and immune to appeals to compromise or restraint in the name of the good of the community. The politics of identity appears to generate conflicts that are 'zero-sum, non-negotiable and resistant to shared political procedures and practices' (Philp, 2000: 170).

Liberalism and the return of civic virtue

In order to examine the merits of these claims about the politics of identity, it is worth giving careful consideration to the character of the liberal case for civic virtue. One of the principal features of this renewed concern with virtue is that it is typically conceptualized as synonymous with civic unity. This conflation underpins some of the most influential diagnostic analyses of the decline of the social culture of democracies and prescriptive recommendations for the renewal of citizenship. One analytic consequence of this association is that particular identities and loyalties tend to be framed as obstacles to the realization of the virtues that political unity requires.

Among Kantian theorists, the purported content of citizens' virtues is typically deduced from supposedly neutral accounts of the principles of liberal citizenship (Macedo, 1990; Galston, 1991; Slawner and Denham, 1998). This involves a move from the elaboration of the basic schedule of liberal rights and liberties to a statement of the moral attributes that such a regime implies. The norms of virtuous citizenship are therefore presented as rooted in the shared understandings that 'reasonable' and public-spirited citizens would be likely to reach. As William Galston put it:

> For a liberal democracy to thrive and not only survive, many of its citizens should develop a shared commitment to a range of political values and virtues: tolerance, mutual respect, and active co-operation among fellow citizens of various races, creeds, and styles of life; a willingness to think critically about public affairs and participate actively in the democratic process and in civil society; and a willingness to affirm the supreme political authority of principles that we can publicly justify along with all our reasonable fellow citizens. (1991: 10–11)

Such interpretations posit a clear antithesis between those forms of associational life that are conducive to such virtues as reasonableness, public spiritedness and reciprocity and those that are not. Identity-based groupings are typically placed in the latter camp.

How useful is this approach to civic virtue in pluralist democracies? David Kahane rightly suggests that it necessarily understates the diversity that is permissible and likely among those partaking in liberal conversations (1998: 105). Kantian approaches, he asserts, are overshadowed by the anxiety that the pool of shared liberal virtues and understandings is evaporating (1998: 106). In order to offset the spectre of social breakdown and the demise of civility, these theorists point to the importance of establishing shared understandings of liberal goods among citizens who are increasingly aware of their differences. But this argumentative strategy neglects 'the actual diversity of stories about liberal citizenship' (1998: 117). Kantians forget that in diverse, pluralist communities the meanings of such values as civility and reasonableness are likely to be open to much greater contestation, and different ways of promoting these ideas are also prevalent (Gutmann, 1993). Positing shared commitments among reasonable citizens to such values as equality or justice can overstate the degree to which particular actors will agree on what these values signify in relation to particular contentious issues. A range of political narratives, culturally mediated beliefs and moral arguments can be generative of democratic citizenship, contributing to 'a diversity that we may be tempted to ignore when we focus on shared liberal pieties about the values of toleration, law-abidingness, critical reflectiveness, civic engagement, and so on' (Kahane, 1998: 117).

Public reason and the politics of identity

The return of civic virtue to the forefront of Anglo-American political theory has been prompted by various intellectual developments, including the proliferation of deliberative approaches to democracy. In these quarters, there is widespread scepticism about whether identity politics is compatible with the kind of deliberation that is required of a political community committed to democracy.[1] In this section I consider how well founded is this deliberative objection to the politics of identity. In order to do so, it is worth taking a short argumentative detour to consider whether John Rawls's particularly influential understanding of public reason is, as has been widely claimed, antithetical to the politics of identity.

Contemporary debates over the content and limits of public reason draw upon long-established ideas about the character and importance of the 'general will' in democratic communities. The Rousseau-esque conception of the group's collective interest as the antithesis of the particular convictions and interests of citizens continues to inform democratic thought. So does the idea that the rationality through which the common good is determined means that good citizens tend to agree upon what constitutes the community's best interests. Liberal-republican theorists have sought to offset this monological conception of deliberation with the recognition that in a free society unanimity upon moral questions is not possible. In recent political theory, this perspective has been power-fully renewed by the later Rawls's account of the character and limits of public reason.[2] Critics see in his ideas a profound argument against the inclusion of identity-based political argument in the public domain. Mul-ticulturalists and other pluralists, meanwhile, reject his account on the basis that it is designed to promote certain kinds of character in prefer-ence to others, and, like other kinds of liberalism, excludes many par-ticular persons and cultures that do not fit this bill. In this section I probe both of these arguments. I consider, first, whether it is correct to view identity claims as incompatible with public reason. And then I ask whether pluralists are right to reject Rawls's conception in particular. In some, though not all, respects, I argue, his version of public reason may well be compatible with some of the ethical claims associated with iden-tity politics.

Identity politics typically gives rise to claims and arguments that invoke the specificity and integrity of group identity. These take the form of the assertion of a special need or particular understanding on the grounds that it is important to a person's or group's identity. Some dem-ocratic theorists are convinced that such an argument is incompatible with public reason (Barry, 2001a; Waldron, 2000, 1993). The latter con-sists of reasons that are, in theory, meaningful to all citizens, and is widely held to be antithetical to arguments founded upon self-interest or 'comprehensive' moral and religious belief. According to Brian Barry, the defence of a practice on the grounds that it relates to a particular culture or tradition does not amount to a proper justification. Practices can be justified only in terms of the reasons for them that arose from within a particular cultural system. By refusing to provide a reason-based argu-ment, identity politics simply evades the democratic duty of providing reasons about which others can deliberate (2001a). On this view, iden-tity groups are intrinsically incapable of offering arguments rooted in shared values because the appeal to unique identity necessarily both delimits the applicability of an argument to a certain group and justifies a refusal to reason. Critics suggest that, when a group or individual appeals to their own identity in order to demand exemption from a law, for instance, what it is really doing is seeking to defend its interest through the rhetoric of authentic identity.

Neither of these objections is unanswerable. Making reference to iden-tity when seeking to ground a particular claim does not necessarily negate the logic of public reason. This kind of argument might well be seen as reliant upon a particular kind of publicly accessible reason. Defending a practice, or making a demand, because of a given identity is, as Jonathan Quong (2002) observes, less contentious than inviting others to evaluate the worth of a given practice from beyond its horizon. The general principle invoked by identity-based arguments – that if practices are integral to identities they merit serious consideration by others – is one that others can understand and that might reasonably be said to apply to all.

The second objection – that identity claims are merely interest claims dressed up in a rhetorical disguise – is also less powerful than it seems. It is insuperable only if we adhere to the notion that a person's self-interest is incompatible with a moral argument. Many good moral arguments are typically founded upon interests, usually ones that are regarded as universalizable (Quong, 2002). Deliberative democracy does not require the exclusion of all interest-based claims but necessitates a distinction between those that should carry moral authority and those that do not (Williams, 2000).

The deliberative case against the politics of identity is, in these respects, less clear-cut than is sometimes suggested. While in abstract terms the politics of identity is not necessarily antithetical to the logic of public reason, there may of course be particular political and cultural reasons for thinking that deliberation freed of the language of identity is more productive and less divisive. Such an objection requires a more thickly contextualized consideration of particular polities and identity claims. Some general observations about the role of identity in democratic deliberation can, however, be usefully advanced. If social identities are a legitimate presence in the public domain, then they are as likely to be the objects as well as the subjects of deliberative interchange and critique. Just because identities are invoked to defend particular practices and demands does not mean that such an argument is necessarily an overriding one when balanced against other kinds of pubic interests and moral arguments. In the case of the Salman Rushdie affair, for instance, the perception of offence to their religion held by some Muslims has to be balanced in a liberal democracy against what many will consider to be a more fundamental public reason – the freedom to write and speak freely on matters of religion. Equally, evaluation of the worth of different identities is an unavoidable part of democratic life. Some proclaimed identities may simply be regarded as too fleeting, offensive or frivolous to require respect and consideration.

Rawlsian public reason

The idea that public reason is incompatible with political arguments based upon identity is also advanced by many of liberalism's pluralist critics. Multiculturalists and other advocates of group pluralism remain sceptical about the notion of public reason. But they may be too quick to reject this paradigm in its entirety. In particular, they have neglected those aspects of the politico-ethical character of the politics of identity that may be congruent with some of the tenets of political liberalism.

Public reason in Rawls's thinking requires that, when dealing with fundamental constitutional issues, citizens argue and vote using reasons that would, in principle, be comprehensible by, and acceptable to, others. Citizens are modelled as reason-giving persons who, when they do justify their views, should do so in terms that their fellows can understand and accept as consistent with their status as free and equal citizens. They should, in particular:

> be able to explain to others why the principles and policies they favour support the political values of public reason. A policy excluding all non-Catholic viewpoints could not meet the requirements of such a duty. Such intolerance violates public reason because it violates the criterion of reciprocity. (Farrelly, 1999: 15)

Through this framework, Rawls balances two potentially contrary ideals: the need for some kind of principled basis to the social co-operation required in a just state; and his sense that, in a free society, a range of reasonable disagreement about moral and theological beliefs and practices – which he labels comprehensive moral doctrines – is unavoidable. This is a model that arises from an acceptance of what he terms 'the facts of pluralism', by which he signalled the ineradicability of moral disagreement about the ends of life. Public reason, in this schema, invokes an ethos of reasonableness which is interpreted in relation to two core virtues. These are the principle of reciprocity and the willingness to recognize the burdens of judgement (Rawls, 1993: 47–89). These, he suggests, are the principal norms governing the organization of the social and political institutions of a democratic society. Deploying a contrast between reasonable, as opposed to unreasonable, conceptions of the good, Rawls is able to set limits to the legitimate plurality of views that ought to protect, and be considered pertinent to, the principles governing the political domain (1993: 174–6). The deeply intolerant, the bigoted and the fundamentalist are therefore ruled out of consideration by this formula (Moore, 1995: 301). Public reason is regarded as integral to the legitimacy of a just state, and is seen as arising from the shared fundamental interests and collective political will of the citizens of a democracy, however divergent they may be in terms of cultural preference and moral belief (Rawls, 1993: 212–16). Through engagement with the political life of the community, and involvement in deliberation that broadly conforms to the norm of public reason, those 'who do not have any identity in common can come to share an identity and thus a will' (Laden, 2001: 12).

Some commentators see such notions as potentially beneficial to campaigns for minority rights or the idea of fair treatment for minorities. As opposed to the idea that liberal citizenship implies the acquisition of a 'standard bundle of liberal protections, of basic rights and liberties' (Laden, 2001: 16), citizenship is conceived by Rawls as partially constituted through the practice of deliberation. By deliberating in accordance with the principles of public reason, citizens come to appreciate the benefits and significance of its norms. As Anthony Laden puts it: 'Deliberation that is reasonable in this sense thus sustains while potentially reshaping our relationships and allows us to form shared wills together' (2001: 97). The attributes of reciprocity and mutual sympathy are generated, deliberative democrats suggest, through the process of formulating arguments that pertain to the general interest. Such a stance allots significance to the enhancement and protection of the deliberative capacities of citizens. Individuals who bear the markings of ascriptive identity may have good reasons to confer legitimacy upon a polity in which such principles prevail, and in which what counts as a determining political argument is not the language of social normalcy, moral character or the norms of the majority culture. The humiliation of some bearers of social identities is a matter of political concern if this is likely to violate citizens' basic rights and form an attack upon their capacities as citizens. The same is true of the treatment of minority groups and cases where individuals are either deprived of their fundamental rights or suffer injuries that prevent them from functioning adequately as citizens.

Pluralist objections to public reason

The idea that political liberalism is pertinent to the political ethics of social identity is, however, not shared by many of Rawls's pluralist critics. Some stress the inadequacy of liberal thought, even in its more pluralist incarnations, to regulate and adjudicate the kinds of deep diversity generated by the emergence of identity-based pluralism. Several generic problems with the Rawlsian account recur in this critical literature.

Bracketing

A common complaint made about Rawls's argument is that, while he attends to the implications of moral disagreement, he does not consider the nature and impact of the social identities that modern citizens possess (Moore, 1995). By considering cultural diversity and group memberships merely in reference to the beliefs of individuals, Rawls may have understated the depth and character of the differences that prevail in democratic society. James Bohman, accordingly, suggests that cultural diversity engenders conflicts and disagreements that undercut easy assumptions about shared interests and values (1995; Gutmann, 1993). Standard liberal solutions modelled on religious liberty and tolerance may well no longer be adequate. These kinds of disagreements resist fair adjudication as they are founded upon differences that go 'all the way down' for individuals and groups, challenging the possibility of agreement on which higher order principles are actually at stake in given disputes (Bohman, 1995: 253; Nagel, 1987). In disputes over whether pornography ought to be prohibited, the liberal ideals of freedom of speech and tolerance that underpin non-interventionist public responses are seen by many feminists as irredeemably saturated with gendered assumptions. Many of the procedures favoured by liberals to determine whether a harm has been committed or a person's autonomy compromised are far from neutral to liberalism's many critics and enemies.

Rawls, these critics suggest, skirts around this problem through his adherence to a thinly constituted self that is possessed only of the twin properties of rationality and reasonableness. His conception of the problematic of 'difference' in terms of the differing moral views held by individuals barely registers the underlying causes and sources of disagreement – notably that 'individuals are taught different religions and values and belief-systems; they speak different languages and have different communal identities' (Moore, 1995: 298). But it is wrong to dismiss Rawls's thinking as irrelevant to the dilemmas of diversity on this basis. In his discussion of the historical emergence of liberal thought, he pinpoints the importance of religious differences and shows an acute awareness of the particular character of disagreements rooted in communal practices and cultural differences (1993: xii–xxv; 2000). His model also suggested that the facts of cultural or group identity are necessarily significant for the political principles of the just state, since these are potentially destabilizing forces threatening the liberal quest for a well-ordered society (Moore, 1995: 298).

Rawls famously argued that, whatever their backgrounds or differences, in the political domain citizens must observe the ethos of public autonomy, treating their fellows as free and equal citizens. This has an important implication for the political life and culture of a liberal polity. Its citizens need to show restraint in terms of the kinds of reasons they give for arguments and political actions, abstaining from reliance upon doctrines on major constitutional issues that their fellows may find contentious. Not only would the principles of justice inform the content of political deliberation, but he further stipulated a number of 'guidelines of inquiry' for debate on matters of major (political) import. These consisted of principles governing political reasoning and various rules of evidence that citizens should use when considering whether substantive principles properly apply in particular cases (Rawls, 1993: 162, 225–6). Underpinning this argument is his distinction between the political and constitutional domains in which the singular logic of public reason applies and non-political realms in which different kinds of rationality and sensibility ought to be tolerated. Critics have queried the merits of these ideas, in terms of both the implausible moral psychology they imply and their political consequences in diverse societies (Bellamy, 2000:

111–27). If somebody sees their religious convictions as integral to the person they feel they are, how can they separate from such beliefs in the political domain (Callan, 1997: 31)? Moreover, it seems perverse not to consider the knock-on effects that the promotion of the value of autonomy in the public realm will exercise. As citizens, Rawls insists, we possess a higher order interest as rational and reasonable beings in our capacity for autonomy 'even though as private individuals we may not see ourselves as having or valuing that capacity' (Kymlicka, 1995: 159). But if children from minority groups are educated in the values of political autonomy, it is likely that they may encounter a profound strain between its constitutive principles and the values they learn at home (Levinson, 1999). Political liberals are either naïve or irresponsible, critics suggest, in their failure to contemplate the inherent spill-over effects of the values upheld in the political sphere for domains beyond it.

Concerns about the unfeasible bracketing of the public from the private self that political liberalism demands are, however, overstated. Rather than demanding a wholesale rupture between a person's convictions and the public reasons they offer, Rawls can be plausibly read as suggesting an ethic of restraint in relation to the identities and beliefs that citizens invoke to justify their arguments in the political domain, and a disposition to present one's concerns in a moral language available to all. As Anthony Laden observes:

> Nothing in this account of political deliberation prevents people from being moved to support a given position as a result of their deep religious faith or their lived experience as a member of this or that minority or excluded group. It merely says that in offering reasons to other citizens in support of such a position, we must attempt to offer reasons we think they would also find authoritative as citizens. Since we are understood to be reasoning together as citizens, public reasons are the appropriate sorts of reasons to offer. (2001: 120)

Such a stance does not rule out partisan and socially informed arguments *per se*. Nor does it require the bracketing of all substantive moral judgements. The ideal of 'public reason' is especially important, Rawls suggests, because of the depth and multiplicity of the ties and identities that individuals possess in addition to their standing as citizens (Laden, 2001: 101; Tomasi, 2001). The idea of public reason does not demand that the garments of identity and contentious beliefs are entirely removed at the door to public life, but stipulates that citizens restrain themselves from addressing their fellows merely within the terms of their own comprehensive beliefs on important constitutional and political matters. Advocates of a fairer deal for unorthodox groups and minorities may well find appealing a normative model that requires a degree of restraint that does not come naturally to those who see human excellence in terms of autonomy or individuality.

Reasonableness

The idea of the reasonable is an integral concept in Rawls's argument. It signals the ideal of a citizen who is a reason-giving person, prepared to justify her decisions, and to listen to, and be persuaded by, the reasons of others (1993: 48–54; Waldron, 1993: 55–6). Presented thus, reasonableness does appear to rule out identity claims as illegitimate. Critics worry that reasonableness is too constricting a value when applied to the ideological and moral diversity that flourishes in democratic society. It is tempting, some suggest, to see in this model an ideological move that fixes non-liberal perspectives as inherently unreasonable (D'Agostino, 1996; McCarthy, 1994). Galston expresses this concern in a more nuanced form, suggesting that, through the exclusionary properties of reasonableness, Rawls is able to conjure up the possibility of a consensus about the basic political principles of a just state where, otherwise, it would be clear that there is none (1995). These criticisms are, however, overstated. Rawls was clear that his aim was not to present liberalism as the hallmark of the reasonable, since such a move runs counter to his emphasis upon the range of contending doctrines that are compatible with the basic principles of justice (2001). Public reason arises from Rawls's concern to specify the principles behind, and limits to, the deliberations in which citizens engage: hence the emphasis upon fundamental constitutional questions, as opposed to other kinds of controversy and policy debate (1993: 227–31). He regarded it as a regulative force upon citizens, serving as a reminder of the merits of presenting arguments in terms that their fellow citizens may ultimately find 'reasonable' (Laden, 2001: 121). Contrary to what some critics imagine, nothing in this conception implies a kind of 'prior restraint law that checks every intervention into a debate that is supposed to be guided by the ideal of public reason' (Laden, 2001: 124–5).

Rawls's critics are on firmer ground when they criticize his notion of what should count as an authoritative and binding public reason. Beneath this notion lurked a veiled commitment to a moral consensus that sat uneasily with his own pluralist ambitions. Here, Rawls's alignment of reasonableness and impartiality looks especially problematic. It may well be possible for persons to meet the criteria of reasonableness while offering highly partial reasons that relate to aspects of themselves that they deem important (Moore, 1995: 302). But the model of rationality that Rawls invoked in this discussion relies heavily upon the concept of impartiality. To determine if a reason that is advanced is a good one, citizens must adopt a public, impartial standpoint – the apparently singular, non-partisan, view 'from nowhere'.

The problem with this idea is that 'reasonable' people may well arrive at different conclusions, even while wielding the same values. By interpreting public reason as consonant with constitutive principles that must be shared, 'and sometimes shared in the same way' (Ivison, 1997: 127), Rawls tempers his commitment to the plurality of reasonable conceptions of the good with a thinly disguised invocation of moral unanimity. Why assume, however, that public reasons are less likely than non-public reasons to generate conflict? This criticism is widely echoed throughout the pluralist and multiculturalist literature. Such is the depth of moral disagreement over various identity-related issues that it extends to the very terms of public reason itself (Bohman, 1995: 255). There is no single public standpoint for working out the reasonable moral compromises that are needed to resolve deep conflicts in pluralist democracies. Some thinkers maintain that Rawls's adoption of a 'consensual mode of public justification' makes him blind or indifferent to the different kinds of political agreement that can underpin political co-operation (Sunstein, 1995). These critics offer a powerful case for the revision of liberal accounts of public reason, stressing the merits of less stringent and more pluralist approaches. They invoke the normative idea of securing co-operation between citizens holding incommensurable views, rather than expecting them to achieve moral consensus.

The idea of the incommensurability of values has been invoked by various pluralists in relation to the proliferation of identity claims in political life. But this is not as obvious an accompaniment to these as is sometimes suggested (Bohman, 1995). Identity claims can also be presented in ways that are consonant with a revised version of the ideal of public reason. Many of the organizations and spokespersons making them invoke universalizable, liberal norms – tolerance and equality above all. While there is no doubt that identity-based arguments can generate new divisions, and lock their adherents into highly particularist moral arguments, this represents only one of the ethical faces of identity politics.

Incommensurability has been deployed by some theorists to justify the idea of *modus vivendi* as the model for pluralist democracies (Ivison, 2000). A guiding assumption of this approach is that, in societies in which identity claims force their way into the political domain, the contestability of values is insuperable, disagreement 'goes all the way down', and there is no neutral ground to which contending parties can refer. Contrary to the hopes of Rawlsian liberals, there exists no non-contentious point from which differences can be arbitrated. The advocates of *modus vivendi* reject the idea of a hypothetical agreement on shared political principles, and propose the notion of a hard-headed political bargain reached by groups and persons with different kinds of public reason (Ivison, 1997). This has become a complex and internally differentiated position in its own right. As Rawls observed in his discussion of mutual advantage theories of justice (1971: 134), however, this kind of argument is faced with the problem that it appears to consecrate whichever particular constellation of interests and forces happen to prevail. Should this equilibrium alter, there is nothing to prevent one party from breaking its word or withdrawing from the bargain. For those worried about the prospects facing marginal and historically subordinated social groupings, this may well represent a fairly hazardous position, rather than the obvious political accompaniment to identity-based pluralism.

Demarcating the political

It is integral to political liberalism, and other leading conceptions of deliberative democracy, that a boundary needs to be maintained between questions of public constitutional concern, to which the norms of public reason apply, and issues that pertain to the domain of moral controversy. This distinction appears to erect an impregnable barrier to the public legitimacy of identity-based arguments. It is important, however, to distinguish interpretative caricature from core intentions in Rawls's argument on this question. While the boundary between the political and non-political is integral to his conception of the just state, he need not be interpreted as propounding the notion that the world beyond politics is secondary. As John Tomasi argues, the Rawlsian conception of public reason makes sense only if we consider the non-public reasons citizens have and the ways in which these prepare them for the ethos and logic of political justification in a democracy (2001: 71–9). Catriona McKinnon suggests that citizens in Rawls's model need to acquire 'the skills of civility enabling engagement in public reason'. This implies that they have relatively deeply held commitments and beliefs (2000: 145). Public reason, these commentators suggest, is best understood as a norm that encourages a degree of reflexivity and restraint among citizens about the reasons they hold, and the capacity to consider whether these might be acceptable to others: 'So long as a person makes a genuine effort do to this, regardless of the reasons she eventually endorses, she acts as a good citizen' (McKinnon, 2000: 157).

Still, Rawls was adamant that 'there are many nonpublic reasons and but one public reason' (1993: 220). Acceptance of the intrinsic diversity of moral beliefs has to be tempered in the political domain by the imperative of social co-operation, expressed through the norms of public reason. But if the political is to operate as a space where citizens debate matters of political importance, then it is implausible to hope that they will detach from the moral, religious and cultural traditions that inform their sense of the purposes and content of politics. Indeed, debating and challenging the boundaries of the political is an unavoidable part of deliberation about the purposes of politics. In a pluralist society, comprehensive doctrines and social identities are more likely than ever to be invoked in the argumentative claims offered by identity-conscious subjects. Rawls's injunction to show appropriate restraint smacks of an attempt to resurrect an arbitrary boundary between the political and non-political that has been submerged beneath the tides of cultural conflict, ideological disagreement and social diversity (Bellamy, 2000: 112–13; Gaus, 1999). The attempt to fix the appropriate boundary prior to political debate between the kinds of claims that count as political and those that do not may deprive politics of some of its most important and necessary ingredients (Chowcat, 2000). Much the same is true of his idea of the separation between the background culture of a society and its public political life. This distinction simply does not hold up in contexts where clashes and conflict over constitutional essentials are frequent, and where various sub-cultures and minority groups are making claims to equal or special treatment (Benhabib, 2002: 111–12). The appearance of social forces determined to pursue a politics of identity is both an illustration and a cause of the inherent contestability of the boundaries of politics. In such contexts, political liberalism's attempt to place political reasons beyond the scope of political deliberation appears unfeasible.

In this respect, the Rawlsian model does appear to grate against the logic of identity politics, and ought to be regarded more critically by liberals (Benhabib, 2002). But there are also resources and insights in Rawls's political liberalism[3] that have been overlooked because of the particularist framework though which the politics of identity has generally been advanced. Rawls took moral disagreement and the group identities that gave rise to it as ineradicable features of the social landscape in a free society, and showed a critical awareness of the pertinence of culture and identity to moral conviction:

> A conception of the good normally consists of a more or less determinate scheme of final ends, that is, ends we want to realize for their own sake, as well as of attachments to other persons and loyalties to various groups and associations. These attachments and loyalties give rise to affections and devotions, and therefore the flourishing of the persons and associations who are the objects of these sentiments is also part of our conception of the good. (1985: 233–4)

Political liberalism offers some important food for thought for liberals keen to take seriously the various dilemmas generated by the realization that injustices are rooted deep within the psychic, cultural and socio-economic structures of democratic society. Whether his particular model offers the right kinds of answers to these problems, not least because of the conception of the boundaries of the political that Rawls invoked, is a more contentious question. But, in one respect at least, his position offers a powerful rejoinder to those calling for a fundamental reformation of the liberal tradition in the context of difference and identity. Rawls demonstrated that the establishment of shared political principles is not only integral to the legitimacy of the liberal state but implies agents who have, to some degree, internalized democratic norms, and are capable of deliberating as free and equal citizens. Rawlsian thinking offers some important guidance for a democracy seeking to balance the requirements of reciprocity with the depth and character of diversity. While the kinds of disagreement arising from the politics of identity may deepen the tensions between these imperatives, Rawls rightly observed that many sources of religious, ethnic and cultural difference, though not straightforwardly liberal in their outlook, generate social goods and values that can contribute to the social capital[4] and political agreement that democracy requires.

'Fraternity': nationhood and welfare

Public reason is not the only possible sticking-point in the relationship between identity politics and democratic citizenship. A different problem for democratic theory concerns the motivations behind the practice of citizenship (Tomasi, 2001; Tully, 2000b). Is the readiness of citizens to bear the costs of citizenship – voting, serving on juries, or paying taxes – imperilled if too much of their moral energy is devoted to encompassing groups (Philp, 2000)? And is the social solidarity that citizenship implies compatible with the centripetal pull of particular groups? The idea that identity politics is incompatible with citizenship on these grounds hinges upon established ideas about the cultural and institutional conditions of solidarity in democratic society. For some recent liberal theorists, the primary cultural source of this mutuality is a sense of nationhood, and its leading institutional expression is the welfare state. It is through debates about nationhood and welfare, and specifically the claim that these are endangered by group loyalties, that we find the sources of the familiar idea that the politics of identity is the enemy of social solidarity.

Regarding nationhood, various authors have drawn a pointed contrast between the moral goods associated with nationality and the centripetal and divisive effects of sub-national group affiliation (Miller, 1995a; 1995b). Nationhood is widely viewed as offering a common sense of moral purpose, drawing from a shared cultural background, that encourages groups and individuals to offset their own particular differences and interests for the common good. The politics of identity, it is supposed, is necessarily antithetical to the construction of a viable, liberal nationalism (Tamir, 1993).

Are national loyalties necessarily in tension with other kinds of group affiliation, as this perspective suggests (Miller, 1995a)? When considering the various moral goods that individuals get from communities, why should we privilege the national community above the other kinds of communal affiliation that individuals have in modern societies (Mason, 2000)? There may well be a historical case for suggesting that a shared sense of national identity and culture has been an important precondition for citizenship, yet the experiences of multinational states are important counter-examples to this view. In any case, observing this historical congruity is a different matter to establishing the case for the moral superiority and singularity of nationalist self-identification as opposed to the sense of worth and meaning individuals may get from identifying, for instance, with their own ethnic group (Kymlicka, 1998; Mason, 2000: 115–47).

A source of deep contention in debates about the ethical character of nationalism is whether national boundaries are a necessary condition for achieving a sufficient degree of mutual sympathy for one's fellows (Hutchings and Dannreuther, 1999). A further contentious issue concerns the spatial scale at which legitimate political boundaries are established. Can this happen at the local, regional and global, as well as the national, level (Mason, 2000)? Cosmopolitan liberals question the case for the ethical singularity of the nation, observing the many instances of sentiment and solidarity that individuals feel towards those with whom they do not share nationality, and stressing the contingent, artificial character of the 'contract' that co-members of national communities make (Held, 1995). These contending positions currently sustain an important debate in Anglo-American political philosophy about the possibility and content of a principle of international justice (Caney, 2001; Pogge, 2002). Liberal pluralists, meanwhile, query the model of a singular national culture in democracies that typically contain peoples from varying national backgrounds. An important question arising from these critical perspectives is whether nationalism and citizenship fit together as easily as liberal nationalists suggest (Vincent, 2002). There are some long-standing tensions in liberal thought between the ideals of nationhood and citizenship, with the former often imagined in particularistic vein and the latter typically represented in the terms of universal moral attributes. For this and other reasons, some liberal philosophers suggest that we regard the nation as a contingently devised, historically transient entity, rather than a constitutive condition for ethical life.

Among liberals, the idea that citizenship can be practised at different levels of community has continued throughout the period of national sovereignty (Linklater, 1998; Held, 1995). Such an idea has been given institutional expression as various regional, local and transnational forms of governance have emerged in the last twenty years, with different kinds of moral and social solidarity emergent at each of these levels. Movements and groupings founded upon imposed or unchosen identity, such as feminism, as well as those that arise around transnational elective identities, such as environmentalism, have played an important role in motivating and exemplifying the ethical de-centring of the nation. Some of the communities and movements associated with the politics of identity are also products of the declining legitimacy of political traditions that elevate the nation-state above other levels of political life. These groupings highlight the idea that ethical life arises in different kinds, and at various scales, of community. It is perverse to present identity politics as antithetical to democratic citizenship on nationalist grounds, therefore, when opposition to the conflation of ethical life with the nation is one of the conditions and causes of their emergence.

Arguments about the importance of social solidarity for citizenship often invoke the welfare state as the institutional embodiment of the principle of universal social provision. The politics of collective identity, in the form of the assertiveness of recent social movements, cultural minorities and intellectual assertions of 'difference', has been blamed for undermining the legitimacy of this principle. Alan Wolfe and Ytte Klausen argue that citizens are increasingly reluctant to share resources with their fellow nationals and connect this development with rising awareness of cultural specificity and ethnic diversity (1992). If identity talk becomes too influential, they suggest, there is a real danger of eroding public understandings of the common interests upon which any credible theory of rights and obligations rests: 'For a welfare state to exist, thick conceptions of citizenship are needed, in which individuals feel a sense of obligation to others whose fates are somewhat like their own' (1992: 241). In this formulation, the imperative of social solidarity and the idea of grounding political claims on group identities are diametrical opposites.

But other, equally plausible ways of conceiving the relationships between these values can be suggested. One possibility is that the 'great community' envisaged by the theorists of social citizenship, such as Marshall and Tawney, may actually be renewed and strengthened through the admission of newcomers (Wolfe and Klausen, 1992: 241–2). Another is that the assertion of group particularities may lead to the healthy renegotiation of the 'common culture' of a state. An important normative distinction for liberals in this context is between the ambition of *integrating* newcomers, or the bearers of newly emergent identities, into a social settlement that allocates them equal rights with others, and the project of *assimilating* them to familiar cultural norms (Kymlicka, 1998: 184; Laden, 2001: 189). While integration may well require newcomers to adapt in various respects to the prevailing language, customs and shared social understandings, it does not necessarily require that they renounce their own cultural heritage and may leave considerable scope for self-government and collective autonomy.

Rethinking citizenship and social identity

Integration and assimilation represent different ways of conceiving the relationship between social totality and group particularity, a theme that is integral to the history of European and American liberalism. Hegel's moral and political theorizing is one of many other, broadly liberal, conceptions that avoid the Manichean presentation of the relationship between these imperatives favoured by contemporary theorists. In

Hegelian thinking, the ethical lives of citizens arise from the moral and social relationships established at different levels of society (Avineri, 1972). This idea was modelled in *The Philosophy of Right* (1967) in his tripartite distinction of family, civil society and state. Within the public domains of law and politics, the ethical character of the citizen surpasses the status of the 'civilian' possessed of a variety of civil and legal rights. But the attributes of citizenship are prepared by these other social roles. Citizens are beings who need social spaces and a degree of freedom to develop and deepen various cultural and moral attachments upon which they draw in their lives as citizens. Cultural and moral diversity are not, therefore, the opposites of the political unity pertinent to citizenship. Instead, Hegel suggested a focus upon the question of what kinds of political co-operation are compatible with a healthy play of social and cultural diversity. Returning to his thought, and that of other figures he influenced,[5] offers an important reminder of the different ways of conceiving fraternity and diversity pertinent to democratic liberalism. The notion that social solidarity means the supersession of other, less significant, differences, and the contrary assertion that particularities are more real than, and prior to, forms of political unity, offer limiting frameworks for conceiving the relationship between citizens and their other identities and affiliations. The false idea that one must choose one of these alternatives has led to a neglect of interesting and pertinent liberal alternatives to them both.

A recent strand within Anglophone political theory has sought to develop further such a conception of citizenship, interweaving universalist and particularistic arguments about its properties and practices. Michael Walzer (1995), for instance, maintains that the status and practice of citizenship should be regarded neither through the lens of universal reason nor, as proponents of differentiated citizenship maintain, through the framework of pure particularity (Hutchings, 1999). Citizens are formed in relation to the constitution of particular political communities, and these in turn rely upon, and generate, a flexible, but shared, moral outlook. While liberal states are distinguished by the pattern of rights and protections that they uphold, the meaning and demands of citizenship vary according to the provisional agreements achieved in different states regarding the capabilities, motivations and qualities that it implies (Smith, 1997; Shklar, 1995).

Walzer makes a strong case for the importance of the various social settings in which the attributes of citizenship are learned, highlighting those 'solidarities with different communities and interest groups, and a dimension of radical democracy, in which the practices of citizenship are essentially practices of self-determination' (1995: 116). Such a view is premised on the argument that commonality is forged from the play of social and moral difference in democratic communities. On Walzer's model, citizens are the bearers of dense personal, moral and ideological attributes. They retain a strong stake in adhering to, and negotiating, the constitutive norms of their state. Democratic citizenship, he suggests, is unimaginable without the variety of cultures and density of associational life that undergirds and enables it. But it also requires the quasi-republican emphasis upon the need to encourage citizens to regard this part of their identity by comparison with their other attachments and loyalties, as special and overarching.

Conclusions

Conceptualizing democratic citizenship and the politics of identity as inherently antithetical makes sense only if we neglect the degree to which the latter invokes universalizable norms and understate the social particularities through which citizenship is mediated. Those who interpret identity claims as signs of the insuperable incommensurability of political values tend to regard the kinds of civic unity and commonality associated with democratic citizenship as distorting myths that harbour and promote particular group interests. But the moral implications of the politics of identity can, I have argued, be interpreted rather differently. Its manifestations generate important questions about how far the content of common citizenship should encroach upon the social identities that individuals inhabit, and whether a more inclusive basis for the common culture undergirding citizenship can be generated. Only when read through implausibly strong universalistic or particularistic philosophical frameworks does it make sense to see these groups and forces as inherently opposed to the project of a principled liberal polity. Members of identity groupings have a considerable interest in achieving and sustaining a democratic community that allows all 'reasonable' citizens to take part in the shaping of the cultural and moral patterning of the public domain.

There remain some undoubted tensions between identity-based political arguments and liberal precepts. Some of these might, however, be regarded as productive in kind and conducive to further mutual adjustment, rather than read as illustrations of a deepening value pluralism in democratic societies (Galston, 1999b). Movements and associations founded upon group identity have helped contribute to a realization that there are different ways of being a good citizen and, more contentiously for liberals, that public reason may itself be pluralized. Good citizens, in the wake of the politics of identity, are not only distinguished by their willingness to obey laws, temper their loyalties in the public domain, or contribute to the common stock of social capital and trust. They are also figures who achieve some kind of balance between their commitment to their fellow citizens and an openness to the variety of identities that can shelter under the umbrella of a democratic political community.

4

Civil Society and the Morality of Association

Introduction

Closely associated with the focus upon the civic culture discussed in the previous chapter is a heightened interest among political theorists in democratic virtues. Two particular questions occupy liberal thinkers engaged with this topic. Where are the seedbeds for citizenship and the sources of the renewal of public life to be found? And what can the state legitimately do in order to cultivate civic virtue? A broad consensus is emerging among liberal philosophers that civil society is a vital domain in relation to the problem of democratic renewal (Gutmann, 1998a). Yet, as we shall see, important disagreements arise when these thinkers seek to pinpoint the moral benefits of particular kinds of association. While some democratic theorists are convinced that groupings founded upon social identity are damaging for the civic culture, other heterodox voices suggest that we ought to broaden our understanding of the groups and processes pertinent to the democratic morality of association. This latter argument, I will suggest, is a more promising one for liberals wrestling with current socio-political dilemmas.

The main cause of the re-emergence of civil society in liberal political thought is the sense that the moral goods associated with it have been mistakenly underplayed in democratic thought. This concern is typically framed in relation to a social narrative that suggests that the integrity and role of civil society as sources of political virtue are imperilled by a host of contemporary developments, including the rise of the politics of identity. The renewal of citizenship is thus typically held to rest upon the regeneration of a dense and pluralistic associational culture. And the principles governing the group life of democratic states are widely viewed as threatened by the proliferation of associations founded upon ethnicity, culture, gender and sexuality (Kymlicka, 1998). In this chapter I consider the merits of these claims and ask whether the relationship between democratic citizenship and civil society is quite as straightforward as the first of these arguments implies. I also consider if a distinction can be sustained between the moral effects of different kinds of identity-based association in ways that are pertinent for liberal understandings of civil society.[1]

Digging up the seedbeds of citizenship

Civic education[2]

The state of public morality and the prospects for the civic culture have emerged as central themes for liberal thinkers in the last two decades. Laments about the decline of public *mores*, the aggressive individualism prized within consumer culture, the erosion of family life and the marked diminution of respect for public life were all, in the recent past, staples of conservative discourse. In the last fifteen years, a marked gestalt shift has occurred within the English-speaking political world. Now, liberal commentators are increasingly preoccupied with such trends, leading some to wonder whether liberal democracy can deal with the various threats it faces in an era of global economic power and the turn towards group identity.

Liberal political theory, we have seen, has mirrored these concerns in its renewed concern for the virtues and motivations appropriate to citizenship. This theme has led to the revival of a long-standing interest in various 'seedbeds' for civic virtue (Glendon and Blankenhorn, 1995). William Galston provides a useful distinction between the different liberal projects that this topic has spawned. He distinguishes between those who regard features of liberal society and culture as inimical to citizenship; those who see civic decline as a contingent problem that the liberal state can remedy; and thinkers reluctant to perceive any problem at all (1991; Kahane, 1998). Among proponents of the first and second of these approaches, emphasis has been allotted to the state as educator of the next generation of citizens. Considerable attention has, in particular, been paid to the schoolroom and the possibilities attendant upon civic education in liberal thought (Callan, 1997; Wingrove, 1998; Kymlicka, 2002: 307–8). Underpinning this focus is the assumption that the school represents a unique opportunity to inculcate appropriate dispositions in the populace at large. Educationalists maintain that social responsibility and civic awareness are easier to cultivate earlier in life, and form an indispensable part of the socialization of future citizens (Crick, 2000). A related reason for the common emphasis upon formal civic education is that the school remains one of the few public locations at which nearly all citizens born within its boundaries can be reached.

But we may wonder whether regarding schools as the sole or primary agent responsible for civic education is appropriate. In both the US and

Britain, inequalities affecting the character and quality of educational provision present an important obstacle to the dream of common citizenship that teachers are asked to instil in their pupils. Equally, a profound difficulty facing advocates of citizenship education arises from the task of balancing the substantive moral commitments that citizenship implies with the prevailing stance of neutrality towards the cultural backgrounds, religious beliefs and moral purposes of the children who arrive in classrooms. The stress upon civics within the curriculum of many American public schools is frequently criticized for its institutional focus and 'thin' approach to morality. But when citizenship education strays towards the cultivation of an informed or responsible citizenry, libertarian critics are quick to raise the authoritarian potential of the state sponsorship of virtue. In Britain, a further complication arises from the prevailing constitutional understanding of citizenship as a predominantly legal status (Crick, 2000). This means that citizens are subjects of the crown and are entitled to rights as established in law by parliament. The idea that citizenship amounts to a set of entitlements that are awarded from 'on high' has been challenged by various intellectuals over the last two decades, yet it remains a powerful obstacle to those seeking to promote a culture of democratic citizenship (Charter '88, 1991). While the tension between a 'thick' understanding of civic virtue and freedom of belief need not be insurmountable, there is good reason to see the schoolroom as only one particular means of promoting civic virtue in democratic society: 'We should think about the means of civic education – the project of shaping citizens – in much broader terms than we usually do. Far too much weight has been placed on formal schooling as the means of promoting civic ends' (Macedo, 1990: 277).

Civil society

Other commentators point to a wider array of social arenas pertinent to the cultivation of the arts of citizenship. In so doing, they draw upon long-standing liberal ideas about the ethical benefits of a rich and dense associational life in societies that are fragmented and pluralistic (Benhabib, 2002: 169; Young, 2000). Like citizenship, the concept of civil society has made a comeback in recent years, and is now an integral part of the vocabulary of Anglo-American political philosophy. The idea that civil society is a vital source of the virtues, dispositions and skills that good citizens need in a modern, complex democracy is a time-honoured one within liberalism (Seligman, 1995). In the wake of the debates between liberals and communitarians that held the attention of many political theorists in the 1980s, two different accounts of the social forms prominent within civil society, and of the virtues associated with each, became prevalent. One of these involved emphasis upon voluntarily constituted association, and the other invoked community as both the source of individual moral purpose and an important means of social integration. This bifurcation continues to inform debate about civil society and citizenship in liberal thought. On the one hand, civil society is presented as a realm in which individuals are free, within the rule of law, to choose between various communities, projects and commitments, and to leave these behind when they wish. Association is typically endowed with a highly voluntary character, and advanced in contrast to non-voluntary social forms, such as the family. Communitarians, by contrast, present this as the domain in which the moral sensibility of the individual is shaped by the community, traditions are handed down, and the habits appropriate to citizenship are learned.

This polarity between liberal and communitarian ideas appears increasingly inadequate as a framework with which to approach contemporary social realities. Considering the ethical promise of civil society in relation to current debates, Charles Taylor observes a deeper, and more significant, fissure in democratic thought. The duality he pinpoints plays an important role in shaping expectations and fears about identity-based association (1995a). He identifies, first, a recurrent conviction that civil society and citizenship are symbiotic. Such an idea was present, for instance, in Adam Smith's argument that, in geographically diverse states, citizens learn the moral qualities and habits that were once formed in the Athenian forum through their involvement in associations. But a rival tradition, Taylor notes, presents civil society and democratic politics as rivals. The spontaneous and organic character of the communities that make up society are, on this view, the source of a legitimate political alternative to the corrupt and bureaucratic world of politics.

Both of these normative visions find expression in contemporary debates, grounding and shaping the hope that civil society, not the state or the market, is the *locus* of the public virtues required to sustain a diverse and complex democracy. The idea of a potential complementarity between citizenship and civil society figures prominently in liberal thought, though few theorists have discussed what are the mechanisms that transform the dispositions generated at the level of association to the relationships that pertain within the polity. This idea of complementarity informs the emphasis given to such values as civility that are represented as ethical bridges between the background culture and political system of democratic states. Stress upon this and related qualities – reasonableness, a disposition to compromise and public spiritedness – means that civil society is regarded by many liberals as 'a social structure which establishes constraints on the pursuit of private interests and provides incentives for individual and collective agents to develop habits of civility' (Bauböck, 2000: 98).

The second, dualistic version of civil society and citizenship lingers in the form of accounts that stress the depth and range of the diversity that has developed in civil society. Some revive the 'classical' Anglo-American liberal heritage in this respect. They suggest that freedom of association is an intrinsically valuable condition of a free society, one guaranteed by the existence of an independent civil society protected by a constitutional state (Tamir, 1998).

Differences aside, many liberal political theorists are united in one important respect in their approach to civil society. This arises from the tendency to posit this domain and the market as opposites. For all its superficial proliferation of competition and choice, the unregulated market is increasingly regarded as responsible for flattening out cultural differences and eroding shared values. Civil society, in contrast, is typically presented as the realm of organic social diversity, an invaluable learning ground for the 'habits of the heart' that a civic culture requires (Bellah, 1996). The experiences gained through participation in common enterprises, even those with relatively narrow or non-political goals, are potential sources of moral development and maturation (Glendon, 1995; Walzer, 1998): it is in civil society 'that human character, competence, and capacity for citizenship are formed' (Walzer, 1991: 109).

The decline of civil society?

These distinct ambitions for civil society have influenced some of the leading accounts of its current prospects. Philosophical advocates of the complementarity of citizenship and civil society have leaned heavily for empirical support upon the assertion of the political scientist Robert Putnam that the character of America's associational life has altered fundamentally in the last twenty years (1993). Like him, they see signs of a deep social pathology in the propensity of citizens to form clubs and groups founded upon such factors as ethnic identity: 'In many ways, large and small, millions of Americans have been steadily disengaging from civil society during the past three decades' (Blankenhorn, 1995: 274). All around us, it seems, are indications of a terminal decline of civility and solidarity among citizens. In the US, the number of people who report attending public meetings on town or school affairs is, Putnam reports, down by more than a third since 1973. Voting has fallen 25 per cent since the early 1960s (1995). Membership of parent–teacher associations has declined from twelve million in 1964 to seven million in 1993. 'Virtually the entire panoply of major fraternal, women's, and service organizations – from the Red Cross to the Boy Scouts to the Jaycees to the League of Women voters – has experienced a steady erosion of members and volunteers' (Blankenhorn, 1995: 274). Putnam emphasizes declining participation within those associations long viewed by democratic theorists as potential sources of civic virtue, especially churches, synagogues, trade unions, civic groups, parent–teacher associations and, most famously of all, bowling leagues (1995; 1993). He stresses the simultaneous emergence of organizations, self-help groups and radical religious sects that deplete the stock of social capital.

This narrative provides much of the empirical meat upon the inter-pretative skeleton of current liberal theories of citizenship. For liberal political thinkers, a concern to elaborate the formal requirements of political membership and the correlative obligations of citizens has tended to displace consideration of the sociological dimensions of citi-zenship (Benhabib, 2002). The lack of engagement with social analysis, other than through the questionable thesis of civic decline, has given Putnam's account an authority it may not deserve. Rival perspectives seek to make sense of the changes he observes, and others he ignores, in a rather different fashion. One alternative interpretation points to such trends as the apparent 'personalization' of political life and the rise of 'lifestyle politics' as indicative of a steady detachment of groups of citi-zens from established collective norms and traditions (Inglehart, 1979; 1997). Less mindful of their social 'superiors' and established canons of morality, many citizens, it is suggested, have opted to engage in identity-based forms of self-discovery and action, as well as localized kinds of social involvement, such as community volunteering. They are more inclined to participate in the affairs of their community but less keen to take part in conventional party politics. As bureaucratic and economic power appear to make representative politics increasingly redundant, citizens, it has been suggested, respond by concerning themselves with issues close to their own life circumstances and identities (Mulgan, 1994). W. L. Bennett synthesizes a variety of empirical findings that chal-lenge Putnam's model (1998). This turn from conventional forms of poli-tics may be far more selective and rational 'than implied by accounts of a social and political withdrawal induced by watching too much TV' (1998: 745). In the United States, while there may be a decline in the membership rates of conventional political groups, volunteering contin-ues to rise in numerical significance, and new kinds of network litter the landscape of civil society.

Equally, advocates of the idea that the civic culture is in crisis have paid insufficient attention to distinguishing cause from effect in relation to this trend. Lifestyle, or identity, politics may well represent conse-quences of the growth of 'anti-politics' rather than independent causes in the political culture of particular democracies. Other plausible social explanations of these trends include the erosion of deference and other cultural and moral traditions in societies in which consumer capitalism has broken free of the shackles of the 'mixed economy'. Many commentators reiterate the depth of the insecurity and uncertainty that economic globalization has brought in its wake (Held et al., 1999). As Bennett notes, this is a period in which, for a variety of cultural, economic and technological reasons, citizens tend to regard themselves as increasingly separated from the control and patronage of the politi-cal class, and society at large is 'characterized by the rise of networks, issue associations, and lifestyle coalitions facilitated by the revolution in personalized, point-to-point communication' (1998: 745). Depending on which account of the current societal paradigm one accepts, trends in civic engagement and social activism assume a differential moral significance. Rather than positing an aggregate decline in civic activity, therefore, some commentators point to the gains, as well as losses, that liberal democracies have experienced as the character of collective endeavours in civil society has altered.

Disaggregating the general trends posited by Putnam, on the basis of group specificity, is also instructive. The changing character of associational participation is more apparent among women, who generally have less to gain from the maintenance of established traditions of group activity than their male counterparts. Membership of long-established groups has fallen in the US among women, and volunteering has attracted markedly more female participants in this period. This finding significantly correlates with the expansion of the numbers of women in full-time paid employment in the US (Bennett, 1998: 746–7). Meanwhile J. Eric Oliver (2001) suggests that Putnam's thesis misconstrues the ambiguous character of the relationship between trust and racial identity in the US. His study of political participation across different ethnic communities emphasizes the variable impact of identity upon the civic culture: 'the particular effects of racial segregation on patterns of civic participation do not lend themselves to any simple conclusions' (2001: 131). In ethnic communities that are separate from others, he reports higher levels of certain kinds of civic activism, noticeably among African-Americans, who are more likely to participate in a range of political activities in inverse proportion to the presence, and influence, of whites in their environment: 'Blacks living in predominantly white places report feeling less empowered and less politically interested. Denizens of racially homogenous places seem to be more socially entangled in their communities than people in diverse locales' (2001: 131). An uncomfortable paradox, Oliver suggests, belies the simplistic conception of social capital favoured by Putnam: that 'suburban segregation may benefit American civil society' and, at the same time, weaken its processes of democratic governance.

This emphasis upon the moral ambiguity of social trends in civil society chimes with the thesis of post-materialism. The shift in the character and content of politics predicted by this paradigm – towards a political culture in which the dynamics of lifestyle, quality of life and identity are central – is echoed in other survey analyses. Inglehart suggests that identity politics be seen as part of a shift towards a political culture that is searching for new socio-political forms and institutional filters (1997). In direct opposition to Putnam, Bennett argues that

> The psychological energy (cathexis) people once devoted to the grand political projects of economic integration and nation-building in industrial democracies is now increasingly directed toward personal projects of managing and expressing complex identities in a fragmenting society. The

political attitudes and actions resulting from this emotional work stay much closer to home, and are much less likely to be focused on government. (1998: 755)

While these sceptical responses to Putnam may underplay the challenges facing the practice and motivation of citizenship in liberal democracy, they illustrate the prevalence of alternative plausible interpretations of the changing character of civil society to the gloomy story told by Putnam.

Interpreting civil society

An integral part of the appeal of the notion of civil society, and a source of its interpretative fluidity, is that it is typically used to combine social description and normative argument. The deployment of a contestable thesis of civic decline in combination with distinctive normative arguments about citizenship offers one such example of the interweaving of these elements. For those committed to reordering the priorities of the liberal state, so that it pays more attention to the cultivation of the character of its citizenry, the idea of civil society as a bridge between the world of social interaction and the demands of citizenship is an attractive one. The belief that there are important moral benefits to be gained from such activities as volunteering, charitable work and involvement in the governance of responsible groups is central to a body of literature devoted to the crisis and renewal of democratic citizenship (Gutmann, 1998a). In this context, civil society is loaded with some potent redemptive ambitions (Keane, 1998c). As its potentiality is juxtaposed with the purported reality of civic decline, it has become something of a holy grail for theorists concerned with stemming the decline of citizenship and worried about the legitimacy and stability of liberal democracy.

But liberal aspirations compete in the marketplace of political ideas with other characterizations of civil society. A number of political traditions offer important rival interpretations. Consideration of these offers some revealing critical insights into the merits and weaknesses of liberal ideas. The virtues of civil society are indeed preached by all of the major ideological traditions. Among socialist thinkers and radical activists, a distinctive understanding of civil society has gained ground since the 1980s (Keane, 1988a; 1998b). This suggests that the spontaneity and dynamics of social interaction are primarily shaped by a new wave of social movements. Civil society has been conceived by left pluralists as the domain in which subordinated needs and hidden collective identities have arisen, and in which heterodox values and alternative political projects have emerged, away from the conventions and dominant assumptions of the political system (Scott, 1990). Some New Left intellectuals have (re)turned to the Italian Marxist theorist Antonio Gramsci. Using his ideas, they have elaborated the significance of this kind of subaltern mobilization, seeing in it a potent kind of alternative to the disappointing trajectory pursued by political parties of the left (Bobbio, 1988). According to Stuart Hall, the constitution of a radicalized civil society arises from the failure of the social democratic project. He points to the

> enormous expansion of 'civil society' caused by the diversification of the different social worlds in which men and women can operate . . . Of course 'civil society' is no ideal realm of pure freedom. Its micro-worlds include the multiplication of points of power and conflict. More and more our everyday lives are caught up with these forms of power, and their lines of intersection. Far from there being no resistance to the system, there has been a proliferation of new points of antagonism, new social movements of resistance organized around them, and, consequently, a generalization of 'politics' to spheres which hitherto the left assumed to be apolitical. (1991: 59)

Civil society has come to be seen by various intellectuals as a set of interconnected sites at which groups and individuals develop their communicative potential. This position is especially associated with the ideas of Jürgen Habermas. In various social domains, communicative norms are invoked in contradistinction to the systematic and instrumentalized logics of the political and economic orders (McCarthy, 1978). In an influential development of this position, Jean Cohen and Andrew Arato distinguish between, on the one hand, those forces in civil society that offer defences and sustenance for newly formed collective identities and, on the other, those movements that expand participatory and emancipatory possibilities in a democratic society and generate new kinds of network and social engagement (1992). The idea that social movements are the primary agencies of the expansion of the public sphere is a view held by many critical theorists. This has generated the expectation among movement activists and sympathizers that democracy itself is being deepened and radicalized by movements that spurn conventional modes of operation and challenge liberal norms about what counts as political (Scott, 1990). In more recent times, this vision has mutated into a form of multiculturalism in which a pluralist democracy is constituted by activist-citizens who engage issues arising from their own social locations and proliferate new, contingent kinds of solidarity (Hall, 1991). Many pluralist thinkers share the conviction that civil society is the preferred setting for the pursuit of the good life. This generic idea has emerged in political contexts that have experienced tremendous dislocation in the wake of the free-market policies pursued by right-wing governments in the 1980s, and in which political life appears to have been hollowed out by the twin forces of technocratic expertise and corporate power. As a consequence, considerable intellectual and political energy has been invested in the promotion of civil society as the domain where authentic forms of togetherness and connectedness remain in place, and in which the human propensity for sociability seems unmediated by the powers of bureaucrats, politicians or capitalists.

Among the different insights and challenges that these radical accounts of civil society offer to prevailing liberal approaches is a more developed sense of the economic and cultural obstacles and resources shaping the networks forged within it. Associational activity reflects the prevailing balance of social forces and the marked asymmetry in standing between social groupings that consumer capitalist society generates. In the face of such arguments, the liberal idealization of civil association as a domain of freedom and an unmediated source of egalitarian citizenship appears to lack a normative edge in relation to current inequalities of wealth and power (Keane, 1998c). Other critics highlight generic ambiguities in both liberal and emancipatory readings of civil society. By positing family life and the market as the opposites of 'the lifeworld', they neglect the insights of some of the major theorists of modern civil society – Smith, Hegel and Marx especially – into the moral significance of these other domains of social life. Civil society represents a more contestable and ambivalent social entity and normative value than current liberal usages suggest (Fine, 1997). In particular, while liberal political thought has focused in the last twenty years on the contest between individualist and communitarian accounts of civil society, social and political changes may well have overtaken both of these alternatives. When these thinkers do attend to the social character of contemporary developments, they reveal a mixture of anxiety and unfamiliarity. To borrow Michael Walzer's paraphrase of Hegel, the realm of fragmentation has never appeared quite so fragmented (1995: 2). To some minds, the prospects for any kind of ethico-political unity appears to be receding beneath the tides of group tribalism.

Nor are such concerns unique to the United States. In Britain, though equivalent social movements may not have been as successful or as prominent, they have had a considerable impact upon public discourse. They have also bequeathed a host of groups, cultural initiatives and associations that are now a familiar part of the social landscape. With the prominence of multiculturalist themes in political life, and widespread public anxieties about the status and character of Islam, British commentators have also taken to lamenting the prospects for indigenous civil society (Gray, 1995a).

Charting civil decline

As a result of these deepening anxieties, the idea that civil society is in crisis and needs renewal has become a familiar refrain (Barber, 1998). As Walzer observes:

> Publicists and preachers warn us of a steady attenuation of everyday co-operation and civic friendship. . . . Our cities really are noisier and

nastier than they once were. Familial solidarity, mutual assistance, political like-mindedness – all these are less certain and less substantial than they once were. . . . The Hobbesian account of society is more persuasive than it once was. (1995: 8)

Attention has thus been directed towards those forces and trends deemed responsible for undermining the civility and social cohesion that democracies require. Among the various parties blamed for the current situation are identity-based communities that violate the principle of free association, diminish the prospects of appeals to public reason and, as a consequence, encourage political demands that erode the stock of civility (Elshtain, 1995). Identity groupings are criticized too for the political logic they impart to their members. Christopher Hitchens's attack upon the language of 'political correctness' articulates this kind of anxiety: 'The real tendency of PC is not to inculcate respect for the marvellous variety of humanity but to reduce each group into subgroups and finally to atoms, so that everyone is on their guard against everyone else' (1993: 562). Identity politics represents a blockage to the pluralistic patterning of social life, restricting its members' incentives and opportunities for cultural innovation and experimentation: 'People are more likely to have some basis for understanding and empathizing with others in societies where they inhabit crosscutting and overlapping roles' (Rosenblum, 1998a: 16). A political culture in which groupings reflect, rather than transcend, cleavages of race, class, gender and sexuality gives undue prominence to apparently ineradicable differences.

These concerns are by no means novel. They were prefigured by earlier liberals' worries about the encompassing identities associated with the cultural politics of nationalism, at least in its vulgar forms, by the appearance of powerful new social movements, especially the labour movement, and the demands of religious organizations upon their members. Concerned at the persistence and appearance of these communities within the heart of civil society, liberal individualists have tended to stress the merits of associations that reflect the complex and shifting dynamics of separation from, and contingent attachment to, one's fellows. This kind of argument is often enabled by a highly selective presentation of the liberal political tradition, in which theorists and schools that stress the social and ethical values of the communities to which citizens belong are removed from view.

Communitarian liberals are in fact equally concerned about these new threats to the integrity of the civic culture of democratic society, and have launched some of the most powerful attacks upon the politics of identity on this basis. Alan Wolfe argues that identity politics is intrinsically harmful to the ecology of civil society (1991: 257). Modern polities generate ineradicable moral dilemmas for citizens. On the one hand, they erode the power of some of the familiar sources of moral and religious belief. But they simultaneously require increasingly individualistic persons to establish commonly acceptable rules of moral conduct and observe obligations to fellows to whom they are strangers. The historical and moral achievement of civil society, therefore, is to broaden our appreciation for, and diminish our suspicion of, our co-citizens. Political claims rooted in collective identity threaten the ecological balance achieved in pluralistic societies and disrupt the natural moral development of citizens. By spurning the language of common political membership in favour of the myth that one's membership of certain groups is a matter of destiny, these social forces teach participants that their duties lie primarily towards those who share their ascriptive designation (Wolfe and Klausen, 2000).

Jean Elshtain advances an even more scathing attack along these lines (1995). Her passionate polemic against the intrusion of identity politics in the American public sphere begins with an emotive analogy between the now waning Soviet threat and the rise of a new enemy within the body politic. She articulates the anxiety felt by many intellectuals that Americans are increasingly prone to see themselves as the inhabitants of separate cultural enclaves, and that they are encouraged to engage with the world outside from within the 'cages' of group identity. As this discourse insinuates its way into the minds of citizens, the suspicion arises that the members of a large national society may have less in common than has been traditionally thought. Identity politics gives vent to a new 'language of opposition', a vernacular of angry demands and absolutist rights, and a 'cascading series of manifestoes' (1995: xii). Recuperation of the virtue of civil society, Elshtain suggests, is the best response to these threats, the main hope upon which the democratic future depends. Healthy forms of civic activism involve open-ended encounters with others, permitting the exchange of ideas and mutual understanding that provides the fabric of a democratic society. It is in these kinds of civil interactions that the skills needed to keep a democracy afloat are learned, notably how to resolve and mediate moral and political differences in an atmosphere of mutual restraint, and the ethos of working with others towards common ends (1995: 2).

New Left advocates of civil society are, likewise, alert to the deficiencies and dangers of identity politics rather than, as their critics claim, unthinking advocates of it (Rajchman, 1995). A widespread contrast is drawn between some of the more culturally conservative manifestations of collective identity and the fluidity and reflexivity that are seen as paradigmatic of contemporary forms of social identity. And conservative intellectuals have also maintained that the crisis of civil society and the rise of identity are linked. Neo-conservative authors in the United States blame such forces as the women's movement for the toleration of non-conventional lifestyles and values (Bellah, 1996). These, it is suggested, are an important cause of the erosion of some of the traditions that sustained coherent national cultures.

This near ideological unanimity about the civic dysfunctions associated with the politics of identity has helped frame the forces and claims associated with it as primary causes of current social ills (Slawner, 1998). The latter include the purported decline of vital moral goods – trust and reciprocity, public spiritedness, civic activism, and respect for politics and public life. Identity politics is often presented as a symptom and consequence of the colonization of social life by the tyranny of either the overbearing state or the overly powerful market. In his powerful societal critique, Christopher Lasch took as a central target the rise of various forms of identity-orientated political argument (1979). These constitute disparate manifestations of a powerful narcissism afflicting the American psyche. Other commentators draw a critical parallel between the marketization of social life and the emergence of forms of politics that promote the immediate gratification of group personages (Worpole, 2001). Formations that encourage a kind of collective egotism can be seen as functional equivalents to the powerful ideal-type of the self-orientated consumer.

A different kind of objection, though one still based upon liberal premises, suggests that demands for the acceptance of unique social identities are the source of a new form of social conservatism. Sheldon Wolin, for example, detects an important paradox at the heart of the politics of group recognition (1993). Its uncompromising language and the deep sense of hurt it expresses rest upon a foundational premise that the political conversation it postulates – between the group demanding recognition and the agency required to grant it – is not one between equals. The desire to be recognized assumes a benevolent state authority capable of intervening within social life to provide the kinds of remedy and support that are demanded. Identity politics deflects citizens from the importance of developing attachments and shared interests with their fellows. Instead, it encourages them to cast their eyes towards the potentially munificent state, and to react angrily when, like the Oedipal parent, this does not provide what is sought.

Given that disagreement is a hallmark of political theorizing in democracies, it is all the more striking when a consensus of this sort – one that stretches from sociologists across to political philosophers, and from the New Left to neo-conservatism – becomes established. The idea that civil society is in decline is often taken as the assumed basis from which learned articles and academic books on this topic begin, rather than a claim that may require examination and defence.

Beyond civic decline: the dilemma of congruence

In order to understand the appeal of the thesis of the decline of the civic culture, it is worth observing the continuing influence of the ideas of

Alexis de Tocqueville (Kohn, 2002). His emphasis upon the role of voluntary associations in generating an ethos of social co-operation and freedom – unique, he believed, to the United States – continues to shape contemporary accounts of civil society (Warren, 2001). Thomas Kohler observes how this view feeds prevailing cultural self-understandings: 'Americans love to refer to Tocqueville's characterization of the United States as a nation of joiners. It fits with our image of ourselves as a self-reliant, can-do people to whom the world turns for lessons about democratic self-rule' (1995: 142–3). De Tocqueville's impact on later democratic thought is apparent not only from his emphasis upon the American propensity for forming groups, but also in his assertion that civic activism naturally spills over into virtuous citizenship. Communities and associations, he believed, are important sources of moral education (Macedo, 1990: 39).

A number of contemporary liberal philosophical arguments about the democratic potential of civil society operate within de Tocqueville's paradigm. The golden age posited in much of this literature is the mid-nineteenth century, the era of the 'rush into clubs' (predominantly churches, unions and lodges) (Rosenblum, 1998a: 100). But, as various historians have shown, this represents a very particular moment within the development of American state and society. Nancy Rosenblum rightly reminds us of the variety of motivations and social dynamics attendant upon association in this earlier era and later (1998a: 100). Contemporary theorists (unlike de Tocqueville) tend to avert their gaze from these in their enthusiastic idealization of this particular golden age. They overlook, in particular, associations that reflect the desire to cut oneself off from, and keep out, undesirable others, as well as the impulse of snobbery and the protection of status. Some of the traits that democratic theorists find most worrying about the politics of identity are in fact long-standing attributes of voluntary groups. The growing recognition of these attributes generates something of a paradox in the literature on association and democracy. Groups that are often exclusionary and hierarchical are nevertheless viewed as an essential ingredient of a liberal democratic polity (Kohn, 2002: 290).

Whether de Tocqueville's notion of the spill-over of civic activism into political life remains plausible is an important question for contemporary liberal political thought. Confident pronouncements about the instrumental value of associational activity for the civic culture in fact reflect only one part of the liberal heritage. As Rosenblum demonstrates, this Tocquevillian idea represents one among various responses that liberals have given to some of the pressing normative questions posed by the existence of liberal democratic polities (1998b). To what degree does a liberal political and legal order require that its citizens mirror its public values in their everyday lives (Galston, 1999a: 869–72)? And what kind of congruity between the public and private domains of life is necessary for a flourishing liberal polity? A second, alternative tradition of theorizing the state–society relationship ought to be brought to the foreground in contemporary liberalism. Here, a greater sense of 'incongruity' is prized. It is the state's role, this view suggests, to provide public protection for the liberties that exist within the social domain, but not to interfere with the lives of citizens beyond what its core moral purposes – maintaining peace, arbitrating disputes, and providing public goods – require. A fertile paradox is integral to this vision of liberalism, in which the individual is seen as free to live as she wishes, within the restraints of the law, often pursuing goals and holding beliefs that are contrary to the spirit of the liberal order.

This alternative liberal perspective presents the freedom to associate as an important secondary liberty arising from the inviolable rights to free speech, conscience and movement. These liberals doubt whether the democratic state can go so far as to shape the character of its citizens by promoting certain kinds of groups and associational activities. Their worry is that 'constitutional democracy suffers when people are legally compelled to become ever more constitutional and democratic in their private relationships and transactions' (Kateb, 1998: 61).

The tension between these two perspectives is pervasive and historically long-standing within Anglo-American liberalism. The current preference of many citizens for non-liberal forms of association has brought it back to the surface of political thought. In normative terms, liberals need to give careful consideration to what they hope for, and expect from, civil society. Applied in contexts where both state and civil society are more internally complex and interwoven, Tocquevillian ideas may well be misleading. They have helped sustain what Rosenblum terms a 'hazy undertheorized conception of the relationships between civil society and democratic citizenship, seeming to suggest that participation in that sector is necessarily democratic' (1998a: 88). By contrast, the second 'classical' liberal emphasis merits reconsideration in relation to contemporary circumstances for two reasons. First, it reminds liberals that one of the main goals of a specifically liberal democracy is to enable the peaceful co-existence of subjects who are in various ways radically different to one another. In this respect, seeking to 'make' egalitarian, democratic citizens runs counter to one of the core ethics of a specifically liberal state. And, second, while a liberal democracy does need to be concerned *to some degree* with the moral disposition of its citizens, the latter can be usefully approached in a more pluralistic vein than republican-influenced liberalism suggests. Concern for the moral disposition of citizens may, for instance, be compatible not only with associations that pursue broadly liberal purposes and are internally democratic (bodies that are in the minority in civil society), but with a range of non-liberal associations and groupings in which various skills and dispositions are fostered and an ethical life developed. Mark Warren's exhaustive account of the 'public sphere effects' of different kinds of association develops this kind of enquiry (2001). He suggests that

'voluntary groups that can maintain homogeneity are most suited to pro-
ducing certain democratic effects.' They are able to 'resist dominant
powers, represent difference, and build a sense of efficacy' (Kohn, 2002:
291).

This shift of attention among some liberal theorists towards a closer
engagement with the moral character of different kinds of group and
community arises from a recognition of the limitations of the idea that
voluntary association necessarily benefits democracy. It also paves the
way for a reconsideration of the ethical character of identity-based association. If Rosenblum is right that a broader range of associations than
liberals imagine generate democratic effects, is it appropriate to exclude
identity groups and movements from these? And, if non-liberal groups
can have beneficial democratic outcomes for some participants, how
should a democratic state relate to them?

These questions are central to some of the hard cases facing law-
makers and constitutional interpreters in this area. They arise, for
instance, in controversies about whether states in the US should support
religious groups that provide social services to their congregations, and
in Britain about the implications of 'faith schools' in the state educational sector. They have also been the subjects of landmark Supreme
Court rulings. On the whole, the court has been reluctant to constrain
associational autonomy, but it has acknowledged a powerful public interest in cases where a grouping appears to violate the civil rights of
members, and sometimes non-members (Gutmann, 1998b). One touchstone case concerns the court's decision in the case brought against the
Jaycees of Minnesota. This arose from the practice of excluding women
from full membership of a Junior Chamber of Commerce (the Jaycees)
in Minnesota. This organization's Department of Human Rights ruled in
favour of the St Paul and Minneapolis chapter's decision to break with
its constitution and admit women as full members (Rosenblum, 1998b;
Tamir, 1998). The court found for the Minneapolis chapter and, in the
widely cited justification provided by Justice Brennan, offered an important moral distinction between associations with purposes that are
private in kind and those that are public in their rationale and aims,
and therefore amenable to wider political norms (Gutmann, 1998b). A
further significant moral distinction reflected in the majority judgement
is between the preaching and practice of discrimination. Associations
that, for instance, declare themselves averse to female equality are per-
mitted to proclaim this goal openly and peacefully. But if an all-male
organization that constitutes a gateway to economic and social opportunity, such as a business organization, practises institutional sexism,
then the state may legitimately curb its autonomy and require that it
observe egalitarian norms.[3]

Some liberal theorists have defended this judgement as a sound basis
upon which to justify state intervention within civil society – the imposition of 'compelled association', as Rosenblum puts it (1998b). But
others, as we saw above, worry about the implicit reliance upon the ideal

of congruence between state and society. Galston raises the question of whether it is really necessary that 'civil associations mirror the constitutional order if they are to sustain that order' (1999a: 869). A range of moral goods can be generated by associations that do not pursue liberal purposes – including the exercise of the liberty of individuals within them and the value of exploring personal and collective identity. Equally, different kinds of community can serve to integrate other kinds of people into a social order. Galston's primary concern is with churches and religious organizations, and the raw deal these have had from liberal theorists who fail to see that the adoption of secular public norms represents a contentious and partisan moral position. Religious groups typically regarded as beyond the pale of liberal tolerance may well be engaged as possible sources of moral sustenance for a liberal polity (1991). Similarly, in their widely influential study of the political cultures of various democratic states, Gabriel Almond and Sidney Verba highlight ways in which involvement in religious groupings enhanced members' capacities for civic virtue (1963). Without abandoning their central normative commitments to toleration and equality, in particular, liberals are justified in adopting a far less censorious approach to religious and other kinds of groups than contemporary philosophers tend to stipulate. There is, then, a strong case for taking religion seriously on the basis of the principles of equal capability and self-respect highlighted in the previous chapter (Nussbaum, 1999; 2000b). Individuals require a measure of self-respect so that they are able to take seriously the moral beliefs that they hold, and so that they are motivated to pursue these. Given the importance of religious traditions as the sources of coherent and widely held moral perspectives, liberals ought to curb their desire to exclude religious argument from the political sphere.

The troublesome place of religious belief in liberal democracy provides one indication of the tendency of Kantian-inspired philosophy to exclude from the public domain morally valuable forms of social practice and, in Rawlsian terms, reasonable comprehensive beliefs. These theorists conceptualize the principles underpinning democratic citizenship as separable from, and prior to, contingent social attachments and forms of belonging. In contrast, Martha Nussbaum and Galston advocate the idea of some overlap between the civic activism undertaken by some religious and women's groups and the liberal order, but both rightly warn against the project of 'maximum feasible accommodation' between state and civil society (Galston, 1999a: 875). This means that, in a liberal society, those who adhere to its constitutive norms must learn to tolerate some practices and values that they may find deeply offensive. Rosenblum agrees that congruence between the public culture and associational life is not a necessary goal of a liberal society, and that this may mean accepting the exclusionary policies of, for instance, churches, fraternities and country clubs, as long as these do not interfere with others' basic liberties and opportunities (1998a: 16; 1994a).

Despite their differences, it is clear that these different theorists of associational life share the Kantian goal of establishing a principled understanding of the ideal relationship between state and society that implies an ultimately non-contentious account of the norms of democratic citizenship. But such an approach may not necessarily represent the most appropriate liberal position. Establishing moral principles governing this relationship beyond the contingencies of political deliberation and judgement means that these commentators draw upon various kinds of comprehensive moral theory that are both controversial and unacceptable to others (de Marneffe, 1998). Rosenblum, for instance, invokes the consideration of social and political stability as an important benchmark guiding the state's dealings with groups (1994a; 1998a). While she argues that the state should restrain its urges to intervene in civil society, a liberal government, she maintains, may well need to intervene to discourage, regulate or ban illiberal groups that threaten the stability of the regime. But even stability is not as straightforward and non-contentious a condition as this may suggest (Gutmann, 1998b: 19). Activities and cultures that will generate violent challenges to the social order are clearly outlawed by this consideration. But what of those that may indirectly threaten the stability of a liberal regime – for instance, the preaching of inveterate hostility to Western society by radical Islamists in Britain? And how to handle cases where stability clashes with the principles of justice, in the case, for instance, of groups that demand that their members recall the experiences of oppression when this may alienate them from the current political regime? And what of the demand that a multicultural syllabus requires that students be taught about the colonial and oppressive actions of a given state? Might this lead to an unacceptable level of disillusion with the current polity? These are necessarily difficult issues, and their resolution may well require engagement with the particular circumstances and deliberative contexts in which they are raised. Much hangs on what is taken to be the guarantor of stability in a given society, and how its laws determine danger and threat. Balancing the burden of state interference with the right of citizens to associational autonomy is an unavoidable task facing liberal institutions and public authorities. And it is one that necessarily involves a disposition to trade off rival values – freedom of speech and the security of the polity, most obviously. Even a value such as stability remains subject to partisan debate in deeply differentiated societies, rather than representing an impartial vantage-point from which decisions about groups can be non-contentiously reached.

The civic effects of identity politics

The roots of prevailing notions of identity politics as alien and threatening to a liberal social order lie, I have suggested, in some influential normative accounts of civil society. Some of these arguments have, in recent years, come under sustained attack in ways that are pertinent for the reinterpretation of the diversity that characterizes democratic society. One important source of theoretical revision arises from the assessment of the democratic potential of associations offered by Rosenblum (1998a) and Warren (2001). Another is located in the arguments of pluralists who question the merits of both republican and liberal individualist theories of civil society. In so doing, they point towards the importance of non-voluntary association for a democratic society.

This latter position is given expression in the influential 'civil society argument' outlined by Walzer (1995). He suggests that adherence to the merits of civil society in the last twenty years is a political and intellectual response to the disappointment and disillusion released as various 'modernist' political projects – including socialism, republicanism, neo-liberalism and nationalism – have failed to take hold in democratic political life. These different ideologies sought to establish a distinctive location and agency for 'the good life' in the guise of the solidarity of the working class, the exercise of the general will, the triumph of the market, or the power of the nation. With the discrediting of these projects, the notion of civil society as the site of the good has increased in appeal, and a more pluralistic moral outlook has been legitimated. In civil society, 'all are included, none is preferred' (Walzer, 1995: 164). A vibrant and dense civil life acts as a bulwark against the ambitious projects developed around class, citizenship, market or nationhood. Although the identities generated within civil society – 'part-time union-officers, movement activists, party regulars, consumer advocates, welfare volunteers, church members, family heads' (1995: 164) – stand outside the republic of virtue cherished by liberal philosophy, ordinary citizens learn to live partially virtuous lives, and balance the moral obligations of citizenship with the benefits and dispositions gained in their associational involvements. Walzer points to the pluralistic conception of civic virtue that civil society engenders, as opposed to the rationalist desire to delineate a quantum of virtue that all citizens require. We should expect ordinary citizens to take different kinds of moral lesson from civic involvement. Walzer, therefore, rejects the notion of radical incongruity between state and society as well as the polar opposite view – that civil society should respect democratic norms. Civil society is sufficiently democratic

> when in some, at least, of its parts we are able to recognize ourselves as authoritative and responsible participants. . . . Civil society is tested by its capacity to produce citizens whose interests, at least sometimes, reach further than themselves and their comrades, who look after the political community that fosters and protects the associational networks. (1995: 171)

Though conventionally regarded as a critic of liberalism, Walzer here points the way towards a more convincing position for liberals on these issues, particularly through his scepticism towards the notion that civic activism necessarily spills over into virtuous citizenship. While a relationship should, and does, exist between both, a state that relates to civil society primarily through the imperative of civic virtue is in danger of eroding the grounds for individual freedom. Walzer's focus upon the complex of needs, interests and identities produced and negotiated within associational life supports a view of citizens who are (potentially) capable of managing the various loyalties and affiliations that membership of multiple groups implies in modern society. Such a conception can be usefully contrasted with the 'classical' liberal idea that state and society are fixed in relations of mutual antithesis, and the republican ideal in which the various affiliations and loyalties that constitute a person's ends are deemed secondary to the overbearing demands of citizenship.

This argument is promising for liberals contemplating the political ethics of movements and claims arising from social identity. Walzer appropriates the insights of earlier generations of social liberals into the various group attachments that shape and obstruct the formation of individuality. Thus, John Stuart Mill saw no logical problem in postulating individuals who have strong and deep communal attachments as well as loyalty to their fellow citizens; and for Thomas Hill Green, social action was made meaningful in relation to the particular ethical goods that communities and groups supplied. Contemporary thinkers such as Galston (1991) and Joseph Raz (1986) have renewed this argument, pressing for a heterogeneous public domain that encompasses the many different cultures and lifestyles that possess moral value. In Galston's case, public norms and laws should reflect and protect a minimal conception of the human good, but the public domain ought to be open to those forms of reasonable flourishing that lie beyond this baseline (1999a: 892–5).

Different challenges to the claims that associational activity leads to democracy, and that civic activism spills over into political virtue, have emerged in recent political theory. Empirical research reinforces the view that the relationship between associational involvements and democratic life should be regarded as open-ended and ambiguous. Remarkably few groups, including many of those that adhere to broadly liberal goals, function as schools of democracy, not least because the effects of distance and technology and the imperative of efficiency mean that democratic internal relations are often counter-productive (Tamir, 1998).

Self-respect

Are there any generic civic virtues that liberals should promote on the grounds of the needs of democratic citizenship? As opposed to both the 'thick' virtues that neo-republicans wish to promote and the civic indifference that some forms of classical liberalism imply, the approach to citizenship suggested here promotes two particular values within civil life – self-respect and civility. Both of these principles are sufficiently elastic to incorporate some of the groups and movements associated with politicized identity. Self-worth has been much debated by political theorists in the context of Rawls's influential discussion of 'the social bases of self-respect'. In his model of the stages of moral development of the citizen, he placed considerable emphasis upon the morality learned in association (1993: 163). Ties of fellow feeling and trust are generated and strengthened, he argued, through participation in a variety of social roles, as well as by learning that others are doing their fair share in a given social enterprise. Moral development hinges crucially upon the existence of a plurality of overlapping and complex memberships in various collective ventures. These expose individuals to different moral ideals and make competing demands upon their loyalty and energy. As our roles within such groups become relatively complex, our experience of the benefits and character of social co-operation deepens. Individuals' capacities to appreciate the values of co-operation at the societal level are thus crucially prepared in the crucible of association (Rosenblum, 1998b: 97–8). As the lessons of co-operation develop, so does the individual's sense of confidence about their own particular beliefs. An important part of the experience of association is to see one's talent and contribution given recognition in the eyes of others. From such experiences our sense of self-reliance and worth grows. Somewhat contentiously, Rawls posited a link between the positive benefits of association and the individual's willingness to bear the costs of social and political co-operation at a societal level.

Not all democrats are convinced that self-respect is this central to the morality of association. Conceptualizing self-respect as a universal human requirement appears to clash with the variety of human needs and aspects of individual psychology. Rawls's account of self-respect, however, offers a valuable riposte to this objection. Based upon a recognition of this diversity within human character, he offered a minimalist conception of the social forms appropriate to self-respect, resting his idea upon an argument about the need for a 'secure sense of our own value, a firm conviction that our determinate conception of the good is worth carrying out. Without self-respect nothing may seem worth doing, and if some things have value for us, we lack the will to pursue them' (1993: 92). Self-respect, on this view, amounts to a basic sense that the goals we pursue are of some worth, and that the expenditure of effort upon them is likely to be worthwhile. In these minimally stated terms, self-respect may well arise from very different kinds of cultural condition and group setting.

If the capacity for self-respect is, as Rawls and other liberals claim, a primary human good, then it follows that democratic states need to pay attention to the social conditions in which this value is fostered and hampered (1993: 82, 106). While it may not follow that self-respecting individuals make good citizens, Rawls plausibly argued that, without a healthy sense of self-worth, moral goals are hard to develop. An important condition of self-respect is met when we regard ourselves as holders of rights and as subjects with duties, but, he argued, we also require a degree of internal confidence to act as purposive agents.[4] 'Individuals need some place where their values and opinions are affirmed, their contributions acknowledged, where the likelihood of failure is reduced and they find support against lurking self-doubt' (Rosenblum, 1998a: 97). While Rosenblum emphasizes the importance of participation as a condition for the growth of self-respect, Rawls's account points towards a less demanding standard – the process of identifying with a group in which an important part of one's self is given some validation. A variety of social groupings and associations appear able to satisfy such conditions, contributing to the self-worth of participants and sympathizers. This idea is powerfully reiterated by Nussbaum (2000b). She urges liberals to engage with a greater variety of communities and moral perspectives that matter to citizens in liberal democracy, offering an important counter-weight to the Kantian tendency to exclude from ethical consideration organizations and groups that relate to ascriptive identities. The liberal principle of moral equality implies that individuals be accorded a measure of respect when they pursue their moral, spiritual or cultural goals, as long as they do so in ways that conform with the wider tenets of reasonableness. Given that many of these goals arise from groupings that partially shape individuals' sense of identity and moral purpose, her arguments suggest that respect may well be due to persons who constitute themselves as social agents deploying the resources and narratives of social identity.

Civility

The second liberal value that is integral to a liberal account of civil society, and is pertinent to identity-based mobilization in particular, is civility. This theme carries an important liberal heritage, and was central to the accounts of civil society developed by figures such as Montesquieu, Smith and Hume. In contemporary debate, it has been used as an ideological stick with which to beat identity groupings and presented as one of the foremost casualties of the culture wars of the 1990s (Gitlin, 1995). Such a view is challenged by a different, more nuanced, account of the relationship between democratic norms, civility and identity-based mobilization (Kingwell, 1995).

An important consequence of a democratic culture in which civility is valued is a willingness to inhabit the public domain alongside those whose beliefs and values are different, and to treat others with the presumption that they are one's moral equals. Feminist arguments for the equal treatment of women in the workplace typically invoke the principle of non-discrimination against various kinds of unjust practice. But they also imply the norm of 'civility' – that women should be treated with a certain kind of respect and presumption of equal worth in terms of the background culture and everyday interactions that shape working life (Nussbaum, 2000b). This idea of civility is closely related to the notion that, in mass democracies, the confidence and sense of self-worth that is a breeding ground for civic friendship are learned from involvement in secondary associations. Our sense of worth is conditioned in part by the kinds of interactions we have with others. The more successful and mutually appreciative these are, the more we learn the value of treating others who are different to ourselves, and being ourselves treated, with civility. Self-esteem, for Rawls, implied the acquisition and exercise of two key skills pertinent to civility: the capacity to acknowledge difference and the ability to feel empathy for others (McKinnon, 2000).

Again, the thin understanding of this value in Rawls's account needs emphasis. The norm of civility does not in itself require that citizens possess particularly virtuous dispositions or suspend their own interests and beliefs for the greater good. It arises from the readiness of reasonable and rational individuals to treat others with a presumption of respect. Presented in this way, this too is a value consonant with a variety of social and cultural differences and purposes. Civility, as in the example of feminist demands for equality, is both the analogue of non-discrimination and a normative condition for compliance to the latter (Banfield, 1992b: xii): 'since whether people have genuinely equal opportunities depends not only on government actions, but also on the actions of institutions within civil society – corporations, schools, stores, landlords, and so forth' (Kymlicka, 1998: 188). Some of the social movements that have developed on the basis of excluded or repressed identities during the last thirty years have exercised a major impact by revealing the consequences and character of profound kinds of incivility – to blacks, women, gays and the disabled, for example. The educative dimension of these social movements has been important to the formulation of legal codes and development of public norms regarding uncivil behaviour and culture in workplaces, private clubs and public places. The dissemination of these ideas across the institutions and organizations of both state and society perhaps represents the most important impact that movements of collective identity have exerted. Their consequences undoubtedly remain the subject of considerable political controversy. As this norm has been disseminated across a range of social domains, the state – in its legal and bureaucratic guises – has become a presence in realms traditionally conceived as beyond its reach: in the bedroom, the corporation and the club. The practice of democratic civility has underpinned a major redrawing of the boundaries between public authority and society in many democracies, as citizens are taught that they 'must learn to interact in everyday settings on an equal basis with people for whom they might harbor prejudice' (Kymlicka, 1998: 189).

Richard Rorty, similarly, highlights how the slow and painful struggle to extend civil treatment to blacks, native Americans and gays in the last forty years has partially helped stem the tides of bigotry and cultural sadism once routinely expressed towards their members (1998). In societies increasingly conscious of their deep divisions, social movements based upon identity have played an important role in legitimating an expansive conception of democratic civility. As the idea that it is the duty of the state and various other responsible authorities to enforce democratic civility has spread, these notions have encountered fierce resistance from libertarians of both left and right, and they have created a new set of legal and moral dilemmas for the democratic state.

Conclusions

The search for the various seedbeds pertinent to the renewal of democratic citizenship needs to adopt a multiple focus. It should incorporate a democratic society's political culture, its institutional norms, the content of its schools' curriculum, the quality and calibre of its associational culture, and the kinds of social and personal interactions this fosters and prevents. The presumption of many political theorists that the sources of citizenship must lie beyond the world of politics has stemmed from an overly romanticized picture of the democratic potential of associations (Rosenblum, 1998a; Warren, 2001). On the other hand, arguments about the rights and duties of citizens that neglect the history, character and cultures of civil society are incapable of grasping the deep cultural roots in which citizenship as a set of social practices, as well as legal relations, has grown. This kind of formalistic approach to citizenship favoured by deontological philosophy neglects the moral dispositions and social attributes that citizens gain from the various kinds of collaborative enterprise in which they are socially engaged. The skills that they need are unlikely to be imparted solely by schoolteachers or the benevolent state.

Debates about the character and content of citizenship have taken on a new urgency in the wake of various challenges to the integrity of democratic political life in the last twenty years. One of these arises from the demands made by movements and communities that draw upon the language of unique group personality. In response, liberal philosophy has relied upon principled accounts of the integrity and specificity of the political and legal domains. Rawls, in particular, provided an important justification for the idea that deeply contentious viewpoints should be kept out of political life, especially when its foundational constitutional and legal ideals are at issue. But the ambition to de-politicize these issues is, I suggested in chapter 3, self-defeating. There are no obviously non-contentious moral ideals to which we can retreat in making these judgements.

Any democracy that is broadly liberal in kind is likely to rely upon the idea of legally enforceable rights and liberties, and will thus have to draw upon some moral and legal principles regarding controversies arising from the character of non-liberal minority cultural practices. But if these problems are approached from the vantage-point of democratic citizenship, the mere elaboration of moral and legal principles may not be enough. A liberal democratic society needs to promote a sufficiency of the values of civility and self-respect, and these are, to an important degree, promoted within civil associations and group life. Consideration of the various motivational sources of and blockages to citizenship, viewed as a set of both social practices and moral obligations, requires some engagement with the trends and character of the political culture of particular democracies, as well as consideration of the social contexts in which citizenship is learned and embedded. The studies offered by Rosenblum and Warren illustrate the limitations of overarching general-izations about the many different kinds of democratic effect and dys-function that groups can generate. An important normative implication of their arguments is that political theorists ought to attend to the complex, micro-level ways in which citizens learn to balance different pulls upon their loyalty. We know far too little about which sorts of group involvements, and what sorts of associational conditions, enable the kind of moral learning that Rawls postulated.

The question of how to establish horizontal communities of meaning and solidarity that cut across locality and social cleavage is a vital one for the political theory of modern citizenship. It may well be the case, as both republican and liberal critics have argued, that the public-sphere effects of the militant rhetoric of exclusive identity can be damaging. But such developments are offset by social and cultural trends that have expanded the opportunities for individual self-development through social participation, and have generated a broad, though not unanimous, social consensus in favour of the idea that democratic civility should be respected in public life. A democratically orientated civil society is not necessarily one in which most associations reflect the norms of liberal culture. But it should perhaps come to be seen, by policy-makers and theorists alike, as one in which the skill-sets of ordinary citizens – as deliberators, decision-makers and the balancers of various affiliations – need careful nurturing and oversight.

The idea that identity politics is incompatible with democratic society is insufficiently nuanced, and an unnecessary position for liberals to hold. The possibility that some of the different moral goods generated by identity-based groups and movements may be conducive to liberal dem-ocratic citizenship, in particular, is worthy of further consideration. In failing to examine the assumption that the politics of identity is the antithesis of the politics of citizenship, liberal theorists lose sight of some potential seedbeds for civic virtue, and mistake a consequence of far-reaching social change for a cause.

5

The Public Faces of Identity Politics

Introduction

In chapters 2 and 3, I suggested the merits of a liberal approach that is sensitive to the differential democratic effects of particular groups, and argued that different normative ideas about civil society have tended to shape responses to new kinds of group mobilization. In this chapter I draw attention to the interpretative concepts that political theorists in general, and liberals in particular, tend to use when they consider the moral character of group activity. First, I explore the prevailing liberal ideal of the voluntary association, and consider tensions that arise from its dual role as a vehicle for advancing social interests and as a source of moral education. The deployment of this concept, I suggest, has tended to diminish the worth and import of those social movements, communities and groups that mobilize non-elective identities. Within Anglophone political theory, the association is typically contrasted with its purported opposite – the cultural community. This has figured prominently within recent pluralist writings. Highlighting some limitations in the deployment of both of these ideas, I propose that liberal theorists consider extending their interpretative range in relation to contemporary civil society, specifically by engaging with the idea of the social movement. This is elaborated further in chapter 6. There, the merits and weaknesses of the interpretations of identity politics framed by some influential contemporary social theorists are considered. There are analytical limitations to the model of the social movement that they advance, but exploring the kinds of collective identity and public-sphere effects associated with such forces may help liberals to bridge the gulf between political theory and contemporary social realities in ways that these other models do not.

Identity politics, interest groups and secondary associations

> I do not see the politics of difference as differing in any interesting way
> from the ordinary interest-group politics which has been familiar through
> the history of parliamentary democracies. (Rorty, 1999: 235)

Does it make sense for liberals to regard associations that arise in relation to a collective identity as a special kind of interest group? To answer this question, it is important to consider what liberal thought has taken to be the determinant features of interest-based associations. Two definitional problems tend to afflict liberal accounts of the social and ethical character of such bodies. The first concerns the different kinds of purpose – be this moral, economic, political or cultural – that associations pursue, and whether common moral effects can be detected in enterprises with such different goals. A second difficulty arises from the different scales of social action at which association occurs – from the most intimate spheres of human interaction to the locality, region, nation-state and international arena. Democratic thought has tended to distinguish between *primary* forms of association, indicating close interpersonal relationships and affiliations – to friends or family, for example; *secondary* associations that permit the expression of an individual's moral, cultural or social purposes and interests; and *tertiary* associations that are more impersonal in character and reflect a broader professional or collective interest. The many different kinds of group and organization based upon collective self-assertion – of ethnicity, gender or sexuality – sit awkwardly in such a schema, straddling the categories of secondary and tertiary association.

Within current liberal democratic thought, as we have seen, much emphasis is given to the moral benefits of secondary associations (Bauböck, 2000). Individual participants within these are usually regarded as the self-conscious bearers of pre-formed interests, and the latter are seen as expressed and amplified through the choice to combine with fellow citizens. The shared interests that such groups articulate are typically represented as partial and contingent in kind. Liberal thinkers have, in the wake of such figures as Adam Smith, tried to unpick the ethical as well as egotistical dimensions of these forms of collective action, stressing the kinds of interdependence and sympathy that they generate among participants. Some thinkers have also emphasized the moral benefits for society at large of an associational domain in which different groupings experience conflicts that are peacefully resolved. Hegel, perhaps more than any other modern liberal thinker, captured the duality of interest-based association in his picture of the articulation of collective forms of egotism and sense of the kinds of moral learning that interdependence, negotiation and regulated conflict can generate (Avineri, 1972; Rosenblum, 1994b: 548–51). Similar ideas were central to the liberal vision of interest pluralism advanced by American political scientists such as Robert Dahl in the decades after the Second World War (1963; 1967). A free and democratic society was one in which a healthy cycle of interest-group formation and erosion occurred, and in which no particular grouping became sufficiently encompassing that it enjoyed a monopoly position on a particular issue.

The plurality of liberal ideas about the sources of citizenship (discussed in chapter 4) is mirrored in its advocates' understandings of the value and character of free association (Kymlicka and Norman, 2000). For some, the morality implied by one's duties as a citizen means that the private concerns and partisan preferences represented by the communities one inhabits as a 'civilian' are set aside when one is called upon to act and think like a citizen (Tamir, 1998). For others, associations are indispensable classrooms for civic virtue, within which citizens come to temper their egotistical natures and learn the arts of compromise, deliberation and civility (Lehning, 1998).

Measured against either of these understandings, the groupings practising the politics of identity appear to fall short. The interests that, say, a women's group advances are not usually understood as partial and contingent. They are typically regarded as integral to a shared identity that is, in turn, usually seen as constitutive of the well-being of group members. But, when a grouping is formed around an irreducible collective personality, there appears little chance of the kinds of negotiative learning and tactical compromise that liberal theorists pinpoint as crucibles of moral development. According to Jeremy Waldron, the notion of a right to unique social identity that such groups promote is simply not amenable to the logic of democratic interchange. It threatens to escalate any kind of disagreement into an argument about the validity of the way of life of a given group (2000).

A further difficulty that these groups pose for these understandings of association concerns their exclusionary and non-elective character. They are often not open to all (though this is not a necessary feature of identity groupings), and joining an identity-based grouping is rarely presented as a free choice. Involvement with a group on the grounds that one is a lesbian, or because of one's ethinicity, is not in itself a problem for liberals, except in so far as these memberships are likely to diminish motivations to participate in groups where one interacts with others who do not share such characteristics, and because some groups appear likely to promote a fundamentalist orientation towards the shared identity. Both of these characteristics undermine the prospects of the horizontal connectedness that liberals tend to regard as necessary for citizenship (Rosenblum, 1998a; Kymlicka, 1998).

The ideal of voluntary association appears unsympathetic to the dilemmas and character of identity-orientated groupings. But it has itself been subjected to a growing body of criticism, some of which suggests that liberals may need to rethink its analytical and normative purchase.

Its critics suggest that it hangs upon an implausible conception of autonomy which makes liberals idealize a narrow band of groups that make exit relatively easy and present their members' involvement as partial, revisable and shallow (Sandel, 1984). A powerful communitarian criticism of liberal notions of association points to the tension between the substantive moral goals that liberal theorists hope will arise from such groups and the lack of trust and moral depth typical of social entities in which a contractarian model prevails.

The key normative question posed by the model of free association is whether groups that are 'voluntary' are of greater moral worth for democracies than those that are not. Beneath the modernist ideal of individuals picking and choosing which groups to join lies the liberal picture of 'autonomous individuals choosing their connections (and disconnnections) without restraints of any sort' (Walzer, 1995: 64). Michael Walzer provides an important counter-view in an argument that reminds us of the value of affiliations and groupings that are not voluntary (1998). Associational freedom need not, he suggests, be understood solely through the metaphor of contract. Many of the collectivities to which we belong are not the results of conscious choice. While it ought to be possible to revoke any such tie – by leaving one's family, or moving to a different state – such a move is not always a healthy or beneficial experience (1998: 64). The fact that many groups are not ones that we freely join, in the sense suggested by liberals, does not necessarily diminish their moral worth. Applying the model of free association to such groupings represents an inherently assimilationist aspiration, implying that they abandon some of their distinctive characteristics and core beliefs by, for instance, making exit easier and adopting democratic internal procedures.

Those choices that are, in liberal parlance, 'free' are not always best understood as such. We operate in a social field in which we are likely to be guided, pressured and persuaded towards certain associations, many of which are hard to leave. Walzer identifies four different kinds of constraint upon our associational freedom. The first is the influence of family and other immediate communal attachments as well as wider social memberships: 'we are members of kin groups defined by nation and class and these forces determine a lot about people we associate with for rest of our lives' (1998: 65). Despite the apparent erosion of some forms of deference and the increased volatility of cultural and political life, most citizens tend to join bodies and involve themselves in enterprises that confirm, rather than challenge, their sense of identity (1998: 65). Although many of these memberships may be chosen, choices take place against a backdrop of social, familial and cultural influence. A second constraint is the lack of influence that most people have over the structure and organizational style of the group they join. This, Walzer argues, illustrates the importance of a continuing cultural norm of imitation and reiteration, as much as innovation and experiment in associational life (1998: 66). A third pertinent constraint is political in kind. Membership of a political community is largely involuntary and foundational to one's sense of identity as a citizen. The voluntary association idealized by some liberal commentators is premised upon a compelled association that they tend to ignore – membership of the nation-state. Walzer points, fourthly, to the importance of moral constraints. These operate as internalized forms of restraint upon the exercise of free choice, aroused by our sense of duty and loyalty to particular groups.

Walzer and other social liberals offer an important corrective to the liberal ideal of voluntary association. A variety of communities have survived and flourished because they meet different kinds of need. Without involuntary association, Walzer argues:

> there won't be individuals strong enough to face the uncertainties and difficulties of freedom; there won't be clear and coherent alternatives among which to choose; there won't be any political protection against the enemies of free choice; there won't even be the minimal trust that makes voluntary association possible. (1998: 72)

The picture that he sketches of a social culture in which family, community and tradition remain constitutive influences is, in some ways, as contentious as the individualist, volitional model that he rejects. In societies containing communities and traditional practices that have been extensively undermined by the twin influences of consumer capitalism and the pluralization of moral belief, Walzer's communitarian vision is sociologically implausible. Some of the constraints that he observes may actually serve to increase the propensity of individuals to engage in certain types of voluntary activity (Warren, 2001: 100). But his argument possesses critical value, suggesting the importance of a less dichotomous understanding of the overlap between association and community, and the inadequacies of modelling association through the ideal of free choice.

The idealization of secondary association has exerted a major impact upon contemporary liberal political thought. Some philosophers have indeed elevated it to the status of an independent norm that should guide the liberal state's engagement with cultural minorities. A version of this position is offered by Chandran Kukathas (1992). In response to arguments for the allocation of rights to some culturally orientated groups, he defends the idea that elective association by individuals is a constitutive feature of a liberal constitutional regime. For Kukathas, the demands for recognition made by minority communities ought to be disregarded in philosophical terms (though he allows that this may not be possible in the political domain) on the grounds of liberal neutrality (1998). 'While liberalism is a term that is properly used to identify a particular movement of European thought, it also denotes a philosophical outlook whose primary concern is to articulate the terms under which different

ways may coexist' (1998: 691). This second, philosophical face of liberalism constitutes the most plausible response, he suggests, to the challenges of moral and cultural diversity:

> Liberalism is indifferent to the groups of which individuals may be
> members. Individuals in a liberal society are free to form groups or asso-
> ciations, or to continue their association with groups that they have joined
> or into which they have been born. Liberalism takes no interest in these
> interests or attachments – cultural, religious, ethnic, linguistic, or other-
> wise – that people might have. It takes no interest in the character or iden-
> tity of individuals; nor is it concerned directly to promote human
> flourishing: it has no collective projects, it expresses no group preferences,
> and it promotes no particular individuals or individual interests. Its only
> concern is with upholding the framework of law within which individuals
> and groups can function peacefully. (1998: 691)

This means that the liberal state should treat all communities as associations, ensuring that the right to exit is not blocked or made unreason-
ably high. As long as such conditions are met, and a group's expressed
purposes do not bring unjustified harms to others, it should be allowed
to run its own internal affairs as it sees fit. The state can in ethical terms
deal only with individual persons, not social collectivities that represent
the decision of different citizens to co-operate in a shared enterprise. Cultural communities rise and disappear, and cannot be seen as subjects
that a liberal state should legally and politically recognize. They are,
Kukathas suggests:

> more like private associations or, to use a slightly different metaphor, elec-
> toral majorities. Both are the product of a multitude of factors, and neither
> need be especially enduring, although they can be. The possibility that they
> might be, however, does not justify entrenching the interests they manifest.
> (1992: 115)

Such communities amount to 'associations of individuals whose freedom
to live according to communal practices each finds acceptable is of fundamental importance' (1992: 116). Kukathas notes the difficulties of
treating, for instance, a settled and geographically based group such as
the Amish as a form of voluntary association. But the imperatives of
liberal democracy are served as long as such a group is treated as an
association in a weak sense: 'Cultural communities may be regarded as
voluntary associations to the extent that members recognize as legitimate
the terms of associations and the authority that upholds them' (1992:
116). As long as this diluted condition of associational freedom is met,
such communities are accorded a large degree of latitude in the way in
which they treat their own members.

Kukathas's argument provides a particular illustration of the limitations of the ideal of voluntary association. First, by requiring only

minimal conditions for an association, it accords a considerable freedom to groups that wish to behave in non-liberal ways towards their members (Barry, 2001a: 239–42). While I have suggested that some leeway between the public norms of a liberal democracy and group autonomy is desirable in a liberal state, this particular assertion of a liberalism that adopts a stance of 'indifference' (Kukathas's own terminology [1998]) is itself indifferent to the content of democratic citizenship to the point where cultural Balkanization is a real possibility. The second weakness of Kukathas's model is its ethical singularity – despite his own avowed intentions. If groups are approached in ethical terms only in so far as they conform with or deviate from this conception of free association, the variety of moral goods that groups can generate and reflect is actually overlooked (as Walzer maintains). The kind of liberal pluralism that celebrates this ideal of association is, in other words, insufficiently pluralistic when it comes to the character, effects and purposes of groupings in civil society.

Schools of civic virtue?

As liberal-republican theorists have increasingly stressed the civic implications of voluntary associations, they have typically turned away from the insights of, for instance, utilitarian theory into the interests pertinent to collective action. These thinkers reiterate, as we have seen, de Tocqueville's idea of associations as breeding-grounds for civic virtue. Groups are approached on this understanding as 'large free schools' where citizens might, as Daniel Bell puts it, 'take a look at something other than themselves' (1998: 240). In de Tocqueville's conception, associations were not only beneficial to the moral character of citizens, but were an important source of social cohesiveness, functioning analogously to the estates of European societies. The most democratic country in the world, he suggested, 'was that in which men have in our time carried to the highest perfection the art of pursuing in common objects of common desires and have applied this new technique to the greatest number of purposes' ([1835] 1969: 514). The associations that mattered most to the establishment of a democratic temper were 'secondary' in kind. They brought participants into direct interaction with fellows who were not members of their intimate, immediate communities. These groups were celebrated for their effects on the cultivation of democratic dispositions, ranging from

> modest law-abidingness, willingness to work, and the self-control necessary to refrain from violence and public shows of disrespect . . . to more demanding dispositions such as tolerance, habits of co-operation, and, if not full blown civic virtue, at least a minuscule of concern for the common good. (Tamir, 1998: 218)

On this understanding, associations and clubs represent the social articulation of particular interests and simultaneously function as 'schools of democracy'. This latter emphasis may seem surprising to contemporary eyes, since many of the groups that de Tocqueville admired – Masonic lodges and secret societies included – were exclusive and hierarchical. The emphasis of contemporary democratic theory upon the importance of a degree of voice and participation in groups for them to have democratic effects is not one he would have recognized.

The historical awkwardness generated by the present-day appropriation of de Tocqueville is worth bearing in mind when we consider the usages to which his thought has been recently put. In the wake of the civic revival among liberal theorists, his ideas have, somewhat ironically, been harnessed to justify a much more interventionist approach by the state towards the internal affairs of social organizations and groups. Stephen Macedo, for instance, argues that it ought to promote civic dispositions by using various mechanisms, such as tax breaks and financial encouragement, to support appropriate associational activities. This means promoting the activities of those groups committed to the value of democratic individuality. A similar understanding of the integral relationship of state and voluntary organization is offered by Joshua Cohen and Joel Rogers (1995).

This reinterpretation of the relationship between state and society worries other liberals, as we have seen, and has emerged as an important fault-line within current political theory. Yael Tamir (1998) rightly cautions against such projects, invoking the second liberal perspective outlined in chapter 4. The principle of the freedom to associate with others emerged in the United States as part of a Madisonian concern to offset the tyranny of majority opinion. If the state begins to favour certain associations over others, the problem that free associations were designed to offset may well reappear. Other theorists remind us that there is something intrinsically valuable about the spontaneous, organic and independent character of association, traits that may well be jeopardized if bureaucrats and political elites seek to impose alien moral purposes upon them. One particular attribute of groups that state intervention imperils, Tamir suggests, is their capacity to reflect and articulate themes and needs within society that pass unrecognized within the political domain, sometimes to the detriment of the state's future stability. If the liberal state and, more worryingly still, particular governments are encouraged to manage the politicization of social life, some of the core principles of the liberal polity are in danger. The conjunction of social and political life in Israel offers a pertinent illustration of the dangers of such an idea (Tamir, 1998: 224–5). Democratic regimes and elected governments need counter-balancing powers, as Madison observed. Only a degree of civic autonomy and the freedom to express dissenting opinion and generate creative opposition offer the requisite bulwark against overarching executive authority. John Dryzek offers a similar argument, reproving radical democrats who want a flow of personnel and an opening of access between civil society actors and state agencies (1996). Such a project opens the way to the incorporation of vital independent sources of argument and opposition, and the neutering and incorporation of such groups by public authorities.

Some liberals retain de Tocqueville's optimism that those clubs and organizations that flagrantly violate the egalitarian ethos of the public culture will, over time, wane in influence and appeal. In the current period such a hope has some basis in that liberal democracy appears to have emerged as the prevailing model of democratic practice across the globe, and because American culture has been exported to its furthest reaches. Some of liberalism's leading philosophical exponents acknowledge that a liberal state inevitably exerts an impact upon the character of the organizations and groups in its civil society. Kymlicka suggests, even more robustly, that it is legitimate and desirable for liberals to seek the liberalization of the societal cultures in their midst (1995; Macedo, 1990: 278–82).

As an empirical claim about actually existing democratic societies, the liberalization thesis is, however, easy to overstate. Groups, ideologies and social movements that feel embattled against particular liberal norms and constitutional principles have flourished in all liberal democracies. Such is the overwhelming anxiety of republican liberals about what they deem to be the inherent dangers of ethnic and moral diversity that liberal political theory has unfortunately strayed from some of the tradition's core insights, including the idea that we regard differences of these sorts as reflections of the diversity of human morality and culture. In the work of Isaiah Berlin, for example, a liberal polity was defined not by the virtues of its citizens but by their willingness and wisdom to devise institutional and legal arrangements that allowed as much tolerance towards the multiple, often incommensurable, goals that citizens hold dear as is compatible with the stability of a liberal regime (Gray, 1995b; Galipeau, 1994). George Kateb, similarly, presents the ethos of a liberal polity in Aristotelian terms, suggesting that this is a political regime uniquely willing to accept the presence of values that are its opposite (1998). In his argument, a liberal regime is characterized by the restraints upon its exercise of public authority.

These counter-arguments to republican and Kantian liberalism challenge the idea that civic unity necessitates a radically novel settlement between state and civil society. These sceptics invoke a deeply rooted liberal belief in the priority of associational freedom and the toleration of difference. The reassertion of the case for freedom of association independent of state purposes is vital to the task of understanding the moral character of social groupings that pursue distinctly non-liberal goals. Tamir, in particular, suggests that liberals return to appreciating and defending forms of collective action and co-existence because these generate a genuine variety of goods and traditions, and urges state actors to heed the different needs and concerns to which social groupings give voice.

Associational pluralism

It is therefore unnecessary and unwise for liberals to dismiss the politics of identity on the grounds that it opposes the liberal state's constitutive norms. Perhaps, however, it is legitimate to do so because it obstructs the diversity that a healthy civil society requires? Associations that are conducive to democratic life are often seen by liberals as socially integrative in their effects and subversive of some of the most entrenched and divisive cleavages of democratic society. No single group should enjoy a monopoly within its particular domain, and individuals should be able to move between various affiliations with relative ease, sustaining simultaneous memberships. Echoing Adam Smith, Mark Warren maintains that 'People are more likely to have some basis for understanding and empathizing with others in societies where they inhabit crosscutting and overlapping roles' (Warren, 2001: 16). The idea that one is part of an embattled cultural minority or an oppressed social grouping may well fatally inhibit such a self-understanding. Such groupings seem to threaten to upset the ecology of a democratic civil society, demanding too much of their members and reinforcing, rather than mediating, divisive social cleavages.

Many liberal accounts of association are premised upon such pluralistic commitments. Though she is critical of Tocquevillian ideas, for example, Nancy Rosenblum is convinced that associations are more conducive to liberal political ends than communities (1998a). The latter are inherently more conservative, while associations can, through their intrinsic fluidity and plasticity, spring up in response to new social challenges and dangers. Rosenblum argues too that those organizations that approximate most to the ideal of democratic association permit individuals to bracket other beliefs and convictions they may have, and come to realize that they share a variety of different interests, each of which links them to different groups. A person may, therefore, come to appreciate the importance of her shared interest in preserving her residential neighbourhood from forms of development that will damage property prices and alter the character of the local environment where she lives. She may simultaneously be battling with a transport company to retain a particular bus route in a campaign that links her to a different sub-set of her fellow citizens – those with a strong stake in public transport. A democratic associational culture is, for many liberals, necessarily subversive of the established ties of class, community and culture. The more that individuals are connected to each other in multiple and cross-cutting ways, the more likely it is that the comforts and tyrannies of community wane in appeal (Rosenblum, 1998a: 46; Warren, 2001).

While this objection would seem to rule out movements and communities that celebrate imposed identities from being valuable and worthy members of a democratic civil society, it does not in fact do so, for two different reasons. First, the claim that self-understandings arising from ascriptively determined group memberships necessarily inhibit persons from joining other groups is a dubious one. Historical evidence might just as easily sustain the counter-claim that, when subordinated groups are granted some kind of political standing, their complaints treated as matters of public concern, and some resources channelled in their direction, intra-group differences and a less defensive collective culture are more, not less, likely to emerge. Analysts of, for instance, the women's movement observe such a process as integral to the cyclical pattern of collective self-assertion (Banaszak et al., 2003; Tarrow, 1994). The flourishing of myriad kinds of feminist argument and politics, including many instances of coalitional activity with liberals, socialists or ethnic minority women, suggests that movements of identity are contributors as much as obstacles to associational plurality. In normative terms, it is not unreasonable to suggest that only when ascriptive group membership ceases to be such a disabling source of subordination are its individual members sufficiently sure of themselves and confident in a sense of fellowship with others to explore the kinds of cross-cutting differentiation that associational pluralists envisage. A second reply to Rosenblum's argument is also pertinent. The more sensitive a public culture is to the discourse of damaged identity, the more likely it is that overarching social groupings will be revealed as, in reality, made up of networks of smaller groupings that can be almost infinitely sub-divided.

The trouble with the freedom of association

The non-voluntary aspects of the identification many individuals feel with particular groups and communities provide an important reason for doubting the applicability of the norm of free association to the experiences associated with identity-based groupings. A further reason for scepticism is the complicated dynamic of exclusion and belonging that arises in groups that form against the background of unchosen identity. Consideration of the processes and structures that create ascriptively based disadvantage illustrates the social contingencies that limit and determine how the freedom to associate is exercised. Liberal philosophers have in recent times been keen to emphasize the democratic consequences of association, but, in so arguing, they have neglected the wider variety of social purposes and motivations shaping the formation of clubs and communities in civil society.

These qualifications to the notion of associations as schools of civic virtue are echoed in various empirical studies of some of the ambiguous moral effects of current associational patterns. Analyses of the spectacular growth of residential community associations (RCAs) in the United States observe that these represent one of the fastest growing forms of association in American life, currently incorporating about thirty-two million citizens in all (McKenzie, 1994). RCAs do not fit neatly into the categories of voluntary or involuntary association used by political theory. They are made up of individuals who make the (apparently voluntary) choice to purchase a house in certain neighbourhoods but are then required to enter into (involuntary) association with others in their local RCA. A marked effect of these social enclaves is to diminish the extent to which members feel tied to the wider community. In several areas, members have sought to withhold the payment of local taxes, on the grounds that most of the services they use are provided by their RCA (Bell, 1998). As Daniel Bell observes, with no little irony, these bodies appear to conform to de Tocqueville's model of secondary associations, encouraging face-to-face interaction and high levels of trust and reciprocity among members. But they also foster a sense of disengagement from the wider community and reinforce trends towards social polarization. The growth of RCAs illustrates that nothing intrinsic to the process of voluntary association guarantees the deepening of egalitarian citizenship. This example suggests a more generally applicable weakness both in Putnam's account and in other similar approaches to social capital: high levels of trust are commonly associated with forms of social exclusivism and withdrawal.

Cultural communities in contemporary political theory

As more critics have come to maintain that the diversity of belief, practice and identity in democratic society is of a depth that liberal thought has not adequately recognized, political theorists have increasingly focused their attention upon the importance of those communities in which non-liberal cultures prevail. The notion of the minority cultural community has been elevated in some writings into the principal agency of multicultural society, and heralded as a new kind of associational paradigm by some thinkers (Kymlicka, 1995; 1989). Two different characterizations of these culturally based groupings prevail in Anglophone political thought. Here I briefly trace these different 'ideal typical' understandings of the cultural community and critically evaluate the normative implications of both.

The primordialist community

The tradition of communitarian theorizing that returned to the fore in Anglo-American political theory in the 1980s has been especially influential in drawing attention to the social and moral importance of certain kinds of community. This paradigm has continued to influence norma-tive discussion of the politics of national and ethnic minority groupings and immigrant groups within Western democracies. Communitarian-influenced theory tends to present the identity around which the cultural and moral lives of such groups are ordered as both singular and pri-mordial in kind.[1] Each shared identity is presumed to arise from rela-tively stable and usually fixed communal interrelations. Nor is such an idea unique among political theorists. Within public debate at large, essentialist communitarian thinking is apparent, for example, in talk of 'the black community' in Britain, even though its members and inter-preters see a myriad of internal differences beneath this term. The ana-lytical combination of a primordialist understanding of collective identity and a sociologically static conception of community generates rather limited interpretations of many of the groups and actual communities pertinent to identity politics (Eisenstadt and Giesen, 1995).

The presumption that a cultural community possesses a core or bedrock identity encourages the misleading idea that group identities can be grasped in isolation from wider social and cultural processes. This neglects the widely documented process whereby a group's identity is in crucial respects formed through a dialogical relation with others. This generates the paradoxical dynamic whereby it seeks to differentiate itself from these, while simultaneously being influenced by them. A second pitfall of such an approach is that it encourages ignorance of the multi-tude of narratives arising within a community. These help form and contest the shared identity that a group possesses (Benhabib, 2002). Communitarian approaches tend to reinforce the self-understanding of dominant groups within them. Finally, primordialist approaches lend themselves to the idea that a group's culture and values are passed intact to their passive, recipient members. Neither identities nor cultures are coherent wholes that can be passed unaltered across time and space. As I suggested in chapter 1, both are better seen as internally differentiated products of many different individual interactions and intentions.

Within the media and public debate at large, ethnic and religious groups are frequently considered in primordialist terms, with the result that particular communities are presented as more coherent and unified than they really are. In conceptual terms, primordialism is a tempting trap for theorists concerned with the politics of race, gender and sexu-ality. Its language of fixity and shared interest appears to give a substance to communal ventures forged upon these bases. But it mistakenly col-lapses particular kinds of socio-cultural mobilization into the imposed identity against which they arise. The impression is, then, wrongly given that there are certain authoritative expressions of 'the gay community' or 'African-American culture', for example.[2] A real problem for the nor-mative interpretation of identity politics is that this framework is so widely used in public discourse that it is almost invisible to those who invoke it.

The affinity group

A very different understanding of collective identity informs the idea that minority communities can be understood as kinds of affinity group (Gianni, 1998; Hoover, 2001; Young, 2000: 155). This model evinces a strong commitment to the different ways in which individual members relate to, and help shape, the dynamic culture of their group or community. The ideal of the affinity groups also gives emphasis to the solace and meanings that participants find within forms of collective interaction, and invokes the centrality of the construction and celebration of shared identity.

In Iris Young's version of the affinity model, identity arises from the interaction between the involuntary sense of 'groupness' experienced by a member of an oppressed group and the subjective value of the interaction that one has within a grouping. She draws attention to the processes whereby people come together and find common interests, and suggests that these are at the heart of affinity groupings (Vincent, 2002: 162). Affinity describes both the ascriptive aspects of membership and the affective kinds of bonding that occur in a group setting. Thus, for an affinity group, a broadly shared sense of its historical past, as well as some understanding of the social relations in which it has figured, are constitutive features. Young describes this involuntary characteristic in less communitarian language than, for instance, Walzer, deploying the Heideggerian idea of the 'thrownness' that is an abiding feature of such formations (1989: 260).

The idea of affinity has been developed in conjunction with a sociologically constructivist approach to the formation and negotiation of group identity, an approach that places emphasis on the dynamism and plurality of its internal cultural system (Gianni, 1998). In multicultural societies, such groups assume a significance, according to Gianni, as 'cultural identity is mainly defined by the existence or the perception of oppressive or alienating relations with the political institutions, values, and practices of the cultural majority' (1998: 38). Such an approach encourages emphasis upon the twin attributes of these groups – their high levels of mutual solidarity and complex internal differentiation. Affinity-style groups shift their outlook in 'accordance with what relations are salient' (Laden, 2001: 157). Such an approach seeks to offset the liberal worry that cultural groupings obviate the principle of individual self-determination, with the idea that individuals are the joint producers the group's culture (Appiah, 1996).

The idea of the oppressed or affinity group is a normatively charged one. It tends to encourage the interpretation of such groupings along the axis of culture, as opposed to economic power or access to political goods (Smits, 2000: 23). It is, as a result, especially attractive to theorists seeking to tilt liberal thought towards the paradigm of difference (see chapter 7). The groups highlighted by these interpreters tend to be those that deploy a confident and pervasive rhetoric of cultural differentiation. Groups that possess the 'thrownness' that Young describes, but that do not articulate such a pronounced cultural politics, figure much less prominently in such arguments.[3]

When brought to bear upon the politics of identity, this framework suggests that affinity-based groups lend themselves to 'progressive' cultural-political initiatives that seek to proclaim and protect identities that are devalued or stigmatized. Melissa Williams therefore urges political theorists to focus on the experiences of 'marginalized' groups denied a proper hearing within the public culture (1998). She defines as marginal those collectivities that are positioned in relations of social inequality, made up of individuals who have not freely joined, and encumbered with negative representations by the wider culture (1998: 16). For such a grouping to mobilize politically, she argues, it needs to generate a shared sense of the injustices that its members experience and a common understanding of the history of its marginalization (1998: 18).

This model has made considerable headway within Anglophone political theory in the last decade, and has helped legitimate the argument that group membership is of particular significance for individuals in culturally diverse societies. But it may not be the only, or best, way of interpreting the social pluralism and inequities associated with group interrelationships. An interpretative problem arises from the tendency to regard the affinity group as the source of a rival culture to the dominant cultural system of the society it inhabits (Fraser, 1995b: 171–3). This generates the culturalist mistake of presuming that cultures and groups align neatly with one another. On this reading, we would expect the members of gay communities to have access to a coherent counter-culture to the hegemonic norm, when in fact its members inhabit an overlapping set of cultures that include various options and hybridized alternatives (Berman, 1996). The cultures of minority groupings interweave with and feed off other cultural norms. And, like all cultures, they are forever in a process of mutation. This obviates attempts to fix 'gay culture' in terms of certain practices and values rather than others. It is indeed questionable whether it makes any sense to talk of, for instance, African-Americans as sharing a common culture, whatever may be the perception from beyond this group (Appiah, 1996). Cultures may be loosely distinct, but, in modern societies, they are never entirely separate (Waldron, 1993).

The affinity-group model also draws attention to the values that arise from involvement in the processes of collective self-assertion. But is it morally sufficient to celebrate individuals' involvement in cultural community rather than, for instance, their efforts to evade the implications of imposed identity, and to achieve respect for their complicated personal identities? Might the assertiveness prized by the notion of affinity reinforce, rather than alleviate, the experience of compulsion built into these experienced identities? This model threatens simultaneously to over- and understate the importance of group membership. By modelling personal identity and well-being as goods that are discovered through the experience of interaction in a 'thrown' collectivity, it underplays the moral significance of individual agency. Individuals are, in part, responsible for developing and managing their own identities, though not in conditions of their own making. We construct and maintain a sense of identity by drawing upon a variety of cultural resources. Merely stressing the moral value of certain forms of collective identity offers only half of this ontological story. It makes more sense to argue, as Emcke does, that

> Collective identities are, after all, something one can never have under control. They are multiple, moving social entities that develop out of traditional, inherited convictions just as they subversively grow out of discriminations. They are constructed groups of individuals who struggle with and against their construction/identity. (2000: 493)

Identity politics as 'ressentiment'?

The frameworks that political theorists use to interpret social interaction are of limited utility when considered in the context of contemporary forms of collective action. This is perhaps not surprising given that the ideas of association and community are categories inherited from nineteenth-century social thought. Neither is entirely adequate to capture the social and moral dynamics deployed by many current forms of collective self-assertion. One particular feature of the politics of identity that neither elucidates is the power and character of the political rhetoric associated with this paradigm. This theme has been highlighted as a distinguishing feature of this new politics in a controversial and challenging interpretation based upon the notion of 'ressentiment'. This draws attention away from its associational or communitarian properties, and towards the political language and public face that these identity groupings present. Such an interpretation appropriates Friedrich Nietzsche's discussion of the centrality of ressentiment to political cultures in which what he termed a slave, or herd, morality prevails among the masses. His fragmentary, but fertile, understanding of the pervasive character of resentment has been appropriated by several current analysts to interpret the character of the righteous anger and unwillingness to compromise that pervades the outlook of many groups (Connolly, 1991).

Nietzsche presented ressentiment as 'the triumph of the weak as weak', an argument that Wendy Brown updates as 'the moralizing revenge of the powerless' (1995a: 23, 66–7).[4] His understanding of ressentiment was lodged within his conception of the tendency for freedom to turn back on itself because it cannot be fully realized (Connolly, 1991: 22–7). This, he suggested, produces frustrations that give rise to various expressions of moralism, guilt and rancour within the political culture (Brown, 1995a: 26). In Brown's version of this argument, resentment gains ground with the onset of two pervasive paradoxes that afflict contemporary democracies. Tensions arise because the modern impulses of individual liberty and social equality prove impossible to reconcile, and an accompanying bitterness grows among members of subordinated groups denied the fruits of modernity's twin promises (1995a: 69–70). She points also to the friction between the radicalized ideal of individuation central to modernity and the artificial cultural homogeneity required for political community. As tensions grow from these strains, there arises among the powerless a rebelliousness that takes the form of the investment of political significance in distinctions of culture and social standing. Brown offers a challenging and fertile account of the character of these dynamics and the problems they pose for current advocates of rainbow coalition-style politics. This interpretation points towards a feature of the politics of identity that pluralists and liberals often overlook: the tendency of its practitioners to become overly invested in the oppressive relationship that they denounce. Brown notes the danger of a double subjugation of ordinary men and women. They may well be oppressed by a hostile dominant culture and burdened by the aspiration of some identity groups to provide, and enforce, an authoritative account of what it means to be, say, black, gay or Christian.

Identity politics is, on this view, a complex social and historical production, as well as the site and source of considerable moral ambiguity. Brown stresses the disappearance from public view of political actors prepared to articulate the envy and anger associated with increasing social inequality. As these themes find fewer political outlets, the anger associated with them is deflected into other proclamations of injustice and resentment (1995b). With the disappearance from political debate of talk of the moral injuries of a capitalist system, 'other markers of social difference may come to bear an inordinate weight, indeed all the weight of the sufferings produced by capitalism' (1995b: 207). The angry replaying of the tension between derided particularity and an abstract and rationalistic universalism embodied in bureaucratic elites and legal codes emerges as both cause and consequence of the politicization of identity. Groups and individuals who subscribe to this political logic adopt a form of argument that endlessly reproaches power, rather than aspiring to take it and reshape the world with it. Such an accusation echoes some of the more nuanced critical assessments of the culture of 'political correctness'. The adoption of a supposedly radicalized stance is effected through a reliance upon a highly fixed, and circular, conception of the ineradicability of male/white/heterosexist oppression rather than a constructive account of how to engage with and transform such relations (Berman, 1995; Cummings, 2001; Dunant, 1994).

Brown observes the danger for the political left of embracing the logic of politicized identity which, saturated in unexpurgated resentment, 'retains the real or imagined holdings of its reviled subject as objects of desire' (1995b: 206). The protests associated with the cultural politics of difference against the ideal of an all-inclusive universal political community are therefore doomed to lament *ad infinitum*, but never transcend, the reified conception of an all-powerful white, heterosexist and masculinist culture: 'politicized identities generated out of liberal, disciplinary societies, insofar as they are premised on exclusion from a universal ideal, require that ideal, as well as their exclusion from it, for their own perpetuity as identities' (1995b: 211).

This interpretation pinpoints some of the absurdities and extremities to which the logic of arguments couched in the terms of identity can lead. It also helps explain such phenomena as the anger and hyperbole invested in some of the demands for the overhaul of the curricula of American universities in the 1990s. And it resonates powerfully with the experiences of various political and campaigning organizations that were convulsed by battles generated by identity talk and the advocacy of extreme forms of 'political correctness'. The politics of resentment describes very well the pathological conversion of righteous anger about, say, the plight of women, into circular and self-limiting kinds of political argument (Brown, 1995a). Rage and anger become self-confirming ends in their own right: the confirmation of a wounded attachment, as Brown puts it, comes to displace the goal of theorizing and working towards those goals that would alleviate the plight of particular groups. An identity that is expressed through the modality of resentment becomes 'invested in its own subjection' (1995b: 216). The political arguments that this logic unleashes quite commonly locate a responsible social or cultural agency and seek sites on which to wreak revenge against a reified enemy.

This interpretation is not intended by its advocates to legitimate the rejection of such perspectives as feminism. The dangers of *ressentiment* suggest instead a regulative standard against which campaigners can test the character of their own arguments. Resentment represents a different mode of political engagement to the rhetoric and morality of, say, feminist-inspired social transformation. When a group succumbs to the temptations of this rhetoric, the identity it maintains becomes premised on, and attached to, its own exclusion.

Other critics echo Brown's critique of the new cultural politics, arguing that campaigners and theorists of social justice should acknowledge the real dilemmas posed by identity politics. According to Barbara Epstein, a political project founded upon the rhetoric of injured identity threatens to reinforce, not transform, the objectification of social identity that the political left has historically tried to surmount (1991). Like Brown, she also locates the appeal of this new politics in wider social and cultural processes:

Many students see identity politics as their only point of leverage in a society with shrinking resources. Faculty members who find the language of 'political correctness' compelling are more often drawn to it by an uneasiness about privilege combined with a sense of powerlessness. (1991: 25)

The charge that identity politics conforms to, and deepens, a logic of pervasive resentment, rather than sustaining a project of social emancipation, is compelling and intellectually challenging. It is most useful, I would suggest, for illuminating aspects of the public rhetoric that such groups deploy within the public sphere, and pinpointing the dangers inherent in identity-based claims.

While the idea of identity politics as a contemporary version of *ressentiment* has considerable appeal, as an explanation of identity politics it is less convincing. Brown presents it as the defining political modality of the contemporary era: with 'the loss of historical direction, and with the loss of futurity characteristic of the late-modern age', cultural politics 'is ... homologically refigured in the structure of desire of the dominant political expression of the age' (1995b). Such an argument stretches a fertile interpretative idea too far, reducing the moral ambiguities of the politics of identity to a brand of late-capitalist angst. If this were its underlying logic, would identity politics really have proliferated in such a divergent set of geographical and social locations? In conceptual terms, identity politics as resentment neglects those other moral goods and social processes at the heart of, for instance, feminist politics. Considered against the characterizations offered by liberal individualists and communitarians of the promise and threat that the politics of identity has brought into being, this approach does, however, bring some of its neglected dimensions to light. Efforts to represent contemporary group politics either in the image of liberal association or as benign forms of cultural community or affinity group neglect the disruptive and angry ways in which some of these groups engage the wider political culture.

Conclusions

Considerable attention has been devoted in political philosophy over the last decade to various dilemmas arising for the state from religious forms of association, the salience of ethnicity, and the impact of feminism. But in terms of normative and analytical discussion of the social forms in which these challenges arise, one cannot but be struck by the paucity of available interpretative models deployed in relation to them. While a more varied interpretative menu is beginning to emerge, the dualism signalled by the models of association and community continues to shape much liberal political thinking. I have argued in this chapter that there are reasons to doubt whether these concepts have sufficient flexibility and range to capture the social and moral complexities of contemporary forms of group life, and the dynamics of identity politics in particular.

Appiah concludes his critical discussion of multiculturalist ideas with the suggestion that political theorists explore the considerable space between the normative reassertion of autonomy and the idealization of group pluralism (1996). His argument lends weight to the deep-seated conviction of many emancipatory and egalitarian theorists that it is politically and morally dangerous to reify the relationship between groups and individual members. In the context of the politics of identity, this means acknowledging that identification with an ascriptive grouping can be conducive to a sense of political agency, but so too can the decision to evade or challenge such an identification. Political theorists have been hampered in their engagements with these kinds of problems because of the continuing influence of particular understandings of association and community. This has obstructed conceptual refinement in comparison with the rich variety of categories familiar to scholars of political culture and social change. In chapter 6, therefore, I suggest the merits and implications for political theorists of engaging with a rather different category – the social movement.

6

Identities in Motion: the Political Ethics of Social Movements

Introduction

Liberal philosophers' attempts to disqualify identity groupings from ethical consideration on the grounds that they do not conform to the ideal of association founder upon the variable ethical implications and the societal significance of the politics of identity. Identity-orientated groupings arise from a multiplicity of moral impulses and political conditions. The social and moral character of groups that employ the rhetoric of injured identity are, I have suggested, neglected by analyses premised upon models that encourage us to view contemporary groups as either democratic associations, societal cultures or affinity groups. In this chapter I develop this argument further by considering whether a more rounded interpretation is made possible if we consider the importance and nature of contemporary social movements.[1]

In order to do this, I will consider the writings of two social theorists, as well as some unorthodox contemporary political ones. I stray across the intellectual boundary between political and social theory in this chapter for two reasons. First, because various social thinkers have begun to theorize the political ethics of current social movements in the context of the challenges posed by cultural and moral diversity. And, second, because their approach to the questions of group identity and individual agency offers empirical and conceptual resources in areas where liberal philosophy has been silent, even though the political ideas of these theorists are somewhat deficient from the point of view of liberal political thought. The institutionalized separation of these different disciplines in contemporary academic life has been intellectually debilitating, reinforcing the hegemony of a form of liberal theorizing that sets considerable store by the parsimony of its analytic logic, and much less by its sensitivity to political contingencies and empirical complexity.

Interpreting social movements

What exactly is a social movement, and what kinds of insights do the empirical and theoretical literatures devoted to it offer in respect of identity politics? Definitions of the social movement abound in the academic literatures devoted to this phenomenon and constitute a subject of considerable dispute in their own right.[2] What counts as a defining feature of a movement depends upon which interpretative paradigm is deployed by a particular analyst. From the 1970s until recently, the academic literature on social movements was organized around a pervasive contrast between the American model of resource mobilization and the West European emphasis upon the cultural implications and hermeneutic meanings of contemporary movements (Tarrow, 1994; McAdam et al., 1988; Kriesi, 1988). Latterly, such a distinction has been considerably muddied, and a range of interpretative theories have been brought to bear upon particular instances of collective action (Rucht, 1991; Cohen, 1985; Canel, 1992; Kriesi et al., 1995: xix–xxi; Klandermans and Tarrow, 1988).

Mario Diani synthesizes the preoccupations of many scholars in the definitional approach that he offers. A social movement consists of a 'network of informal interactions between a plurality of individuals, groups and/or organizations, engaged in a political or cultural conflict, on the basis of a shared collective identity' (cited in Tilly, 1994: 1; Diani, 1992; Tarrow, 1994: 3–4). In a similar vein, the historian Charles Tilly suggests that a social movement differs from a group, representing a 'complex form of social interaction . . . logically parallel to a loosely-choreographed dance' (1994: 1). Central to the idea of a movement is a sense of temporal motion and dynamic interaction among its constituent parts, meanings that the concepts of group or community, for example, do not necessarily convey. Such a sense of dynamism and internal flux are alien to the ways in which contemporary political theory conceptualizes social interaction: 'To be in motion is to be at odds with many of the criteria on which serious politics has come to be judged. Like rivers that cannot be stepped into twice, social movements cannot be pinned down, cannot keep their powers in place' (Walker, 1994: 677).

Despite a welter of theoretical and conceptual differences, scholars of social movements tend to agree that the formation and sustenance of an identity within a movement is a multifaceted and contingent process. One of the most influential theorists of contemporary social movements, Alberto Melucci, has contested the idea that a movement can be treated as a unified empirical object, highlighting the various analytical levels at which its significance and character might be explored: 'Social movements . . . should not be viewed as *personages*, as living characters acting on the stage of history, but as socially constructed collective realities' (1995: 110). The interpretative approach that figures in Melucci's work is geared especially towards hermeneutic understandings. This idea is widely echoed in West European research into the cultural and symbolic meanings of these forces – for their individual participants, the social collectivities they bring together, and the social order as a whole (Buechler, 1995; Canel, 1992).

What might engagement with various strands of social movement theory offer to liberal political theorists contemplating the new group pluralism? One important claim associated with the interpretation of social movements in Western Europe is that a variety of identity-orientated social mobilizations have become increasingly important and energetic as a representational crisis has developed in liberal democracy (Offe, 1985; 1998). This is typically conceived as the product of deep-rooted tensions between political and bureaucratic elites and a disillusioned, increasingly demanding and fragmentary public. Some commentators have turned to a variety of apparently novel social forces, such as the women's or peace movements, as symptoms of the breakdown of the system wherein social interests are represented within the political sphere (Bickford, 1999: 90). Others suggest that they are signs of the emergence of new kinds of social concern and political issue that are slowly being incorporated within the political system as mainstream political parties appropriate, and dilute, such issues as gay rights, environmental concerns and feminist politics (Melucci, 1988). Underpinning these emancipatory, communicative interpretations of social movements, as we have seen, is a distinctive conception of civil society as the habitat of new kinds of collective social expression and resistance to the logics of market and the state (Keane, 1998b). This idea underlay the notion that civil society was being reshaped in the image of such forces as the women's, anti-racist and gay rights movements. While the political hopes associated with this view may have waned, the idea that civil society has become the home to the main agencies of radical democratic development and renewal is widespread among left intellectuals.

Research into social movements typically deploys a descriptive language that stresses the importance of informal networks (Della Porta and Diani, 1999). The sociological analysis of these forces often presents a disaggregated picture of the webs of interaction that underpin collective action and the particular repertoire of protest activity deployed in a movement's lifespan (Della Porta and Diani, 1999: 16). Much of it was, until the 1990s, slanted towards the analysis, and idealization, of selected left-libertarian currents. But, more recently, a wider range of forces have been the objects of analytical attention (Jasper, 1997).

In the different empirical and theoretical literatures devoted to social movements, the problematic of collective identity takes centre stage (Melucci, 1989). This is approached both in terms of its instrumental potential for movement activity and for its independent importance within the wider cultural field. A shared identity, and the cultural and symbolic processes through which it finds expression, means that a movement can offer participants a new, or different, sense of collective belonging, even after a specific initiative or campaign has terminated (Della Porta and Diani, 1999: 20). Below, I pick out three thematic concerns in this literature that are of particular pertinence to liberal conceptions of the political ethics of identity politics.

The expressive character of the politics of identity

One theme that arises from various commentaries and theoretical treatments of modern social movements concerns the importance of their expressive dimensions for the political domain. An intriguing way of interpreting these forces is through the idea that they gain hermeneutic meaning and social impetus because they are so orientated towards expressive themes within political systems in which technocratic processes and instrumental reasons have become pervasive (Habermas, 1971).

In both the United States and Britain, such a claim echoes the complaint that the democratic state and its leading institutions are often justified by liberal political theorists in rationalistic philosophical terms that disqualify arguments founded upon emotions, passion and experience. This is a normative claim often made by proponents of the politics of difference. It trades, however, upon a simplified picture of liberal thought. While Kantian thinking is a leading influence in liberal political philosophy, it is by no means the only voice within it. Such influential figures as Hannah Arendt, Isaiah Berlin and Judith Shklar have, in the last half-century, discussed the place of emotions within public life, the potential for the manipulation of cultural and emotional needs in mass society, and the place of cruelty within modern society (Levy, 2000; Shklar, 1985). The suggestion that liberal politics is justified solely by a bloodless kind of rationality, and that emotions and cultures are relegated to the domain of the private, remains an integral feature of the caricature perpetuated by many of liberalism's critics. As an observation about contemporary democratic politics, however, this representation is not entirely without foundation. The contrast between the tepid and often technocratic 'official' discourse of party politics and policy-making, and the clamour of marginal voices demanding that questions of 'the good' be given a political hearing, rings true of various democratic polities. As democracy is increasingly interpreted in terms of a set of supposedly non-contentious procedures, it may well be that the partial, partisan and moralistic arguments that emerged from subaltern movements in the 1960s and 1970s represented the first wave of a much broader revolt against the triumph of a technocratic and instrumentalized approach to political life. As Todd Gitlin argues, the contrast with proceduralist approaches to political life helps explain why the movements of the 1960s are so important:

There is a specific reason, of course, why 'the Sixties' are still so heated a subject. To put it briefly, the genies that the Sixties loosed are still abroad in the land, inspiring and unsettling and offending, making trouble. For the civil rights and antiwar and countercultural and women's and the rest of that decade's movements forced upon us central issues for Western civilization – fundamental questions of value, fundamental divides of culture, fundamental debates about the nature of the good life. (1993: xiv)

Movements and communities based upon social identity can constitute defensive, conservative and parochial enclaves, fiercely resistant to outsiders, as their critics are quick to observe. But they are also fired by contentious and deeply held feelings about what is of value in life. These sentiments may not always gain a ready hearing within the dominant political discourses of liberal states. Movements for gender equality and gay rights have campaigned for the extension of established rights to particular groups. And they have raised questions about what it means to be free in everyday life, what kinds of ethical behaviour we can reasonably expect from our fellow citizens, and what constitutes social normalcy in societies where, for instance, conceptions of masculinity and femininity are the objects of dispute and renegotiation. In information-mediated democratic societies, we might regard identity politics as helping sustain a continuous argumentative babble, mostly coming from marginal social arenas (Bickford, 1999). While liberal philosophy seeks to establish principles and rules governing which of these issues can legitimately be constituted as political, others suggest that the drive to bring social relationships and 'private' matters into the public spotlight is an integral element of modern politics. Andrew Gamble suggests that the question 'who are we?' and the various answers it elicits are central features of a political order. This dimension of the political he characterizes as

the space where choices have to be made between values and principles, where people define who they are, where they embrace or acknowledge an identity, and take on a particular set of commitments, loyalties, duties and obligations. Choosing or affirming an identity means seeing the world in particular ways, and such identities are necessarily defined in relation to other identities. Politics is here about understanding the world in terms of us and them, of friends and enemies. (2000: 7)

Political parties and state institutions cannot control or close down this expressive dimension of politics. Various social actors and cultural forces play roles in relation to it. The desire to politicize identity, from this perspective, may be better understood as an integral feature of democratic life in the conditions of modernity, part of an ongoing attempt to order the relationship between social identity and formal politics.

In terms of social movements themselves, Melucci's (1989) research points to the importance of their hermeneutic function as agents raising questions about prevailing cultural and moral values, and as sources of various alternative social experiments. Such an understanding also informs the thinking of some political theorists. According to such figures as Jürgen Habermas, Jean Cohen and Andrew Arato, new social movements 'represent the main vehicle by which a non-instrumental rationality can be brought into public life' (Tucker, 1991: 75; Habermas, 1981; Cohen and Arato, 1992). A sense of the expressive dimensions of social movements suggests an important theme for political theorists to consider. They typically use the term 'identity politics' to denote both a particular sub-set of group activity – the formation of ethnic associations as opposed to neighbourhood groups, for instance – and a particular style of group organization that deploys a rhetoric of injured identity. But, among scholars of contemporary social mobilization, the politics of identity is often seen as a mode of group behaviour. This can be deployed by movements instead of, or alongside, other modes, such as bargaining (in the case of interest groups) or publicity (as with groups committed to campaigning against injustice). Such an approach is especially fertile for the theorizing of the democratic potentiality of contemporary social change.

Alain Touraine

Several of these themes are raised in his recent elaboration of the social impact of identity politics by the French social theorist Alain Touraine.[3] His argument merits consideration because of the distinctive way in which he interweaves sociological insights with a challenging, though contentious, account of the political tribulations facing the liberal democratic state. In his most recent work, Can We Live Together? (2000), Touraine makes social identity central to his discussion of the moral pluralism affecting multicultural states, and stresses the erosion of the moral and cultural bases of national citizenship. He points to an epic, ongoing struggle within various democracies between those who react to new uncertainties and anxieties by seeking refuge in communalist enclaves, on the one hand, and the difference-friendly, post-nationalist responses of cosmopolitans, on the other (2000: 89–106). Observing the rise of identity-based groupings, sects and cults in civil society, he suggests that these share a common ambition to bring a given polity and culture into line with an established ethnic or political authority. These projects tend towards forms of identity politics that enforce singular conceptions of the good, and seek firm boundaries to exclude views and parties that are perceived as alien (2000: 31–6).

Touraine worries that the political left will embrace the idea that political radicalism should orientate towards the particularist insistence upon special rights and immunities for minority groups. Such a development neglects the emancipatory principle of inter-group communication. This is in decline 'because we no longer recognize that we have anything in common except a refusal to prohibit the freedom of others and a common involvement in instrumental activities' (2000: 4). Like many other democratic theorists, Touraine is concerned about the prospects for generating a sense of common values and social solidarity in deeply divided societies. Connecting the rise of identity with the growth of uncertainty attendant upon the radical disembedding of economic activities from the nation-state, he highlights an increasingly vicious circle. Economic flux generates a responsive desire for the security and certitude of fixed identity. But the new political economy simultaneously makes such a response inappropriate in an age of fluidity and flexibility. The only way to break this cycle is to enhance one of the other trends immanent within the modern social order: specifically to realize the modern ideal of individuals who take moral responsibility for their life-choices and contribute to the self-governance of their polity. This means becoming, in his parlance, a 'subject' (2000: 52–88). To become a subject, the individual must see herself as an independent social agent and a stable point of reference in a world of permanent and uncontrollable change. To recognize oneself as a being capable of critical reflection is, Touraine suggests, the precondition of the achievement of subjecthood, and requires in turn that one recognizes the moral status of one's fellows (2000: 76–81). This quasi-Kantian position is combined with a Habermasian stress upon the merits of intersubjective communication. Those who have achieved a healthy degree of subjecthood will communicate with others to deepen their understanding of themselves and those around them. They demand institutions that safeguard their individual rights and equip them to develop their own individuality.

In Touraine's eyes, without the generation of autonomous and rounded individuals willing to question authority and sensitive to the needs of others, progressive social change is unimaginable. Social movements are integral to his vision: they are actors who can provide alternative forms of identification and purpose to the principal options of contemporary political life – the espousal of a vacuous moral cosmopolitanism or new kinds of communalism (2000: 98–124). They occupy an inherently ambivalent moral role in Touraine's thinking. He posits a stark dualism between those forces determined to produce closed communities founded upon charismatic authority and those that seek to deepen and develop political dialogue. The first kind of movement has a tendency, he suggests, to become a social 'anti-movement' in which the preservation of a threatened identity becomes an end in itself. One face of identity politics takes the form of the protection of a communal tradition against the cultures of modernity. Its other aspect is to be found in those campaigns, networks and movements that seek to expand the possibilities for subjects to live autonomous lives: legitimating new ways of living, questioning established traditions and offering resources for participants to enhance their sense of self-worth. These kinds of social movement 'call less and less for the creation of a society or a new social order, and more and more for the defence of personal freedom, security and dignity' (2000: 70). In a context where political narratives founded upon progress or the triumph of reason have waned, and when conventional politics appears to have been colonized by instrumental rationality, social movements can enhance citizens' capacities to reflect independently upon the social order. They are no longer the servants of political utopias or the objects of elite manipulation.

In ideological terms, Touraine's reflections have, in comparison with his earlier writings, drifted into the territory of liberalism (see, for instance, Touraine et al., 1984; Touraine, 1981). But he retains a sharp critique of liberal culture throughout this text, lamenting its capacity to deliver on its commitment to the values of self-development and equality (2000: 26–31). Without the realization of these values, he warns of a worsening social Balkanization and violent inter-cultural conflict. Read from the vantage point of political theorizing, a distinguishing feature of this position is Touraine's assertion that a liberal polity should be justified without recourse either to moral principles rooted in claims of universal truth or to the philosophical embrace of difference. His alternative is democratic dialogue in general and inter-communal communication above all. Facilitating these should be guiding concerns when devising political institutions. The communicative ideal must be reflected in a political community's public culture and become the regulative principle informing its institutional and constitutional design (2000: 137–44).

This recourse to deliberation in response to the dilemmas generated by identity politics echoes some of the positions central to the recent upsurge of interest in deliberative democratic practices in Anglophone political theory (Fishkin, 1991). By comparison with these, the absence of a clear sense of the principles that ought to guide these dialogues in Touraine's writing is not reassuring. Moreover, his confidence in the likelihood of satisfactory compromises and deliberative outcomes sits awkwardly with his gloomy views about the social and moral effects of mass culture (2000: 53, 83). Underlying these tensions are two generic problems that are familiar to the proponents of deliberative democracy: how to ensure that participants possess the appropriate characteristics and skills for the dialogues they develop to be meaningful, and on what basis should we be confident that inter-cultural debate will protect the 'primary goods' that make a particular state a recognizably liberal democratic one? These are extensively theorized problems in contemporary philosophy, but are glossed by Touraine's optimism about the possibility and consequences of dialogue.

A different weakness afflicts his, and other sociologically informed, accounts of political transformation. Touraine reproduces a schematic model of the successive social forms common to Western modernity, one he shares with other European social theorists (Hannigan, 1985). This can encourage a reductionist approach to political ideas and traditions, and relies heavily on a postulated contrast between those political ideas that are deemed applicable to the industrial age and those now pertinent to a 'post-industrial' era. One debilitating normative consequence of such an approach is that the bulk of the liberal and socialist traditions are presumed to be relics of the past. Studies of the evolutionary and adaptative capacities of ideologies suggest, more plausibly, that these be regarded as evolving systems of belief that particular actors use in relation to different kinds of social and political challenge (Freeden, 1996; Gaus, 2000). An unspoken assumption in Touraine's argument is that the dilemmas engendered by the twin forces of globalization and identity require a novel political mind-set. Such a position not only overplays the discontinuity of the present from the past, but also deprives us of a host of intellectual resources with which to understand and interpret recent developments.

Such faults are magnified when these works are read in the context of Anglophone political theory. But there is still much of value and interest in Touraine's blend of social and political theorizing for liberal political theory. Above all, his sense of the rival ethical trajectories of contemporary social movements, and his conviction that mobilization based upon collective identity is foundational in contemporary political life, offers food for thought for political theorists interested in a richer social understanding of the contemporary 'facts of pluralism'.

The character of collective identity

As well as their stress upon the expressive dimensions of politics, many European-based scholars of oppositional movements emphasize the constitutive importance of struggles to establish a sense of shared identity for particular groupings in civil society (Hannigan, 1985; Canel, 1992). Some of these accounts, and the theoretical reflections upon which they are based, have an important bearing upon discussions of the character of the politics of identity.

Alberto Melucci

Much theoretical discussion of the collective identities marshalled by social movements takes a lead from the Italian scholar Alberto Melucci. His wide-ranging account developed from an examination of those 'marginal counter-cultures and small sects whose goal is the development of the expressive solidarity of the group' (1989: 49; 1984). The solidarities generated by such currents as the peace, women's and environmental movements in the 1970s, he argued, emerged from a strong 'commitment to the recognition that personal needs are the path to changing the world and to seeking meaningful alternatives' (1989: 49). Melucci presents movements as shaped by a tangle of ideational, cultural and political processes. In his best-known work, *Nomads of the Present* (1989), he focuses upon the importance of networks, personal contacts and informal interchanges. These constitute the bedrock upon which the public face of a movement rests. His study of peace activists in Rome in the 1970s illustrates the significance of these submerged networks. They served as springs from which movement activism flowed and as seedbeds for further activity (1989: 43, 70; 1984: 829–30; 1985: 789–90).[4] This underlying tissue of attachments, affiliations and relationships is as integral to the formation of a shared identity in a movement as the public slogans, activities and pronouncements that it makes.

The social currents that burst into public view in the 1960s in Western Europe were, Melucci argued, poorly comprehended within the terms of conventional movement analysis. These forces should be seen as 'nomads' in a disenchanted world, harbingers of quite profound changes in the sub-cultures of modern society and a turn away from the patterning of social identity that prevailed in the 1950s and 1960s (1989). Earlier generations of social movement placed themselves under the emancipatory banners of religion, nation or class. As each of these projects has waned, social ferment has sustained its power and impetus by encouraging an inward, reflexive turn – towards the self, the body and culture (1996a). Central to this shift, Melucci argues, has been the desire to secure the revaluation of some of the identities that have been the subjects of marginalization and oppression. A new kind of reflexive politics has arisen as a consequence, in which the desire to control one's own self-definition and construct positive self-representations are integral (1996b).

One of the features distinguishing these currents from conventional forms of political protest, Melucci argued, is the investment that their participants place upon the symbolic and cultural politics of identity (Melucci, 1985; Lustiger-Thaler and Maheu, 1995; Sassoon, 1984). Being part of a widely held identity, and experiencing the thrill of belonging that this involves, is, he suggests, integral to the experience of participation in such ventures. For Melucci, the common identity that a movement develops is typically a fragile, open-ended and internally plural construction. Collective action is always 'built' by social actors. Its analysis requires attention to the processes through which individual participants 'communicate, negotiate, produce meanings and make decisions within a particular social field or environment' (Keane and Mier, 1989: 4). Through these processes and experiences, participants develop a shared frame of reference and a collective self-understanding. These provide 'a moveable definition of themselves and their social world, a more or less shaped and dynamic understanding of the goals of their action as well as the social field of possibilities and limits within which their action takes place' (1989: 4). A collective identity, on this understanding, lies somewhere between a settled and roughly coherent communal value-system and the formal rules that govern the actions of an association. It is 'nothing else than a shared definition of the field of opportunities and constraints offered to collective action' (Melucci, 1985: 793). It approximates more to an ethos that is both shared and internally diverse, a set of codes that its members develop and observe and over which they may disagree (1985: 798–9). The various kinds of collective action that a movement undertakes arise from the conjunction of the decisions and choices made by individual agents as well as the character of the group's identity. It is a mistake to see them as straight-forward manifestations of an already established collective will (Melucci, 1996a). Moreover, relationships with various significant others – competitors, allies and adversaries – 'define a field of opportunities and constraints within which the collective action takes shape, perpetuates itself, or changes' (1989: 4).

Developing these insights, John Keane interprets Melucci's character-ization of these social nomads, suggesting that they

> focus upon the present wherein they practise the future social changes they seek, and their organizational means are therefore valued as ends in themselves. Social movements normally comprise low-profile networks of small groups, organizations, initiatives, local contacts and friendships submerged in the everyday life patterns of civil society. These submerged networks, noted for their stress on solidarity, individual needs and part-time movements, constitute the laboratories in which new experiences are invented and popularized. (1998c: 172)

Within his own writings, Melucci has tended to avoid the triumphant proclamations of emancipatory potential that other analysts perceive in today's social movements. But his interpretative framework does in some respects lend itself to such readings. This is principally because his account is premised upon a disjuncture between the cultural and symbolic orientation of social mobilization in the contemporary period and the strategic-instrumental character that prevailed before the 1960s (1989: 12). One consequence of this dichotomous approach is that Melucci tends to separate the cultural initiatives of movements from the political and social goals they pursue.

In a more recent work, *Challenging Codes* (1996a), Melucci specu-lates about the political implications of the symbolic practices of social movements, and considers what these mean in terms of the morality of a democratic society. In this book a clearer picture emerges of the ethical character of social movements. As 'nomads', these forces are typically marginal and fleeting, but they are also free to move across the moral, sexual and cultural landscapes, questioning shibboleths and attracting dissident individuals. They are also prophets, calling out from the pol-itical wilderness. In so doing, they draw attention to issues that will become prominent in years to come. Melucci remains sceptical about attempts to align these forces with grand projects of social emancipation or political reform. Their primary function is to act as social signs, point-ing towards deeper contradictions within a social culture and occasion-ally hinting at their possible resolution – as in the case of the introduction of the ideal of sustainability to European publics as a result of different kinds of environmentalist agitation (Melucci, 1989: 75; 1988). In liberal democratic contexts, these mobilizations are especially important symp-toms of, and intuitive responses to, the demise of established moral codes. Such movements generate a range of effects upon the systems that provide homes for them. They increase the differentiation and fragmen-tation of the social world, and they frequently elicit defensive or hostile responses from those troubled by the challenges they proclaim to estab-lished moral precepts or cultural practices. The political fall-out from movement demands, and the tensions they generate, cannot be regarded, Melucci suggests, as generalizable. Social mobilizations may generate roughly coherent political demands and programmes, but they are not primarily designed to do so. They play a vital role within the social system – above all as alarms warning society of emergent problems (Plotke, 1996).

Like Touraine, Melucci interprets these phenomena using various theories of macro-societal change, and these have a similarly distorting effect on the political aspects of his argument.[5] His adoption of the model of the information society and enthusiasm for cybernetic metaphors tilt the focus of his argument, most obviously in *Challenging Codes*, towards an accent upon the communicative and symbolic dimensions of con-temporary movements. In so doing, he removes them almost entirely from the world of political ideas and ideological contestation. Yet, as in the case of Touraine, there are some valuable insights to be gleaned from this body of writing. Melucci's sense of how identities are constructed in cultural fields has an analytical bearing upon philosophical debates about the merits of group or cultural rights. His sophisticated and agent-centred analysis of the collective identities through which groups and movements come into being highlights the limits of the idea of the group as a plural person (1989: 4). His framework suggests that movements and identity-orientated groups do not possess identities in the same way that persons do, and that it is misleading to expect them to be the repos-itories of coherent value-sets. A striking normative implication of his work is that social movements are better considered as forums and inter-active systems wherein individuals negotiate and develop their own self-understanding, as well as that of the wider group.

As for movements that make the rhetoric of identity central to their outlook, Melucci observes the dialectic of commonality and difference through which, say, the women's movement has developed in the last thirty years. Movements frequently develop various forms of connect-edness and solidarity as well as new kinds of internal division and dif-ferentiation. A further analytical implication of Melucci's argument is that the dynamism of social movement activity tends to destabilize the idea of clear and fixed boundaries between established social groups, as they bring together persons from a range of backgrounds. Like Touraine, Melucci is no cheerleader for the politics of identity. He too worries about the prospects for public debate of an increasingly difference-conscious citizenry (1996a: 186).

Melucci's analytical commitment to the delineation of the depth and character of social individuation in what he terms 'complex' societies is combined with a strong sense of moral individualism. Unlike those who make major claims about the ethical and ontological significance of groups, his focus on movements as social signals is underpinned by the argument that they address 'individuals as individuals, and not as members of a group, a class, or a state' (1996b: 288). In a recent text, he has pinpointed the centrality of the tension between the desire that moderns feel for greater control over the circumstances that shape their lives and the increasing capacity and imperative of the state to order and regulate their existence (1996b). This is a clash that has now extended to the manipulation of the biological and genetic natures of individuals.[6]

The focus upon the provisional and complex character of efforts to develop shared identities in modern societies is a familiar theme within the sub-field of social movement studies. An important effect of the inter-pretative turn signalled by Melucci's work has been an emphasis upon the informal and submerged relationships that underpin and precede the public manifestations of group behaviour. Melucci's extensive engage-ment with the social dynamics and socio-cultural forms pertinent to the politics of identity offers some fertile insights for theorists contemplat-ing the sources and character of moral diversity. His detailed delineation of the conceptual and empirical complexities pertinent to group identity suggests the merits of a more nuanced social and psychological picture of how individuals interact with groups than is typically offered within Anglophone liberal political theory.

Public spheres and the politics of identity

A final generic theme can be extracted from the extensive literatures devoted to the interpretation of social movements of the past and present. This is perhaps the most directly 'political' in content, and touches upon some central themes of modern democratic thought. It con-cerns the character and prospects of the various public spaces that social movements have helped establish in civil society, specifically the idea that

> social movements contribute to the creation of public space – social set-tings, separate both from governing institutions and from organizations devoted to production or reproduction in which consequential delibera-tion over public affairs takes place – as well as sometimes contributing to transfers of power over states. (Tilly, 1994: 1)

Accounts of contemporary social movements are replete with claims about their actual and potential effect upon the generation of new public spaces, as well as assertions about the significance of their challenge to established norms (Scott, 1990). These concerns have given rise to three distinct arguments regarding the democratic impact of movements that arise outside the world of conventional politics. First, among those intellectuals excited by the emancipatory potential of, for instance, the women's or environmentalist movements, one of the most appealing attributes of these forces is the diverse range of viewpoints and arguments they include. In some accounts, this was taken to be a sure sign that these forces were conducive to radical democracy (Scott, 1990). A related 'virtue' that supporters observed in them was their propensity to establish new public spaces on the margins of the established culture. In these, it has been suggested, new kinds of social experiment and a sense of collective self-confidence were established (Melucci, 1989).

A rather different normative account of the relationship between heterodox movements and public space has also emerged. This concerns the impulse at work within various social movements and minority groups to disrupt conventionally established boundaries between the political and non-political. This generates the desire to bring into public view questions and practices hitherto regarded as private, such as domestic violence or marital rape. On this view, the politics of identity is motivated by the desire to challenge and disrupt established ideas about what politics is about, rather than to set up parallel institutions and spaces.

A third, distinct conception of the implications of social movements for public space is offered in the accounts of civil society developed by, among others, Habermas (1981; 1971) and Cohen (1985). They interpret these forces as repositories of the logic of practical, as opposed to instrumental, reason. Emancipatory social movements defend and advance communicative logic within the public life of democratic political communities (Tucker, 1991: 75). This argument echoes throughout the social movement literature (Tilly, 1994). Many authors have been influenced by Habermas's historical account of the emergence of the public sphere (though some have questioned its historical accuracy), and especially the idea that it functions as 'a kind of political thermostat' (Young, 2000: 177). Iris Young expounds the notion that public spheres provide a means of transferring information about problems and unmet needs from the realm of everyday experience to a wider public consciousness, and sometimes into the legislative and bureaucratic parts of the state system.

The notion that these marginal and dissenting voices are pertinent to the conceptualization of public spheres is widespread, though somewhat variable in implication. Common to such arguments is the claim that a variety of spaces and sites are pertinent to the public space and culture of a democracy (Taylor, 1995b). The first and third views have sustained the idea that subaltern groups play a vital, and largely unacknowledged, role, carving out oppositional counter-spheres from which different voices have made claims upon the public culture at large.[7] Jane Mansbridge argues that this development is especially pertinent to the rise of identity politics (1996). She draws attention to the development of

> different forms of protected enclaves, in which members legitimately consider in their deliberations not only what is good for the whole polity but also what is good for themselves individually (their private lives and well-being, in Arendt's words) and for their group. (1996: 57)

Finding and legitimating space for these identities to be asserted, and the various perspectives associated with them to be explored, is, she argues, important for a democracy: 'the present reigning hostility to "identity politics" does not recognize the value to democracy of deliberative enclaves in which the relatively like-minded can consult easily with one another' (1996: 57). Nancy Fraser, similarly, points to the role in democratic politics, since at least the early nineteenth century, of 'subaltern counterpublics' in fostering demands 'from below' (1999; Young, 2000: 172). These are spaces forged by oppositional or subaltern groupings, 'through which are invented and circulated counterdiscourses, which in turn permit groups to formulate oppositional interpretations of their identities, interests and needs' (Mansbridge, 1996: 57). This kind of argument resonates among recent interpreters of social movements – for instance, Paul Byrne's observation, based on his discussion of protest in Britain, that

> one of the prime objectives of social movements is to open up new 'spaces' in politics – to get issues and ideas, previously ignored, on the political agenda, and to win cultural and political acceptance of the method used to propagate their message. (1997: 27)

The notion that groups propounding the merits of a particular identity are continuing a lineage of subaltern mobilization that has been integral to the articulation of democratic demands is a striking one. In normative terms, some theorists are especially attracted to the idea that this lends historical weight to the pervasive call for the pluralization of the public domain to reflect the many different voices and styles of public talk that multicultural democracies include. For this reason, the idea of interlinked, but separate, public spaces, as opposed to the republican ideal of a common single political conversation, has been celebrated by various pluralists. Charles Taylor hails the appearance of a set of 'nested public spheres, shaped by movements beyond the political system, that play a vital role as conduits between the public sphere and the political system' (1995b: 279). This notion appeals especially to thinkers keen to postulate a pluralized deliberative democracy in which no single source of authority or political agent can assume control. Increasingly such an idea is presented as both a precondition for, and a product of, a radicalized version of representative democratic government (Keane: 1998c).

These accounts of the 'heterogeneous public sphere' expand the interpretative repertoire of analysts contemplating the impact of recent assertions of collective identity. But they raise, in normative terms, the problem of whether diversity really can, or should, be the regulative norm for the democratic public sphere. If the public sphere is subdivided into its group parts, it is likely to be overloaded with too many voices and claims. It may also lose its capacity to constitute a public with a sense of shared moral priorities and commitments.[8] Many democratic theorists remain justifiably suspicious of a conception of democratic praxis that appears to evade, rather than reformulate, the problem of the 'general will' (see chapter 4).

Not all advocates of the importance of subaltern mobilization are committed to the ideal of the heterogeneous public. The second view outlined above, by contrast, suggests that we consider movements as the bearers of messages to the wider polity. In this role they dramatize growing social frustrations and unmet needs and highlight potential societal dysfunction. Such ideas have been most influentially expounded by Habermas, in his writing on social movements from the 1970s and early 1980s (1971; 1981): 'In the last ten to twenty years, conflicts have developed in advanced Western societies that, in many respects, deviate from the welfare-state pattern of institutionalized conflict over distribution' (1981: 33). The social and political crises of that era were interpreted in these as products of the expansion of the scope of capitalist society's steering mechanisms at a time of social and economic dislocation. These developments, he suggested, disrupted pre-existing patterns of social integration. Habermas identified the women's and student movements as important reactions to these intrusions by the state, and subsequently the market, into hitherto non-commodified arenas of social life (1981; 1971). Although his own arguments about such movements have shifted somewhat as his complex *oeuvre* has developed, this position has remained influential. Thus, Grant Farred stresses the significance of the attempt to achieve a voice and gain a public hearing by groups whose members are culturally, rather than formally, disenfranchised (2000). He points also to the role of ethnic groupings and anti-racist politics in contesting the terms in which marginalized voices get aired in a frequently hostile and derogatory public environment. In a variety of ways 'identity politics gave cultural articulation to the achievements of the Civil Rights, Black Power, Stonewall, students', and women's movements of the 1960s and 1970s' (2000: 631).

The politics of identity, on such a view, involves a necessarily combative engagement with the assumptions underpinning what is 'normal' and what is 'deviant' in a given political culture. Farred suggests that this aspect of identity politics be regarded as the source of a potent 'politics of embarrassment' in democratic life (2000). The public spokespersons of cultural minorities are fired by the aim of revealing the bad faith and hypocrisy of the liberal state that promises universal equality for all, but in fact supports those who conform to the cultural norm more fully than those who do not. Rather than collapsing into a circular and self-defeating *ressentiment*, this stance, Farred suggests, can be the source of important political and legal changes within liberal polities. These states should be shamed into delivering on their egalitarian promises, redressing the historical injustices experienced by particular groups: 'Publicly reminded of and embarrassed by its inability or refusal to deliver on its basic ideological premises, the liberal state can be made to confront the consequences of its racist or homophobic or misogynistic or class-based inequities' (2000: 644). This interpretation draws attention to the different kinds of impact that such forces as the civil rights coalition or the women's movement have exerted upon the expectations of various segments of the population in democratic states.

This suggestion appears to conflict directly with the idea of identity politics as a form of late capitalist *ressentiment* (discussed in chapter 5). But both claims may well be partially valid and analytically combinable. There is a propensity in such groups for righteous anger to be pathologically converted into self-confirming, and sometimes self-aggrandizing, resentment. But the possibility is also present of a re-formation of a society's understanding of the cultural, moral and political character of citizenship in the wake of the discussions of injustice that groups promote. This suggests an inbuilt indeterminacy, and perhaps instability, in the political outlooks pertinent to many forms of identity politics. The fury, pent-up frustration and sense of injustice that forms of cultural politics release can be channelled into different kinds of political project and public rhetoric. They can either lead to a divisive and blame-orientated politics of resentment or contribute to a transformation in the understandings of the social relationships in a democracy.

Practising identity politics in the public domain

Empirical investigation of the ways in which particular groupings understand themselves and use political rhetoric bears out this bivalent characterization of the politics of identity. A single group can inflect the language of identity in either of these general directions. Paul Lichterman's study of the public discourse of various gay activist groupings exemplifies this dual possibility (1999). He observes a marked distinction between two different kinds of 'identity talk' in the groups he studies. Each rhetorical mode is deployed depending upon context, audience and political situation. Participants switched between a 'more multivalent critically reflective identity talk' in contexts where members felt secure with each other and away from the public gaze, and a more 'narrowly affirming' rhetoric of group solidarity and need (1999: 101–2).

This discourse was deployed in coalitional work with other kinds of groups. In this second mode, which he labels 'community interest' talk, a harsher, more instrumentalized rhetoric of friends and enemies prevailed. Such findings lend support to the argument that theorists of the public sphere need a more sensitive appreciation of the different cultural frames and repertoires available to groups and movements in their public lives. Lichterman's argument is highly pertinent to ongoing debates about civic renewal in democratic states. Rather than perceiving the state's duty in terms of the bolstering of sources of social capital in general, this analysis highlights the democratic benefits of establishing social and institutional contexts in which groups feel sufficiently secure to engage more in the first kind of self-reflexive and alliance-building public talk.

For some liberal advocates of civil society, as we have seen (in chapter 4), the democratic state ought to promote as diverse an associational life as is possible. The hope is that this will undermine and marginalize identity-based mobilization (Warren, 2001: 3). The arguments of the social theorists considered in this chapter, however, suggest that the shift towards identity-based politics is a more integral feature of contemporary social development than some political theorists imagine. Their different analyses also have a bearing upon the notion that liberal civil society is the antithesis of the politics of identity. These movements reflect important and deep-seated social changes. They are the sources of various ethical goods for individual participants as well as potential causes of social Balkanization and division. In macro-social terms, they play an important role, providing messages for the political system about needs that are unmet or ignored.

Conclusions

This brief engagement with the copious literature devoted to social movements brings to the surface empirical and analytical arguments that are of considerable pertinence to liberal political theorists. These include a sense of such forces' temporal contingency and evanescence, their internal dynamism and pluralism, and their capacity to dislodge and reinforce the established boundaries between social groups.

For all their fertility and suggestiveness, such theoretical accounts are deficient as treatments of the dilemmas generated by these developments in respect of political ideas and democratic theory. The institutionalized divorce between the communities of political and social theorizing within Anglophone intellectual life appears unfortunate in this regard. Political theorists have much to gain from an enhanced sensitivity to social context and the complex character of collective identity. Social theorists, on the other hand, might usefully heed the arguments of political philosophers about the epistemic, moral and political difficulties facing those seeking to legitimate a liberal polity in a deeply divided society. The current separation of these theoretical genres represents a break within the historical unfolding of the liberal tradition, whose leading intellectual exponents have more typically interwoven social with political ideas – for instance, the pronounced sociological sensibilities and interests of early twentieth-century American and British liberals.[9] Current philosophical practitioners have also departed from the propensity of earlier liberal thinkers to combine empirical enquiry with high theory. As John Gray puts it, liberal philosophers such as Smith and Mill

> were deeply concerned with the cultural and institutional preconditions of liberal civil society, preoccupied with threats to its stability and anxious to understand the deeper significance of the major political developments of their time. The strange death of this older tradition has gone oddly unlamented, as political philosophy has come to be dominated by a school ... whose intellectual agenda is shaped by a variety of liberalism that at no point touches the real dilemmas of liberal society. (Gray, 1995a: 10)

The idea of the social movement should not be considered as an alternative to other familiar social categories, such as the association, the interest group and the community. It represents, rather, a possible addition to the conceptual repertoire of political theorists. Indeed, for many nineteenth- and twentieth-century liberal thinkers, what are now labelled 'new social movements' were highly familiar features of the social landscape – in the shape of the suffragette campaign or nationalist movements, for example (Tucker, 1991; Calhoun, 1995). A sense of the vitality and ethical importance of collective action is deeply embedded in the lineage of liberal theory, but has been somewhat forgotten in recent theorizing. The tasks of establishing a legitimate basis for a political regime and understanding the forces that may contribute to, and threaten, a liberal polity require a more nuanced social understanding as well as the skills of the philosopher.

7

Liberalism and the Politics of Difference

Introduction

A significant intellectual accompaniment to the interest of many contemporary political theorists in cultural diversity and the politics of identity is a revival of theorizing about the subjectivities of modern citizens (Katznelson, 1996: 149). For some thinkers, social pluralization is a further sign and cause of the inadequacy of liberal conceptions of the self. Some of the main attempts to recast liberal thought against the background of cultural diversity have, therefore, been built upon the foundations of alternative accounts of the (post)modern self. I examine two such endeavours in the next two chapters. The first, considered below, involves an attempt to persuade liberals and other radicals that the ideal of impartiality should be replaced by its opposite – a politics in which the ontology of difference takes centre stage. The ideas of Iris Young are evaluated in relation to this concept, as she offers an unusually sustained and thought-provoking version of such an argument (1989; 1990; 2000). I also consider the rather different approach of the theorist William Connolly. He embraces and justifies the principle of difference on the basis of an extensive engagement with post-structuralist thought (1991). His radical rethinking of the meaning of liberal citizenship, using the idea of alterity, is considered in the second half of this chapter. In chapter 8 I consider attempts to derive a politics of recognition from the new cultural politics of identity. Liberals, I suggest, should be wary of the various legal and political reforms that proponents of difference and recognition suggest, even though these perspectives offer some valuable critical insights into some of liberalism's blindspots and prejudices.

Their intellectual merits aside, one reason why an engagement with these theoretical projects is significant is that they overlap with some of the claims and self-understandings advanced by various political activists, community spokespersons and policy-makers. The philosophical theories of difference and recognition are organically related to some of the leading ideas of Anglo-American political debate, notably through arguments about the moral value of cultural diversity and the assertion that democracies should be made more inclusive (Young, 2000).

The notion that both culture and difference should be integral to democratic political theory is widely held to be anathema to the prevailing version of analytic liberal philosophy. Theorists in this philosophical school have increasingly declined to engage in metaphysical debate when developing accounts and justification of the basic rights that free individuals should possess. A liberal constitutional regime, according to such figures as Rawls and Dworkin, is one in which no particular version of the good life is promoted over any other. It is distinguished by its protection of the rights and liberties that permit individuals to pursue their personal moral goals (Rawls, 1971; Dworkin, 1978). The communitarian critique of the liberal self that emerged in the 1980s served to highlight that deontological philosophy rested upon an untenable account of the detachment of modern subjects from the ends that they choose to pursue (Sandel, 1984). In the wake of these communitarian-inspired controversies, as well as the growing salience of republican and feminist challenges to liberalism, 'self-craft' has once again become central to Anglophone political theory (Digesner, 1995).

Iris Young's politics of difference

Young's contribution to these debates is one of several attempts to flesh out the idea of a differentiated liberalism. Her ideas have achieved a deserved salience due to the extended critique she offers of the ideal of impartiality, and because of her challenging attempt to translate this alternative perspective into a radical political programme (1990; 1986). The foundational premises of her pluralism are an ontological commitment to the importance of social groupings in relation to the personal identities of individuals in democratic society and a critique of the inadequacy of liberal reasoning in the face of this reality (1989; Tebble, 2002). Liberal ideals require the assimilation of minority groups to powerful norms protected and disguised by the universalist robes in which they are adorned. Young sets out to debunk the claim that the differences associated with group membership can be fairly handled by treating everyone as if they were the same. This rings especially hollow, she argues, in the context of groupings that are founded upon a nonvoluntary aspect of social identity – on the basis of skin colour, ethnicity, sexuality, gender or class. These differences are screened away from political and moral consideration by liberal arguments that are built upon individualist and universalist premises.

The ideal of impartiality, which liberal philosophy holds dear, denies its adherents critical tools with which to engage the processes of structural and cultural oppression that constrain many individuals' self-understandings and opportunities (2001). Groupings are, in fact, resources and bulwarks for their members, offering important sources of solidarity, consolation and hope. Liberal individualism fatefully neglects 'the deeper existential wellsprings of cultural life forms, the fact that cultural groups are defined not by extrinsic attributes but by "a sense of identity," that is, by shared practices and by shared historical experiences and agonies' (Dallmayr, 1996: 282). For ordinary citizens to gain a sense of worth and of political agency, they require more than the acquisition of a basic schedule of rights or the sense of recognition provided by national membership. They need some measure of public acceptance of their particularity from the society at large (Hoover, 2001: 205). This implies that liberal citizenship be reformulated so that it no longer evades the collective commitments and affinities that are integral to the lives of actual citizens.

A sense of the social goods that groups offer to individuals underpins Young's conviction that emancipation is wrongly conceived as the transcendence of social context and particularity, as liberals and socialists have often argued (1986). Re-engagement with the 'positivity and specificity' of group difference (1986: 535) is a prerequisite for a political project that marries social emancipation with pluralism. In its failure to grasp the significance that groups have for their members, and through its lack of engagement with the consequences of group-mediated inequality, liberal thought actually legitimates the position of dominant collectivities. It does so by making a fetish of a procedural neutrality which frequently works to generate an inbuilt majoritarianism in political life, and by presenting the outlook of leading groups in Western democracies as universalizable moral truths.

Although critical of the liberal tradition on numerous grounds, Young is committed to its central values. In order to be just, a liberal polity needs to develop structural and cultural strategies to remedy the disparity between groups (1990: 118). Liberals are similarly urged to jettison the ideal of uniformity that pervades their understanding of the public sphere. Instead, they should embrace a more heterogeneous appreciation of the many different kinds of person who should be able to participate in public deliberation. An important consequence of such a shift would be to introduce a degree of cultural reflexivity into the outlooks of dominant groups. As Jeffrey Hoover argues: 'Only if the particularlist perspectivalism [sic] of dominant groups is revealed can the interest-laden nature of the supposedly "difference-blind" or "neutral" nature of traditional liberalism be properly understood' (2001: 202). The recurrent dream of much liberal and republican theory of a public sphere in which group-based and cultural differences are set aside is unrealistic and morally unacceptable (2001: 204). The normative correlate of this position is that, the more inclusive is a polity towards the culturally marginal and socially subordinate, the greater the likelihood that it will redress structural and cultural forms of disadvantage.

In a recent essay, Young offers a clearer distinction between the ontological significance of groups and the particular form of group behaviour associated with identity politics (2000: 87–92). The latter, she argues, constitutes only one mode through which collective interests are asserted. The social pluralism that the proliferation of groups has engendered ought to be distinguished from the 'logic of identity' applied by supporters and critics to group life in general. Individual persons do not simply inherit fixed and stable identities from these communities of fate. Identity is forged in relation to various structural and cultural influences: 'Social relationships, institutions, and structures are prior to individual subjects, both temporally and ontologically. A person encounters an already structured configuration of power, resource allocation, status norms, and culturally differentiated practices' (2000: 99).

Individuals remain the sources and *loci* of moral and social agency, but the materials and resources through which they come to understand themselves and exercise their capacities are shaped, above all, by the groupings to which they belong. In her recent writings, Young places a greater accent upon the structural axes along which inequities between groups are operative. These are as important as the peculiarities of cultural differentiation and distinction. Both dimensions, she maintains, are pertinent to the politics of difference: 'Whilst they are often built upon and intersect with cultural differences, the social relations constituting gender, race, class, sexuality, and disability are best understood as structural' (2000: 92). This understanding is counterposed to that of multiculturalists, who mistakenly conceive of groups as static and coherent totalities that determine the identity of their members. Such arguments rely upon the notion that groupings can be defined in terms of a substantive core – of beliefs or interests. Young's own approach to these collectivities is relational in kind. She stresses the contingent relationships forged by their constituent members and the fluidity of boundaries between a group and others: 'Any group consists in a collective of individuals who stand in determinate relations with one another because of the actions and interactions of both those associated with the group and those outside or at the margins of the group' (2000: 89).

On this basis, Young offers the case for a reformulation of the ethos and character of liberal citizenship. She calls for a pluralization of the ideal of the citizen so that a range of attributes, traits and selves come to be viewed as legitimate subjects in the public sphere. This argument is captured within her advocacy of the ideal of the heterogeneous public sphere as a guiding framework for the realization of social justice (1989: 263–5). Modelling this notion in terms of the differentiated and anonymous character of urban life, she argues that political thought needs to contemplate a public domain without the comforting ideals of social homogeneity and unmediated face-to-face deliberation. Citizens are akin to city dwellers who do not know everyone in their neighbourhood but need to forge agreements to advance contingently shared interests (1990). In order to ensure that the voices of marginal or oppressed groups are aired in the political dialogues modelled on this urban ideal, it is a duty of public authorities to ensure that members of minority or oppressed groups are supported in their endeavours to take part in public discourse. In such a model, 'the perception of anything like a common good can only be an outcome of public interaction that expresses rather than submerges particularities' (2000: 119).

This approach to citizenship has implications both for the rules and rights that determine citizenship as a formal status and for the idea of citizenship as social practice. Young makes a case for the readjustment of the rules regarding representation in the liberal democratic order, and suggests that a broader, more inclusive approach be adopted towards the particular backgrounds from which individuals engage each other as citizens. This conception is presented as a stable middle ground between two rival trends in political debate: liberal models that invoke the stance of impartiality, and the worrying separatist impulses that Young observes within various subaltern movements. Her unease with this latter move tells us much about her own intellectual and political intentions. She observes the implausibility of separatism in contexts where groups are deeply intertwined with others, and, in moral terms, she fears the consequence of a strategy that is likely to render one version of a group's identity the dominant or legitimate one. Equally, she accepts that this mode of group behaviour can be judged negatively by the standard of civic unity: 'If a politics of difference requires such internal unity coupled with clear borders to the social group, then its critics are right to claim that such a politics divides and fragments people, encouraging conflict and parochialism' (2000: 88). This is an important point in her argument, a moment when she invokes a norm usually associated with her republican and liberal critics.

Young is relatively unusual within this field for her willingness to translate ontology into policy. She suggests, for example, the merits of overlaying the existing structure of legally enshrined rights and duties with protections for groups that have been oppressed and remain important for the self-identity of many citizens. Among such groupings she names 'women, blacks, Native Americans, the disabled, gay men, lesbians, and Spanish-speaking Americans' (1990: 206). These groups might be supported in the form of public funding and through the requirement that policy-makers consult them when important decisions are likely to affect their interests. Just as controversially, she argues for the inclusion of group representatives within legislative bodies, and for according these some kind of veto power over policies that affect their constituencies. These ideas are interesting in various respects, not least because they chime with proposals and practices that have been much debated in various democratic states.

Evaluating Young's politics of difference

The idea of the 'heterogeneous public', according to its critics, is a recipe for the transformation of democratic politics into a divisive contest between rival groups. This model gives to these collectivities incentives to proclaim and hype their differences (Barry, 2002: 211). A related criticism is that models of differentiated citizenship renounce the constitutive hope of modern democratic thought – that citizens may learn to adjust their arguments in accordance with a wider notion of the public good. Even Young's sympathetic critics worry about the consequences of negating the republican insight that

> democracy also includes a vision of people coming to perceive the limits of their own specific interests and concerns, learning to recognize the potential conflicts between their own position and that adopted by others, and acknowledging the wider community to which we all ultimately belong. (Phillips, 1993: 117)

Young addresses these worries at some length in her recent work. In this she attends to the implications of group pluralism for deliberative democracy and emphasizes the 'need to build shared understandings that are sufficient to create the conditions for democracy' (2000: 209). Here, she brings to the surface the theme of civic unity that is a muted presence in her earlier work. She retains the ideal of deliberation orientated towards an appreciation of the common good, but distinguishes between political agreement reached by different persons who hold differing moral beliefs and the ideal of unanimity associated with liberal models of public reason. The common interests of a community can only be discovered through an open dialogue in which different styles of political rhetoric and argument are accepted as legitimate. They do not arise from the realization of moral principles that are established independently from politics. Young's aim in this text is to persuade those who share her own deliberative predilections to renounce the dream of rationally determinate consensus. Our sense of what counts as legitimate public talk needs to be pluralized:

> Those who lack self-esteem or self-confidence in the political arena – those who, for example, are less well-educated or are non-professionals – may be disadvantaged by a process that emphasized the rational, face-to-face, assertive debate among political constituencies. (2000: 209)

A key normative question raised by Young's arguments is whether the mixture of radical democratic practice and ontological pluralism that she presents is a stable or a combustible one. Throughout her various writings, she repeats the claim that the public good and the various principles pertinent to citizenship are the provisional and contingent outcomes of democratic processes. It is wrong to regard either as prior to, or conditions for, concrete deliberative interactions. A real difficulty with this stance is that, for public deliberation to occur, a public needs to be constituted and some sense of the rules by which it will be governed, and its appropriate scope, established. Young says little about who should constitute this public, or what would be the remit or character of the 'constitutional convention' that, she implies, will be required to provide a legitimate sense of common citizenship (Meyer, 1998: 68). Moreover, her commitment to the dialogic constitution of shared interests means that there is no space in her model for the possibility of any foundational or constitutive needs that a democratic polity is bound to reflect and defend – such as its citizens' interest in peaceful co-existence and ineradicable need for political community itself. In her strong reaction against attempts to fix the core moral purposes of the liberal state in the guise of impartiality, Young mistakenly abandons the possibility of shared values and norms that arise from the social contingencies and uncertainties generated by shared co-existence in an established state.

Viewed from the vantage-point of the requirements of liberal democratic practice, Young's proposals for group-based representation in political life are also troubling. These appear likely to engender the kind of divisive and competitive political culture that makes any discussion of common interests difficult, and perhaps impossible. The idea of granting extra representation or the power of veto is, in fact, likely to exacerbate group-mindedness and social envy. A public that engages in political interchange as members of competing groupings is one in which reified and essentialist group identities are more, not less, likely to develop. Once groups are invited to select representatives and offer a collective voice on policy matters, there is a good chance that their internal character is likely to alter. Strong incentives arise for leaders to cement their own positions and to encourage a more unified outlook, as well as to police dissent and difference more firmly. Such collectivities may well become subject to the same pressures as political parties, increasingly required to have 'a line' on particular controversies and to respect hierarchical and bureaucratic organizational principles. Such a programme may also render a group's interests less negotiable, a development that may have 'debilitating political results for consensus-building' (Hoover, 2001: 208).

Groups merit public support, Young suggests, when it can be demonstrated that they have, in historical terms, been the victims of both domination and oppression.[1] Through this idea she seeks to incorporate a moral intuition that is very widely shared among liberals, social democrats and socialists: that some ethnic and cultural minorities, and women more generally, deserve public support in order to reverse entrenched patterns of inequality, or as a form of restitution for past wrongs. But her proposals for group-specific provision are troubling despite her confidence that we can distinguish between those groups that count as deserving and those that are not (Macedo, 1995: 468–70). Young's historicist and relational commitments might just as plausibly lead to the judgement that what may appear to be a cohesive social grouping in need of restitution may actually turn out, on closer inspection, to be made up of a mosaic of complicated sub-groups that vary in terms of the oppression they suffer. And, if so, what is to stop us differentiating further between the collectivities that make up a sub-group, a process that may have no logical end point until we are left with the plight of individuals (Tebble, 2002)? Once the fluid nature of social group membership is presented as a definitional feature, 'it seems difficult to deny the importance of sub-subgroups . . . and even ultimately of the domination and oppression of individuals' (Tebble, 2002: 267). Her emphasis upon fluidity and indeterminacy when she theorizes the ontology of groups is, oddly, replaced by a more fixed and reified understanding when she engages with politics and political institutions (Jaggar, 1999).

Young's focus upon degrees of domination and oppression as determinants of a group's desert does not help her evade this kind of criticism. She defines domination as institutionally based constraints upon the self-determination of individuals, and oppression as obstacles to their self-development (Tebble, 2002: 260). Consideration of the ways in which these processes affect individuals tends to undermine the idea that the social group is necessarily the appropriate level at which to locate and remedy the injustices perpetuated by both oppression and domination. In her discussion of oppressed and dominated groups, she has in mind such collectivities as African-Americans, many of whose members have been subjected to both processes. Yet they have clearly not experienced them in the same way and to the same extent. One reason for this differentiated experience is that African-Americans are simultaneously members of other ascriptive groups – men and women, straight and gay, urban and rural dwellers, and inhabitants of northern and southern states in the US. Unpicking the processes of domination and oppression requires a fairly refined sense of the ways in which different group identities intersect. Thus, the black unemployed or, more specifically still, unemployed black women may well constitute sub-groupings of greater moral purchase for liberal egalitarians than African-Americans in general.

The idea of sustaining a distinction between 'deserving' and 'undeserving' groups in terms of the oppression they have suffered is also rendered difficult by the proliferation of groups claiming victim status. The dissemination of the rhetoric of injured identity within political life has considerably clouded the issue of deciding which claims are legitimate. This is a tricky issue for those who advocate group-specific support on the basis of oppression. Various forms of counter-identity politics – for instance, the mushrooming of organizations and networks aiming to promote traditional or family values, or the recent growth of a transatlantic 'men's movement' – ape the rhetoric of damaged identity introduced to the body politic by the left-libertarian movements of the 1960s. Such developments illustrate that establishing an acceptable criterion of subordination is necessarily a contentious affair, and that Young's confidence in the 'facts of oppression' is misplaced: there is likely to be a legitimate plurality of views regarding the desert of different groups, and sub-groups, that confounds such a project.

Critics suggest that the inadequacy of Young's conception of moral desert is a reason to reject the totality of her theoretical claims. But it is possible, and for liberals advisable, to accept the idea that group-based inequalities matter without adhering to the group-specific remedies that Young and others propose. One reason for this is that, if one believes, as Young herself does, that the real problems with oppression and domination are their malign effects upon individuals and individuality, then it is questionable whether group-specific remedies are necessarily the appropriate means of providing the restitution and empowerment that individuals need. Moreover, the distinctions Young makes between group types possess considerable analytical merit. She defends the possibility of distinguishing ethically between groupings that are in certain respects constitutive of the identities of their members and those that operate as either 'aggregates' or 'associations' (2000). By an aggregate she means a classification of persons in terms of a shared attribute that is not necessarily of social significance – eye colour, for instance (Miller, 2002a: 178). Both this idea and the notion of an association are inadequate to the comprehension of groups that exercise a constitutive influence upon an individual's 'particular sense of history, affinity, and separateness, even the person's mode of reasoning, evaluating, and expressing feeling' (Young, 1990: 45). Her conception of the relationship between groups and persons is a useful corrective to that offered in some communitarian theory. She points to the considerable overlap between collectivities that philosophers tend to ignore and the inherently porous boundaries of identity-based communities: 'The practical realities of social life defy the attempt to conceive and enforce group difference as exclusive opposition' (cited in Tebble, 2002: 262). Only a conception of the group in which fluidity and the absence of fixed boundaries are stressed, she suggests, is appropriate to justify a differentiated, democratic polity. Young labels this anti-essentialist understanding of groups a 'structural' approach because it underlines the importance of the social and cultural relations between groupings but avoids over-reliance upon the idea of fixed or reified cultures (2000: 85).

In her more recent study *Inclusion and Democracy* (2000), Young switches focus from the character of groups themselves to the institutional conditions necessary for an inclusive public conversation. Some of the tensions affecting her ontological account of groups surface too in her recasting of the principles and practices of deliberative democracy. She returns here to her earlier elaboration of the case for group representation:

> Representation should be designated whenever the group's history and social situation provide a particular perspective on the issues, when the interests of its members are specifically affected, and when its perceptions and interests are not likely to receive expression without that representation. (1989: 266)

In the deliberative context, she suggests that a group merits assistance 'when its perceptions and interests are not likely to receive expression without that representation.'[2] But this principle is not straightforwardly consonant with the twin criteria of domination and oppression. In societies where there has been a massive proliferation of media outlets and opportunities to gain some kind of publicity for marginal views and issues, giving expression to group demands and concerns is not in itself always difficult. Getting a proper hearing, rather than mere expression, is the problem that oppressed and subordinate groups face. And this may well require an ethos of trust, or goodwill or respect towards others – values associated with the kinds of liberal and republican arguments that Young rejects. She is certainly right to insist that some groups, such as the unemployed or elderly, are almost entirely without voice in public life, and that attention to their representation is an important challenge for those championing deliberative democracy. Yet her attempt to develop a normative principle whereby groups are given representation when otherwise they would not be heard belies her own anti-essentialist understanding of groups. Her argument is prone to a troubling circularity. Social groups do not possess identifiable essences. They are constituted through relationships, including that with the public at large. But a group thus constituted has, it would appear, represented itself publicly in some form or other, and does not appear to need representation on this criterion.

Young's emphasis upon inclusiveness as a condition for democratic debate echoes widely in contemporary theorizing (Dryzek, 1996). By including group-based perspectives within public deliberation, a greater array of viewpoints and social needs are given consideration, and a sense of the common good that reflects a wide range of interests is made possible. A familiar problem besets this stress upon inclusion: is it compatible with the need for agreement and sense of common purpose that democratic citizenship requires? For Young, the moral priority of inclusiveness means that a democratic polity must devise ways of ensuring that groups 'attend to the particular situation of others and be willing to work out just solutions to their conflicts and collective problems from across their situated positions' (2000: 7). One consequence of such inclusiveness would be an improvement of the chances that those who make proposals will transform their positions from an initial self-regarding stance to a more objective appeal to justice, because they must listen to others with differing positions to whom they are also answerable. Even if they disagree with an outcome, political actors must accept the legitimacy of a decision if it was arrived at through an inclusive process of public discussion. (2000: 52)

In other words, through experiencing the dynamics of deliberative interchange, an agent will learn to present a particular argument with reference to the good of all. A condition favouring this outcome, Young suggests, is that parties in these dialogues are 'answerable' to one another. Even when they disagree, they must accept the legitimacy of a decision on the grounds that it was arrived at because an inclusive dialogic procedure was followed.

Young's understanding of the relationship between inclusion and the public good is not entirely convincing. There is nothing within her scheme to instil confidence that individuals will accept the legitimacy of votes and decisions with which they disagree. Her confidence that a degree of 'answerability' is required of citizens by dint of their mere involvement in public debate is offered as an alternative to liberal accounts of 'public reason'. The latter invokes a distinction between legitimate and illegitimate ways of presenting arguments in a democracy that Young regards as overly stipulative and biased towards modes of expression favoured by dominant groups. In liberal democracies, she suggests, the favoured ideal is one that requires citizens to stand aside from their own cultures and identities.

Instead of such a requirement, Young argues that merely feeling included within a discussion, and then being called to account for one's beliefs and values in a respectful way, offers a basis for the recognition of putative agreements. But are these conditions sufficiently stringent? If we accept her view that some of the defining features of one's identity arise, as Thomas Spragens puts it, from a 'concatenation of external accidents on one's being' (1999: 88), what plausible grounds are there for believing that mutual sympathy will arise from inclusion in a debate when differences of moral outlook are so firmly embedded in differences of social and cultural background? If crucial aspects of our identity are the products of this kind of 'social imprinting' (Spragens, 1999: 88), then very little mutual understanding may well be possible. Nothing intrinsic to the ideal of inclusiveness guarantees the move from the holding of a particular view to a sympathy for the particularity of another. 'Answerability' is just as likely to make people resort to reasons grounded solely upon their own culture, history and unique experience, or to dress these up as arguments for the common good. Young's emphasis upon the special characteristics of social groupings also undermines her case here. Because efforts have to be made to meet the conditions of inclusiveness *in relation to social groups* – not neighbourhoods, regions, sub-groups, moral perspectives or ideological traditions – there is a strong likelihood that the character of any such dialogue will reflect this group-specific mode of representation. The chances of enhancing inter-group rivalry and reinforcing the insularity and defensiveness of groups appear high.

A final difficulty that Young's inclusionary emphasis raises is whether the idea of displacing hegemonic notions about what counts as a 'rational' contribution to public discussion is in fact rather self-defeating for subordinated groupings. Young extrapolates from her particularist and pluralist understanding of groups to the claim that a variety of modes of communication and public discussion ought to be regarded as equally valid. The damaging myths of consensus and impartiality extend, she argues, into assumptions about how democratic speech and debate should occur. Thus, forms of address typically seen as irrational or manipulative (such as rhetoric, greeting and story-telling) are to be regarded as intrinsically valuable within deliberative dialogue (2000: 52–80).

Young's suggestion that Enlightenment rationalism has determined what counts as legitimate public talk leads her towards the self-defeating argument that established forms of political reason should be regarded as outcrops of the historical dominance of certain groups. A real danger of such a stance for powerless groups is that, if they heed this advice, they may become locked within modes of communicating that will not count as effective or legitimate forms of argument because they are not designed as forms of public reasoning. To assume that social differentiation means that women or African-Americans can *only* reason in women-specific or African-American-specific ways is to fall into the trap represented by the logic of identity that Young herself criticizes. Equally, she fails to notice that the political rhetorics deployed in democratic societies are, in practice, far more variegated and plural in kind than her argument allows. The conceptual resources and political vocabularies that democratic politics engender have enabled the advance of subordinate groups as much as they have hindered them. In some historical accounts, the procedures and rules shaping public debate have indeed been presented as the products of agitation and political campaigning from below, as much as the preserve of elite groups. The historian Edward Thompson, for example, demonstrates the importance within English radical politics of the eighteenth and nineteenth centuries of the blend of rational argument, political passion and righteous anger – the fusion of reason and desire – that animated the struggles to create public spheres (1961; Kenny, 1999). In normative terms, encouraging groups to speak *only* from within their own vernacular threatens to leave them stranded in the politics of the enclave.

While Young advocates a politics of group difference on the basis of her ontological ideas, it is worth considering other ethical and political conclusions that may be consonant with them. A more plausible egalitarian position would be to suggest that an engagement with groups represents merely one path towards the creation of a more just society.

Though sometimes classified under the heading of multiculturalism, her analytical conception of groups actually undercuts some of the central assumptions and ideas of this paradigm. If oppression and domination are the most compelling problems facing individuals, then the valorization of, say, Islamic culture and belief, or granting its adherents representative rights in the British legislature, may well be inadequate. These measures may do little to combat the particular combination of pressures and inequities faced by, for instance, working-class Muslim women.

The ethos of pluralization: William Connolly

Young is one of a number of philosophical voices calling for a fundamental reorientation of liberal political thought in the wake of the challenges generated by social pluralization.[3] Although these are often presented as allies in a joint intellectual endeavour, some important differences of philosophical stance and political vision underpin liberal pluralism. This is apparent if we consider the influential ideas of another contemporary American theorist, William Connolly (1991; 1995). As with that of Young, Connolly's work is challenging in its own right, but it also carries a wider, indicative status. His appropriation of post-structuralist thought gives a particular quality to his critique of liberal universalism and sustains an unusual justification for liberal institutions. Critical engagement with his writings leads to an encounter with figures and traditions that lie beyond the boundaries of Anglo-American political philosophy.

Connolly agrees with those cultural and social theorists who regard difference not simply as a description of a plural social world, but see it as a dynamic integral to the formation of the self in (post)modern society (1991: xiii–xxx). Such ideas lead these thinkers to favour those forms of social expression and political opposition that challenge and contest established norms and identities. Social movements are frequently regarded as agents of a new iconoclasm, undermining sources of social authority – the patriarchal nuclear family, for instance – and bringing into view the contingencies and particularities that lurk beneath the universalist pretensions of liberal humanism. Both of these emphases are intertwined in Connolly's writings (Spragens, 1999: 96–102). Conceiving the modern self as a fragmentary and incomplete being, Connolly draws heavily upon Nietzsche and Foucault in his presentation of subjectivity as a matrix that is continually remade as agents move within complex fields of discursive meaning (1991). He draws from Foucault a sense of the various performative practices through which selfhood is generated. The self is constituted within a variety of arenas and in relation to multiple traditions. Selfhood, on this understanding, is both provisional and open-ended, and critically depends upon the configuration of relationships between one's own groups and those cultures and values that are deemed 'other'. The regulation of alterity becomes a defining attribute of selfhood, as my sense of who I am is crucially mediated by an understanding of that which I am not (Connolly, 1995: 69). Self and other are configured in a symbiotic, interdependent and porous inter-relationship, an idea that is extensively explored within psychoanalytic writings. This anti-essentialist account of the self implies an emphasis upon the contingent and partial character of the relationship between groups and individuals, and a marked hostility to political projects and claims that purport to reflect or express fixed identities. Social identification is plastic, contingent and infinitely complicated, open to a never-ending dynamic of articulation and reinvention (1995). From such a perspective, the politics of identity enjoys a distinctly ambiguous status. Insular, essentialist kinds of cultural politics appear to vitiate, rather than embrace, the sense of the indeterminacy and contingency of being that these theorists enunciate. Thinkers such as Judith Butler have led the way in stressing the importance of a deconstructionist approach to some of the deepest cultural dualities – gays as against 'straights', black as opposed to white, and female as against male – through which the social order is structured (1990). None of these categories is immutable or 'natural', as each is produced and negotiated with reference to its purported opposite.

In ethical terms, these themes tend to translate into an individualist normative orientation, as critical emphasis falls upon those differences and particularities that make social collectivity almost invariably oppressive. There is a marked scepticism in these quarters, however, about the liberal model of the sovereign, autonomous self, capable of exercising a singular will and stepping outside traditions, cultures and relationships. Intellectuals influenced by postmodernist and post-structuralist thought share the multiculturalist ambition to expose the hubristic character of liberal claims to cultural and ethical neutrality. As Gianni puts it:

> Just like other kinds of institutions, the liberal ones create strangers and enemies of those who do not fit into their categories; their functioning is based on a process of normalization, which ends up in the denial and the exclusion of the 'Other' as deviant or abnormal. (1998: 41)

Like Young, Connolly wants to tear away the universalist mask of the liberal citizen and reveal the subjects who stand to gain most from 'his' normative power. But he adds a distinctive note of alarm and urgency to his analysis of the effects of liberal culture. Those whose social standing and cultural background mean that they do not conform to the values of liberal humanism are increasingly alienated from its cultural norms: they are 'told to leave their bags of faith at the door when they enter the public realm', while 'Dworkin and his buddies are allowed to bring several suitcases in with them' (1995: 124). Connolly is especially critical of liberal responses to the politics of identity that invoke a distinction rooted in Enlightenment culture between legitimate perspectives that adhere to the norms of universal reason and those that cling to pre-modern traditionalism or communitarian monologism (Young, 2002). Dividing up the political field in this way is an unwise move. Liberals' invocation of state neutrality, and their underlying belief that their institutions and way of life are superior to others, produces alienation, frustration and anger from immigrant communities, cultural minorities and religious groups. Identity politics is neither an accident nor a historical anomaly, but a response to the hegemony of liberal culture. The inroads forged by various fundamentalist, anti-liberal currents in American political life in recent years – neo-conservatism and the Christian right, for example – can be partially explained by profound resentment at 'attempts to impose a liberal creed upon others in the name of a universal reason, a natural subject of rights, a neutral state, or a fictive contract conveniently skewed in favour of liberal presumptions and priorities' (Connolly, 1995: 123).

Invoking Carl Schmitt's critique of representative government, Connolly argues that a liberal state, just like any other political regime, produces a series of friends and enemies. The reproduction of a liberal political order relies upon various processes of normalization – the building of a common national identity, for example – that lead to the denial and the exclusion of the other as deviant or abnormal (Gianni, 1998: 41). With their hubristic belief that liberal democracies are havens of tolerance and inclusion, liberals are unable to take seriously the reasons of their opponents, condemning them as atavistic traditionalists. Liberal individualism cannot appreciate that it too is a social construction (Rorty, 1999: 237) and therefore needs to tailor its hegemonic ambitions. While much post-structuralist critical theory is ambiguous in political and ideological terms, Connolly is unusual in deploying its insights both to critique liberal theory and to provide new grounds for a democratic polity, though one without the moral foundations that liberals have generally sought. In a similar vein to Richard Rorty, he argues that liberalism must acknowledge its contingent historical and cultural roots. Unlike Rorty, he takes anti-foundationalism to imply an abandonment of liberal hubris and the adoption of a stance of humility in its dealings with other cultures.

But on what basis is a liberal polity to be justified, given the radical indeterminacy and differentiation that, Connolly suggests, shape the character of selfhood? His answer is that liberalism needs to divest itself of many of its foundational moral claims and develop an open-ended, agonistic democratic order (1995). Because we are increasingly likely to regard our identities and interests as changeable and multivalent, it is inappropriate, and potentially damaging, to draw rigid boundaries around what counts as political. Connolly therefore recommends an agonistic kind of politics in which no issue can be excluded from public consideration on an *a priori* basis. The political domain should mirror the plasticity and mutability of the self, and the liberal polity no longer comes to rest upon values that are meaningful and appealing to only some of its citizens. A defining feature of this *agon*, according to Connolly and other contemporary theorists, is that it will strive to avoid the fixing of unnecessarily restrictive boundaries to the content of politics (1995). A political culture in which no single value-set is promoted by the institutions of the society, and in which different identities are negotiated in a peaceful and open-ended fashion, requires a deliberative framework that supports the idea of negotiation and a non-judgemental approach towards others.

Connolly posits an essential ambiguity in persons towards cultures and values that are not their own. We possess the capacity to respond openly towards the other, and also to flee from and reject it. But the liberal idea of tolerance is inadequate as a basis for a democratic culture (1999). A society which requires no more than tolerance encourages nothing more than indifference towards the fate of others. In an argument that carries interesting analytical purchase in the context of the upsurge of anti-immigrant populism in both the US and Europe, he suggests that the idea that 'our' culture is tolerant, while various others are not, serves to generate a profoundly intolerant response to minority cultures, on liberal grounds. Such processes figure prominently in Connolly's analysis of the libidinal forms of group aggression that generate bouts of inter-group hostility and rivalry in pluralist societies in which 'difference' is culturally devalued. In any democratic society, there is the potential for social differentiation to become overloaded with symbolic significance and reduced to the most brutal kinds of racial or cultural determinism. His case for the liberal *agon* relies on an unusual mixture of ontological heterodoxy and political caution about the shallow foundations of liberal democracy. Being responsive and open-minded towards difference emerges as the central value of the agonistic democracy, an attribute that the state needs to cultivate and promote.

This version of a radically pluralized liberalism differs in some important respects from attempts to promote a politics of group identity or recognition. Connolly suggests that there is no authentic core to the self that can be realized through particular political or social arrangements. The interplay of identity, difference and desire within the self is disruptive of any such project. There is no ultimate self for the state to recognize in order to ensure a stable democratic order. Liberal theory instead needs to come to terms with the idea of selfhood as 'a contingent formation modestly open to further strategies of craftsmanship' (1995: 69). The self is always a work in progress, its author requiring the modesty, wit and sensitivity to modify its constitutive elements in response to the circumstances she inhabits.

A striking normative implication of this argument is that the state should cultivate among its citizens a sensibility appropriate to a world in which social and cultural difference are regulative principles. Modern citizens need to become far more aware of the degree to which laws, institutions and cultural norms favour certain groups and exclude others. Connolly also advocates the dissemination of a Nietzschean sense of the inescapably tragic character of moral choice, since there is no rational basis from which to distinguish between legitimate moral options (1995). In political terms, he regards further democratization as the most appropriate vehicle for the promotion of a political culture in which a sense of self-effacement, openness to difference and cultural moderation can be established (Spragens, 1999: 98). These are virtues especially appropriate to postmodern society, because they undercut those desires – to punish, preach and control – always struggling to find expression in modernist projects. Self-effacement arises in a culture in which our openness to others leads to an ethos of mutual care and respect and the growth of meaningful forms of reciprocal generosity (Spragens, 1999: 99). Connolly seeks a justification for a democratic political order without resort to the traditional moral and epistemological foundations that liberals have deployed. In so doing, he takes the deep differences associated with cultural inheritance and social identity, rather than the clash of moral beliefs, as the central problematic facing liberal thought.

Evaluating Connolly's liberalism of difference

The bulk of Connolly's arguments are pitched at the epistemic, ontological and ethical levels. Their implications for political institutions and practice are lightly, and not unambiguously, sketched. A rather telling absence from his account is a discussion of a putative mechanism or agency that might legitimately encourage citizens towards the kinds of mutual respect and sensitivity to difference that he advocates. Some sort of institutional device seems necessary because, without it, we have only his intuitive claim that the recognition that one's personal identity is a rather open-ended, multivalent and fragmentary affair is likely to produce a more open and generous spirit to the 'other'. This confidence appears, at best, optimistic. Uncertainty and fragility just as typically find expression in collective desires to deal more roughly with those deemed 'alien' – illegal immigrants and asylum seekers, for example.

Equally, we should ponder the merits of an argument that regards difference as of such constitutive significance for individuals and groups that notions of commonality and agreement come to appear inherently coercive and manipulative. Such is Connolly's philosophical nominalism that the very idea of generalizing about the political terms upon which social co-operation emerges in a liberal democracy, or about the generation of commonly held moral beliefs through dialogue, vanish from the normative horizon. Instead, he invokes 'difference', both to interpret social pluralization and as a yardstick to reinterpret such values as equality and justice. Through this concept he is able to overlay an account of social change upon the ontological claim that difference is a condition of identity.[4] Connolly also subscribes to a strong version of the idea of the incommensurability of values, and joins other liberal theorists in observing the unavoidably 'tragic' implication of this situation on the basis that no one person can adhere to all the ideals that inform a valuable life. Incommensurability implies that individuals must learn to manage the tensions arising from the clash of competing values, as well as the tragic necessity of compromise. Rationalistic liberalism, he claims, does little to prepare its citizens for these conditions.

But his advocacy of the thesis of value pluralism weakens Connolly's strong attachment to democracy. On what grounds can he be sure that a democratic polity is the most appropriate for a society characterized by moral disagreement 'that goes all the way down'? An elitist form of rule or the control of an enlightened despot appear just as capable of delivering on the social conditions that Connolly sees as pertinent to any functioning democracy – social peace and the space for diversity to flourish. His belief that radical democracy is most conducive to the values and practices of diversity and pluralization relies heavily upon the hope that, through democratic interchange and participation, reciprocal understanding and trust are deepened, and that these provide fertile conditions for the kind of openness to the 'other' that he celebrates. In the agonistic polity, the stance of ironic self-effacement should supplant liberal hubris. The idea that these are likely outcomes of democratic interchange, however, appears to be founded on an optimistic disposition, and little else. Why should we share his conviction that democratic institutions are appropriate to the realization of the sense of awe at the diversity of life that he celebrates? And on what grounds are we to believe that an agonistic political framework can capture the loyalties of its citizens? Democracy within his model can be justified only contingently, and, presumably, just as contingently abandoned. Participating in joint enterprises and learning the arts of negotiation with others are presented as potential sources for the cultivation of an ironic, self-effacing citizens' culture. These values, however, may well depend upon the prior establishment of such goods as reciprocity, social capital and trust, all of which appear in short supply in democratic societies. In such contexts, the unyielding language of differentiation, and the renunciation of the idea that democracies require a shared moral horizon, appear more likely to diminish than enhance the democratization of representative democracy.

Connolly's (and others') emphases upon pluralization and differentiation as the conditions for, and goals of, democratization should make liberal democrats uneasy (Spragens, 1999). There are good reasons, for instance, to suggest that differentiation has produced various novel kinds of shared interest and forms of connectedness, but these are missed by the particularist outlook that these thinkers favour. New senses of localized and regional belonging, the slow but steady move towards toleration of some 'differences' in liberal cultures, and the increasing willingness of many leading religions and cultural groups to accept the 'burdens of judgement' in democratic societies all suggest that the uni-dimensional emphases upon difference and incommensurability skew our understanding of contemporary social and political dilemmas.

Conclusions

Connolly's account of the agonistic polity arises from a more radicalized stance towards difference than that adopted by Young. Though his is an unusual and heterodox voice within debates about multiculturalism, he does speak in relation to a swathe of cultural and social theory that asserts the ontology of difference. He argues that, in the context of marked social and moral differentiation, liberals should jettison their universalist pretensions and advocate the cultivation of a sense of open-ness towards, and reciprocity with, the other. But such is the totalizing character of his attack upon the veiled intolerance of liberal democracy that he leaves little room in his argument for any account of citizenship as an organizational principle of representative democracy (Gianni, 1998: 43).

Young, on the other hand, argues for the public domain to be made more amenable to many different groups in civil society, and makes a case for public intervention on behalf of oppressed subjects. She believes that the values dear to many other liberals – social justice and equality – remain pertinent if they are divested of the myths of impartiality and deliberation based upon unanimity. In her model, difference emerges from an ontological account of groups, and this is deployed to justify the idea of a heterogeneously constituted public domain, as well as a more inclusive and plural political conversation.

Though different in many respects, both of these positions illustrate the increasing influence of heterodox ontological and metaphysical ideas upon current liberal theorizing. On the whole, rationalistic philosophers tend to ignore or dismiss the challenges laid down by these attacks upon the intellectual architecture of liberal thought. But, despite some of the weaknesses that afflict these authors' conceptions of the political, their arguments deserve a considered, critical engagement. These positions derive momentum and inspiration from the belief that the hubristic ele-ments of liberal theory need to be tempered. Equally, the idea of a dif-ferentiated citizenship is one that chimes with the outlooks of various social and political forces within democratic settings, and more gener-ally with the idea that liberal democracy constitutes a 'pragmatic exper-iment for reaching a better political integration in deeply culturally divided societies' (Gianni, 1998: 43).

Through a critical engagement with these projects, political theorists come face to face with some important contemporary social intuitions and pluralist claims. Yet the central arguments of both of these thinkers merit scepticism on liberal democratic grounds. The political recommendations they propose are hampered by the strongly particularistic ethical approach that they adopt, preventing them from adequately theorizing the problems of social co-operation and political agreement without which democratic citizenship is impossible. Neither gives a plausible answer to the question of when the institutional, moral and political requirements of a democratic order can legitimately infringe upon social identity. And neither considers that, in morally and culturally diverse societies, it may have become *more* important to differentiate between the duties we possess as citizens and the loyalties and obligations we feel towards the sub-national groupings to which we belong.

8

Liberalism and the Politics of Recognition

Introduction

As well as such terms as difference, diversity and identity, the idea of recognition has once again become a familiar presence in the conceptual vocabulary of Anglo-American political theorists. It is widely claimed that the politics of identity finds its natural political expression in the increasing number of demands for recognition made by various social groups (Tully, 2000a). One of the foundational impulses for normative accounts of recognition is scepticism towards the notion that the state can or should be neutral towards the culture, language and values of its citizens (Bader, 1997: 784; Bennett, 1999). Recognition is, therefore, typically advanced as the antithesis to the liberal idea of cultural neutrality and suggested as the basis for a liberalism that is sensitive to the diverse values bound up in different group cultures.

Charles Taylor is one of the leading thinkers to suggest that the liberal ideal of public neutrality is inapplicable in culturally diverse societies and should be displaced by the principle of the equal worth of cultures (1994: 62; Baumeister, 2000: 134). The idea that a neutral ground exists on which 'people of all cultures can meet and co-exist' is one that he repeatedly dismisses (Nicholson, 1996: 7). He rejects, in particular, the proceduralist liberal argument that a set of institutions and procedures can be determined independently from arguments about the ends of life. Such a claim serves to normalize outlooks and practices consonant with the values of North American liberalism. The lure of neutrality has successfully diverted critical attention from the *Kulturkampf* that liberal states have pursued in the guise of their various nation-building endeavours and the assimilationist impulses these have engendered towards minority cultures (Kymlicka, 1998).

The concepts of recognition and neutrality, I will suggest, however, do not have to be configured by liberals as opposites. A rather different liberal approach takes neutrality to imply an even-handedness that can accommodate some forms of public recognition without subscribing to the culturalist claims advanced by Taylor (Carens, 2000). This position takes its cue from attention to the various asymmetries of standing and power between groups, especially those that arise from the experiences associated with imposed identity, and considers how these affect the liberal principles of equality of concern and respect (Patten, 2000: 200–1). It emerges into view through consideration of Nancy Fraser's work. She and others suggest that many group differences are not solely graspable along the dimension of recognition, but are also pertinent to the more familiar axes of distribution and equality (Fraser, 1995a; 1995b; 1997; 1998). Avoiding the positions inhabited by advocates of a cultural politics of recognition, on the one hand, and versions of neutrality that imply an indifference to group membership, on the other, these thinkers suggest that the problematic of recognition can be usefully incorporated within the framework established by liberal theories of justice. This idea suggests the possibility of a reformulation of the politics of recognition beyond the culturalist preoccupations of parts of the liberal intelligentsia. The notion of recognition as an aspect of justice relies upon the idea that this value might be considered as a kind of currency distributed to those who seek it, and hence as akin to other goods, such as resources or power, that are the subjects of a more or less fair distribution among individuals (Emcke, 2000: 484). This is a distinct approach to recognition from demands for group rights or the public recognition of cultures. These latter measures may well be only partially beneficial to individual members of subordinated collectivities since the cultural politics of recognition may not be sufficient to deal with the damaged self-esteem or the absence of capabilities generated by complex relations of social inequality. More generally, the emphasis on recognizing cultures may crucially underplay the degree to which individuals forge a sense of self by working with, and in reaction to, various cultural materials, rather than through deep immersion within a single cultural system.

One further sense of recognition has also become prominent of late. This too offers some promising insights for those seeking to explore overlaps and synergies between liberalism and recognition, rather than presuming that they must be opposites. This argument postulates democracy, rather than justice, as the major political value that recognition illuminates, a position elaborated by, among others, the Canadian theorist James Tully. Rejecting end-state notions of the fully recognized person or group, he suggests that we consider recognition as one of the conditions for a genuinely democratic dialogue that will enable citizens to come to understand each other more fully and to generate different kinds of 'recognition capital' (2000a: 470; 2000b: 215–17, 229).

The multiple politics of recognition

The way in which the concept of recognition is deployed by a theorist tends to shape their conception of what is required to satisfy the demand for it. Three different kinds of project can be connected with the constructions of this value considered in this chapter, although this is by no means an exhaustive taxonomy. Taylor's intersubjective focus tends to encourage examination of the social and cultural preconditions that produce or vitiate recognition. This idea has been taken to support the multiculturalist claim that an individual's well-being requires that their culture be publicly validated. Second, Fraser's approach leads its adherents to consider how groups seek to gain various goods for their members as part of a wider and continuous struggle for advantage and standing. Though the idea of an encompassing collective identity can figure in such analyses, it does not have to, as individual members can be regarded as identifying with various groups in order to gain material and symbolic benefits. The third sense is striking because, in Tully's formulation, it promises to disconnect the question of singular group identity from the struggle for recognition:

> what is at issue is whether or not there are open processes or practices of critical negotiation and modification of the identities under which we are led to recognize ourselves and others as members of a fair system of social co-operation, so we are not unnecessarily and arbitrarily subject to an imposed identity. (2000a: 479)

By following fair and inclusive deliberative procedures, a pluralistic democracy can generate negotiative practices in which a variety of different identities are aired and given degrees of legitimacy and recognition, and individuals confidently develop various kinds of interdependence with, and difference from, others. One of the constitutive aims of such negotiations is to strengthen and deepen the sense of belonging that culturally diverse citizens feel towards their polity. Inclusion, it is claimed, is deepened when individuals feel that they have played some role in shaping the decisions by which the norms and values of their community are determined.

Recognition as intersubjectivity: Charles Taylor

Taylor's is the best-known contemporary political theory of recognition, in part because of his skilful importation of insights lodged within the fields of ethical and psychological thought. In both of these disciplines, the claim that the social practices through which recognition occurs are integral to the formation of the self is a familiar one, developed by, for instance, leading authors such as Axel Honneth (1995) and Jessica

Benjamin (1998). Taylor is among the first theorists to deploy such ideas in a political context, offering an extended and influential intervention in debates about the implications of multiculturalism for liberal thought and politics. His essay 'The Politics of Recognition' (1994; first published 1992) has become the major text within the emerging literature on this topic and has achieved an audience beyond the world of academic political theory. His contention that democracies need to take the claims of indigenous peoples, linguistic minorities and other kinds of social groups far more seriously resonates powerfully with political debate beyond the academy. Underpinning his argument is an account of the historical formation of some of the leading notions of the self in Western society (1989; Smith, 2002; Horton, 1998). Taylor's understanding of the origins and development of distinctively modern conceptions of selfhood have stimulated an important set of intellectual enquiries in their own right. His thinking is explored here with a view to establishing if he succeeds in demonstrating that recognition is valuable for the reasons he suggests, and if the thesis of intersubjectivity translates into a political programme that can safely be regarded as either liberal or democratic.

One of the main foundations for Taylor's theory of recognition is the claim that our sense of our own well-being and moral goals depend critically on how we see ourselves reflected in the eyes of others (1994). Since our notion of who we are arises from social interactions, the experience of repeated disapproval or stigmatization in the gaze of significant others may well compromise our sense of self-worth. 'Since each person is intersubjectively interwoven with others, he or she is dependent on the reactions of others for his or her self-image and identity' (Emcke, 2000: 484). This argument is typically combined with the suggestion that such harms can amount to moral injury if humiliation or damage to self-esteem result from them (Carens and Williams, 1996). The establishment of healthy and rewarding interpersonal relations is thus postulated as a condition for the development of the independence and sense of worth of individual citizens. Taylor's communitarian leanings lead him to consider social relations through the social framework of the communities to which individuals belong (Horton, 1998: 160–2). Being in a group whose culture is reviled and devalued is to be prone to this kind of moral harm. To make effective repairs to damaged identities requires that the internal self-dislocation generated by malign intersubjective relations be overcome. The despised group must be revalued and publicly acknowledged as a legitimate presence within the body politic.

A challenging and contentious feature of this argument is the assertion that moral, as well as psychological, injuries arise from misrecognition. Taylor's confidence in this proposition stems from his distinctive account of modern understandings of the self (Vogel, 1993). The desire to achieve an identity that is authentically one's own has emerged as a central ideal of modern selfhood. This means that we typically feel ourselves to be the unique possessors of various qualities and potentials, and deserve some respect in relation to these (Taylor, 1994: 29–33). In his major study of the genealogy of modern constructions of selfhood, *Sources of the Self* (1989), Taylor charts the emergence of this sense of personal authenticity, connecting it to the dissolution of established forms of moral, theological and social authority. Modern approaches to identity are characterized by their radical turn inward, as the notion that the sources of our beliefs and passions lie in some externalized cosmological or theological notion of the good is weakened. With the steady decline of such traditions, and the propagation of the idea that we are each responsible for our distinctive natures and endowed with the capacity to determine our own moral goals, the need for recognition comes to the surface of contemporary political life (1994: 37–44). It provides a functional replacement, Taylor suggests, for the quest for honour in the medieval social order (1994: 26–7). In the conditions of modernity, the ideal of authenticity intertwines with the notion that we each fashion our own personhood.

Combining these emphases upon intersubjectivity and authenticity, Taylor develops the argument that to achieve a stable identity I require recognition from my peers for my particularity, being granted recognition in respect of my own qualities and attributes. The quest for recognition, however, carries a dual meaning. On the one hand, the need for authenticity encourages the belief that I should demand to belong to a society that is prepared to hear my voice, and that recognizes my capacity to forge an identity worthy of respect (Vogel, 1993: 328; Seglow, 1998). And yet, I also need protection and rights in respect of my shared status as a citizen. These needs are typically reflected in various legally enshrined rights and liberties that give expression to the norm of the equal worth of persons. They are granted irrespective of the many particularities and unique qualities of individuals (Taylor, 1994: 37–44). The principle of recognition therefore unfolds along two different axes: both as a reflection of the need to have our particular moral goals and aptitudes accorded value, and as an expression of the idea of the universal dignity of the person (1994: 44–51). Some of the most important demands made by contemporary cultural groups – over such issues as language, culture and ethnicity – can thus be seen as collective expressions of individuals' needs for recognition (Honneth, 1995; 1997). The politics of difference that has come to the attention of intellectuals and policy-makers alike is underpinned by the yearning for cultural authenticity and the refusal to submit to the moral injuries that arise from assimilation to the cultural practices and preferences of the majority.

One difficulty posed by this normative model concerns the potentiality for the proliferation of group conflicts if the discourse of cultural authenticity is publicly legitimated. What of situations where two cultures regard their own traditions as legitimately furthered by practices that are deeply offensive to the 'authentic' traditions of another (Benhabib, 2002)? Recognition theory is haunted by a compossibility problem that few of its adherents acknowledge. It is impossible to imagine according positive value to all of the cultures that co-exist in a democratic state, because many of these are rivals (Levy: 2000: 31–3). The explosive character of the question of whether Loyalist parades in Northern Ireland ought to run through Catholic areas illustrates such a difficulty (O'Neill, 2000). Adjudicating fairly between these different claims to recognition is well nigh impossible if they are to be judged primarily in relation to the authenticity of the experience and identity they offer to participants. Adjudicating conflicts generated by group cultural differences inevitably invokes claims about such values as justice, desert and equality, which are, of course, integral to liberalism (Benhabib, 2002: 57).

But, in Taylor's account, liberalism enjoys a troubled and ambiguous relationship with this emergent ideal of recognition. Its commitment to the notion that each individual's way of life is of equal potential value implies that it regards a range of moral perspectives and cultures as valid sources and objects of individual choice. But philosophical liberalism typically frames this commitment to 'difference' within a normative framework that stresses the equality of right that individuals possess in relation to the different goods and ends that they pursue. This points towards the idea of treating persons irrespective of their differences (1994: 43). Taylor is famously critical of Kantian versions of liberalism that claim to prioritize the principles of 'the right' over 'the good' and posit an ideal constitution founded upon purportedly non-contentious moral principles (1995a). A liberal polity, in his view, does indeed require 'difference-blind procedures for interpreting and redeeming individual rights (by judicial review)' (Smith, 2002: 155), but it also needs a substantive sense of common moral purpose forged out of the interaction of the different cultures subsisting within it. Different 'expressive possibilities' (Smith, 2002: 156) are compatible with a system of equal basic liberty. At the level of the laws and constitution, equality generally implies the uniform treatment of all citizens. But in terms of public policy, and by implication the public institutions and norms of the state, the recognition of cultural differences is integral to the sense of purpose and prevailing moral understandings of a political community.

For this reason, Taylor is a strong proponent of multiculturalist educational provision if this is designed to enhance mutual cultural understanding, rather than merely represent incommensurable perspectival differences (1994: 63–9). The ground for this, he stresses, is neither the claim that all cultures are of equal value, nor the relativist idea that it is impossible for anyone to judge whether another culture possesses value or not. He combines a pluralist sense that every culture of a certain longevity is likely to possess some contribution to and understanding of 'the good' with a call for restraint in the judgements we make, both individually and collectively (1994: 66–7). Some degree of knowledge of the operative meanings and totality of another cultural system is a necessary feature of responsible judgement and the possibility of greater mutual understanding. The need to offer moral evaluation is a fundamental aspect of human well-being, but such judgements are best made against the backdrop of respectful dialogue with members of other cultural groups and 'out of a reasonable presumption that we have much to share: an ultimate horizon in which we all participate' (1994: 68). Such an interpretative engagement, Taylor hopes, will produce a more reflexive sensibility towards the partiality and contingency of the majority's culture and, beyond that, a putative 'fusion of horizons' as new kinds of hybrid perspectives and vocabularies of cultural comparison emerge (1994: 67). Justice demands that respect be awarded to a diversity of actually evolved cultures within the boundaries of the political community (Deveaux, 2000a; 2000b; Poole, 2000).

Observing the many political conflicts generated by the tension in liberal societies between the politics of dignity, usually translated into a regime of individual rights, and the impulse towards cultural differentiation, Taylor is adamant that a proceduralist response to these dilemmas is inadequate. A multicultural, liberal society is one in which individuals are accorded respect in so far as they are adherents of a particular cultural heritage, as well as a distinctive kind of legal-constitutional regime in which the basic structure of rights and liberties is preserved. Partisan debate and moral judgement are intrinsic features of the political life of such a state. There is no neutral ground that individuals can occupy, beyond the scope of their various identities and attachments, in order to determine the rules of the just society.

The sources of 'recognition' in Taylor's thought

Different commentators have suggested that, in order to understand the principal features and purposes of Taylor's argument, it is necessary to consider a variety of religious, political and philosophical influences upon his thinking.[1] In terms of his understanding of the role of culture in political life, his experiences in Canadian politics have rightly been emphasized (Smith, 2002: 183–92; Laforest, 1993). Less widely observed, though also important, is the impact of anti-colonial struggles upon his embryonic thinking. This influence was absorbed in part while he was a central participant within the first phase of the British New Left (Smith, 2002: 172–83). While a postgraduate student at Oxford University in the late 1950s, Taylor was a contributor to the debates and ideas associated with this current. A central inspiration for many of its participants was the rising tide of anti-colonialist agitation during this period (Kenny, 1995). The writings of, among others, Frantz Fanon were embraced by a generation of young radicals captivated by the ethos of radical nationalism and by the moral importance of the struggle for an authentic post-colonial nationhood within the 'third world'. Fanon's account of the psychological and socio-cultural dimensions of this kind of 'nation-building', and his analysis of the ways in which colonial social formations relied as much upon internalized subordination as on the formal apparatus of imperial rule, was widely discussed (1965; Taylor, 1994: 66). Taylor was also influenced by, and took part in, debates about the usages and significance of culture as a system through which hegemony was exercised and the alienation of man, in the language of the early Marx, was effected (1957; 1958). This particular experience is worth bringing into view as it provides some important clues to the complex fusion of philosophical, ethical and political ideas in Taylor's work, and, specifically, his sense of the emancipatory potential of culturally orientated political projects.[2] It also illustrates one of the organic links between New Left thinking and contemporary liberal pluralism, highlighted in chapter 1.

Taylor's formulation of an explicit theory of recognition was developed above all, however, through his particular experiences of the divisive politics of federalism that emerged in Canadian political life in the 1980s and the arguments surrounding the 1982 Canadian Charter of Rights (Taylor, 1994: 51–61). He sought to square his commitment to the significance of Canada as a political community, in which different national and indigenous groupings might co-exist, with his support for the rights of those committed to the preservation of Francophone culture within the Quebec region. The divisive debates that arose in this conflict, and the apparent gulf between the demands of the English-speaking minority in Quebec, on the one hand, and radical elements in the Quebecois community, on the other, informed his normative argument for a liberal polity in which different identities were to be regarded as sources of value. Given these experiences, it is perhaps not surprising that the model of the national and linguistic minority figures prominently in his understanding of the injustices that democratic states can effect upon minorities. Contrary to the accusations of some critics, this is not the only kind of grouping that Taylor has in mind when he considers the idea of group recognition (Lamey, 1999). Yet there is some merit to the claim that, because, in his eyes, the paradigmatic instance of a group seeking respect is an ethno-national community, the ethos of recognition makes more sense in relation to some social struggles than others.

In normative terms, the idea of adopting a moral framework that generalizes from the particular, and perhaps peculiar, struggles of beleaguered national minorities to the experiences of other kinds of group represents a major source of contention. Linda Nicholson, for instance, historicizes the shifting meanings of both recognition and social identity that have emerged since the 1960s (1996). Some groups, she notes, demand recognition less on the grounds of their authentic cultural individuality, but so that the burdens of ascriptive group memberships can be lessened for members. Many develop a dual political outlook: at certain moments they want to proclaim their unassimilable differences, and at others they want to evade or transcend the idea that they are different. Taylor's political model threatens to corral these into one, potentially inappropriate, political framework.

Evaluating Taylor's politics of recognition

Culture and identity

This kind of criticism is best located in the context of the wider controversy occasioned by the efforts of some contemporary pluralists to assert the value of culture as a theme of intrinsic moral and political significance for liberal political thought (a position that is discussed in chapter 2; Kymlicka, 1989). This kind of argument raises the considerable problem of how to understand the relationship between the identities achieved by individual citizens and the cultures to which they belong. Taylor advances two claims in regard to this relationship that appear to fit awkwardly with his commitment to the integrity and values of whole cultures. The first is his suggestion that in crucial respects the particularity of individuals arises from 'the ways in which they integrate, reflect upon, and modify their own cultural heritage and that of other people with whom they come into contact' (1991b: 7). He elaborates this position in several major works, observing the importance to the self of its immersion in, *and interaction with*, what he terms webs of social and linguistic interlocution (1985: 13–76; Benhabib, 2002: 55–6; Horton, 1998: 157–9). The second important claim that Taylor makes about this relationship is that identity should be conceptualized as the product of dialogical interactions – between self and a variety of different others.

Yet neither of these commitments sits easily with the stress upon the coherence and depth of a group's culture that Taylor regards as sources of its claims to recognition and respect. According to the first stipulation, modern individuals are uniquely possessed of the capacity to modify and reflect upon values, and to relate simultaneously to a variety of cultural resources (1985). When considering the needs of individuals, it seems that Taylor has in mind a more de-centred, fragmentary and pluralist conception of cultural life. His understanding of the different sources of meaning and webs of interlocution through which individuals develop also implies, in normative terms, that it is erroneous to privilege any particular level or kind of community when considering the ethical formation of individuals. But when he turns to groups, Taylor defends an ethic that appears to obviate these social conditions for modern individuality and his own strictures about the self. The multiculturalist demand that value be accorded to minority cultures may actually worsen the chances for sub-groups and persons within that minority from developing their own individuality.

Taylor's second claim implies that the intersubjective character of self-hood naturally lends itself to the idea of the political re-evaluation of marginalized cultures. But in the cases of those cultures that are founded upon ascription (as is the case with some of the examples he himself considers), it may be more appropriate to reflect the desires of individuals to be recognized on the terms they choose – and this may imply a refusal to be defined predominantly as Hispanic or gay, for example, as much as a desire to have that identity valued more widely (Appiah, 1994). Underpinning Taylor's argument for recognition is the dubious proposition that members of subordinated groups are inherently prone to moral harm because of the process of misrecognition that liberal culture produces. Such a claim radically underplays the degree to which individuals forge a sense of themselves as much by rejecting and refining collective identity as by immersion within it. This idea is also politically damaging because it inflects its adherents towards the idea that contemporary injustices can be overcome primarily through struggles designed to achieve the restitution of derided or stereotyped identities, as opposed to devising strategies that aim to secure equality of respect for all.

Moreover, if, as Taylor claims, dialogue and interaction with the other are to be regarded as constitutive of a person's identity, on what grounds can we be confident that a polity which seeks to provide the kinds of group recognition that he advocates will promote the right kinds of dialogic interaction? One of the major difficulties with Taylor's formulation of recognition is the implied analogy he offers between the recognition that individuals require and that which some groups seek. In fact, 'Individual claims to authentic self-expression need not run in tandem with collective aspirations to cultural recognition. They may even contradict one another' (Benhabib, 2002: 52). Once cultures, as opposed to individuals, are regarded as the *locus* of value, the latter can become the moral servants of the former.

Behind these particular tensions in Taylor's position lies the wider and recurrent problem of determining what a culture actually is, and what kind of moral weight it should carry for those who belong to and partake of it. In the debates about the ethical and social character of cultures that have developed among political theorists, it has become increasingly clear that 'characterizing the "identity" of a culture is itself a politically and ideologically charged issue' (A. O. Rorty, 1994: 152). What counts as the legitimate expression of a group's culture or the official version of its history inevitably form the subjects of disagreement. But, in Taylor's model, there is little space for the possibility that such debates and differences are constitutive of the collective identity that any group establishes. This version of recognition also underplays the potency of the recurrent dilemma that a liberal political system poses for outsider or oppositional groups – to comply with or rebel against its core norms and values. Marginalized and oppressed groups react to this dilemma in different ways, and it is these reactions, rather than the postulated cultural essences that underpin them, that help shape how individuals relate to the wider political culture and system they inhabit. Without such a distinction, the different stances adopted by identity-based groups towards the liberal polity – a spectrum that is not captured by the duality of for/against liberalism – make little sense.

In his desire to establish both the independent moral significance of cultures and the diverse ways in which these connect individuals to 'the good', Taylor tends to disconnect the cultural from other dimensions and modalities of power. To explain human behaviour, however, we need to understand the totality of circumstances of which culture is an aspect (Appiah, 1996: 83; Benhabib, 2002: 7). The influence of the romantic heritage upon his thinking is perhaps most marked in this respect. It encourages a conceptual counter-opposition in his thought between the authenticity and belonging that culture can supply and the individualism, instrumentality, and shallowness of liberal society. But such a duality deflects attention from the heteronomous and hierarchical character of many cultural communities, and sustains the myth that struggles for recognition pursue a trajectory that is entirely independent of other kinds of egalitarian campaign. This restricts the adequacy of this model for those seeking to understand and overcome the complex character of injustice. As Iris Young argues:

> Where there are problems of lack of recognition of national, cultural, religious, or linguistic groups, these are usually tied to questions of control over resources, exclusion from benefits of political influence or economic participation, strategic power, or segregation from opportunities. A politics of recognition, that is, usually is part of or a means to claims for political and social inclusion or an end to structural inequalities that disadvantage them. (2000: 105)

Finally, Taylor's conception of culturally based politics is overshadowed by the problem of authenticity. What exactly determines the authentic character of a cultural system, and its consequent moral significance, is a much more troubling issue than his account of recognition implies. The very quest for a stable or objective distinction is confounded by the open-ended nature, dynamism and de-centred character of modern cultures. While Taylor may well want to dismiss such cultures as partriarchalism, heterosexism or consumerism as insufficiently authentic to merit respect and recognition, for many of their adherents these are experienced as rich in meanings and are as authentically experienced as any other cultural formation.

The problem of authenticity

This brings us to the second class of problems that critics have observed with this model – the notion of authenticity, and its relationship with and bearing upon autonomy. The ideal of authenticity that Taylor sees as central to modern notions of the self finds expression, he believes, in the assertion of irreducible group differences. These sustain a reassertion of the particular demands for recognition that bump against the egalitarian logic of equal dignity. This is a fascinating and challenging historical thesis, but is it also a normative argument to which contemporary liberals should adhere?

Other theorists of recognition suggest that these impulses may be more mutually intertwined and symbiotic than Taylor suggests. Axel Honneth's interpretation of Hegel's thinking reminds us of an alternative conception that has exercised some influence over the project of designing democratic institutions and legal systems (Honneth, 1995; 1997; O'Neill, 1997; Spång, 2002). In this, recognition is conceived as immanent within the legal and social relations realized in the liberal state. For Hegel, the particularity of the group life shaped within civil society also possessed an immanent quality of universality (Avineri, 1972). The system of needs prefigures and implies the principle of right and the unity of the political community. These imperatives find their fullest expression at the level of the public life of the citizen. Our standing as citizens generates a sense of security founded upon the recognition we bestow when we regard our co-citizens as worthy possessors of rights and duties. Honneth highlights Hegel's conception of 'a form of recognition that allows subjects to esteem one another in those attributes that contribute to the reproduction of the societal order' (1997: 21). Recognition is, on this model, integral both to civil society, the realm of 'difference', and to the laws and norms pertinent for the citizen, and is one of the ethical values through which the particular and universal are inter-imbricated. While Taylor regards recognition as embedded within the unfolding logic of the particular, other democratic theorists suggest the fertility of conceiving this value through the push and pull of similitude and difference.

A similar argument has been made by various critics of the ideal of authenticity (Habermas, 1993). Maeve Cooke detects an ambiguity in Taylor's alignment of the politics of difference and the ideal of authenticity, 'whereby each individual is thought to have a unique identity, an original way of being human, to which she or he must be true' (1997: 260). But what does being true to oneself involve? Some sense of one's unique attributes or potentiality is part of the answer, but so too is 'the individual's power to determine for herself a particular understanding of the good life' (1997: 261). This suggests a moral conception that approximates closely to the value of autonomy (1997: 261), and is rooted in the premise that individuality is 'equally worthy of respect in the pursuit of its own self-realization' (Benhabib, 2002: 56–7). Taylor unjustifiably removes autonomy from his account of the politics of group identity, when in fact his conception of the individual self relies upon such a notion (Habermas, 1993: 131).

Taylor's account of recognition as a moral imperative that liberalism needs to accept has commanded wide attention in political theory, not least because it captures a mood of scepticism towards the stance of cultural agnosticism favoured by leading Anglo-American liberal philosophers. His argument poses some important questions about the capacity of individuals to pursue the quest for individuality in societies traversed by powerful and unyielding patterns of subordination and marginalization. His position is especially pertinent in political contexts where many liberal-minded citizens are acutely aware of the tension noted by Richard Rorty – between the impulse to embrace diversity and a growing unease about the shallow roots of the consensus underpinning the liberal rights and liberties of democratic citizenship.

But, with his ultimately unconvincing analogy between the kinds of recognition that individuals need and those that some groups demand, Taylor's position slides from ontology to advocacy in a way that is worrying for liberal democrats. The politics of recognition can very easily slip into an illiberal bolstering of certain communal scripts and identities over others (Appiah, 1994). While this is clearly far from Taylor's own intentions, it is a danger attendant upon the ideal of cultural authenticity. His position does have critical bite, however, in its critique of the cultural agnosticism of proceduralist liberalism. He and other critics point to the collusion between such a position and the influence of a pervasive, hegemonic kind of cultural individualism that is founded upon the myth that an increase in choice necessarily enhances the prospects of freedom.

Recognition and justice: Nancy Fraser

One of the most controversial aspects of Taylor's account of recognition arises from his suggestion that the politics of recognition has been historically subsumed beneath the redistributive ambitions associated with the traditions of social democracy and social liberalism. Some commentators see in his arguments an important illustration of a much broader attitudinal shift among liberal and left intellectuals towards an embrace of cultural diversity and identity, and a consequent abandonment of the progressive tradition of social reform and justice (Barry, 2001a; Fraser, 1995b: 166; 1998). Richard Rorty captures and laments this move in his delineation of the rise of a cultural left more committed to a therapeutic concern with the cultural and psychological obstacles to selfhood. The idea that thinkers such as Taylor have made a fateful choice in their focus upon 'sadism' rather than 'selfishness' is bound up with the continuing intellectual and political fall-out that has accompanied the recent weakening of socialism and social democracy as political traditions (Rorty, 1998: 76). As we have already seen (in chapter 1), such broad-brush characterizations of those intellectual trends are rarely innocent: they are best treated as argumentative devices through which ideological leverage is sought. Nevertheless, Rorty's complaint resonates widely. From these debates, various rival accounts of the character of group-based inequality and oppression in liberal capitalist society have emerged. One such argument figures in the work of Fraser (1995a; 1995b; 1997; 1998).

Fraser rejects the culturalism latent within Taylor's arguments but retains his insight into the psychological harms and social inequities that are perpetuated through the marginalization and stigmatization of some social groupings. She begins by asking whether the emergence of a new cultural politics of recognition has contributed to the disappearance from the mainstream political agenda of egalitarian arguments for redistribution (1997). Like others, she worries that the politics of difference is advanced in ways that encourage separatist, patriarchal and authoritarian tendencies. By replacing a concern with the material and structurally embedded sources of injustice with the problem of cultural diversity, advocates of 'difference' or 'recognition' may indirectly be contributing to the marginalization of the problem of economic inequality (1997: 11–39; Barry, 2001a).

Fraser does not, however, reject the value of recognition claims entirely. She proposes instead a normative framework that seeks to bring the demands associated with recognition into the parameters set by established notions of social justice (see also Tully, 2000a). She also challenges egalitarians to heed voices proclaiming forms of hurt and injury that they may not as yet have considered. At the heart of this framework is the idea that, although neither recognition nor redistribution are entirely subsumed within each other, it is possible to offer a theoretically ordered account of how they might interrelate as moral imperatives (Fraser, 1999–2000). In her account of recognition, the language and logic of 'identity' is replaced by the Weberian notion of status. Individual members of groups whose identities are devalued or ridiculed by the majority culture are prone to injuries to their status as equal members of, and potential participants in, the life of the political community (1997).

Following Weber, Fraser suggests that it may be possible to consider such harms in relation to those generated by inequities arising from socio-economic standing and power. This position complements the discussion of self-respect and humiliation, which I suggested were germane to contemporary liberalism, in chapter 2. An adequate theory of social justice, Fraser suggests, requires attention to the character of cultural hegemony in liberal society, as well as an analytical sense of the continuing and deepening divisions associated with social class (1995a). Based upon this dualistic framework, she critically engages contemporary political theories of recognition and justice. Adherents of cultural politics are wrong to read all manifestations of inequality purely through the lens of culturally mediated difference. Marxists and liberal egalitarians are similarly mistaken to interpret status harms through the lexicon of class. While such a double focus may be analytically advantageous, by itself it is not enough to guide understanding of those cases in which the logic of recognition clashes with the ethos of redistribution – as, for instance, when a minority demands recognition for its cultural practices that are premised upon the denial of equality to women within its ranks. Fraser is well aware of this tension and argues that we should heed the demands of minority groups and communities as long as they are combined with 'the social politics of equality' (1995a: 69). The politics of identity is morally significant in so far as it conforms to the parameters of status and class inequalities.

Across the communities of movement activists and sympathetic intellectuals in which talk of recognition and identity prevails, Fraser detects two contrasting strategic-political outlooks associated with, respectively, recognition and redistribution (1995a: 80–92). The first consists of an affirmatory stance towards a particular group identity. One such example involves campaigners for gay equality who seek to gain for gays and lesbians public goods and rights enjoyed by others, and to remove unjustifiable burdens upon individuals affected by these imposed identities. A rival approach suggests a fundamental rearrangement of the cultural field in which the marginalized identity is produced. The development of 'queer' theory and various instances of radical gay activism illustrate the ethos of such a transformative aspiration. Demands for redistributive justice in the political realm likewise divide into two contrasting strategic orientations: those who seek an affirmative remedy for particular inequalities – advocates of the welfare state, for example – and those who seek to attack the causes of these inequalities – radical socialists and, in today's terms, anti-globalization protesters.

Returning to her dualistic conception of social justice, Fraser highlights the various normative combinations of this fourfold matrix that have been, or might be, forthcoming. She argues the case for an as-yet unrealized politics in which both transformative approaches are conjoined (1995a). Some common assumptions underwrite such a potential overlap or alliance, not least that it is possible to do justice to certain claims for recognition without accepting that this invariably entails accepting a group's own account of its history. Benhabib sees such a fusion as consonant with a democratic politics that emphasizes the importance of transforming social patterns of representation, interpretation and communication, as opposed to the furthering of specific group agendas (2002: 70). Certainly the idea that the politics of recognition can be taken to imply a deepening of democratic interchange, the airing of intra-group differences, and a more reflexive dispensation by groups towards their cultures is a promising one for liberals. Fraser adds an unusual note to some increasingly standard multiculturalist claims: the politics of recognition needs to be inflected away from the image of the cultural enclave and deployed as the basis for a political culture in which identity figures as the source and object of dissent, debate and contestation.

Recognition and democratization: James Tully

One of Fraser's main aims is to expand the social and moral horizons of contemporary social and political theorists regarding the dimensions along which inequality arises. The bifurcatory normative model that prevails among egalitarian political theorists is insufficiently adept, she observes, to unpick the combination of socio-economic and cultural pressures experienced by, say, Hispanic-Americans in California or Bangladeshi immigrants in the UK (1995a). In her discussion of particular groups and the moral dilemmas they pose, she reserves a special place for those 'bivalent collectivities' that suffer along the axes of both recognition and distribution – women and African-Americans, for example (1995a: 74–82).

Fraser is one of a number of contemporary theorists who stress the interrelationship of recognition and redistribution and see these as the twin normative pillars of a contemporary theory of justice. James Tully suggests that we should regard current political struggles as typically driven by both imperatives (2000a: 469). His thickly contextualized approach to these issues generates an important warning about the whole genre of argument in which Fraser is engaged. Attempts to elaborate moral principles designed to guarantee the achievement of social justice prior to our engagement with the particular social forms and political contexts in which they are applied may distort understanding of the particularity of group demands and suggest the imposition of inappropriate legal and political measures in response. Tully conceives of recognition in a distinctive fashion: as a process that contributes to the broader instantiation of democratic relations (1995). Recognition does not constitute an end-state or a finite good that one either does or does not wholly possess. It is achievable to differing degrees, and is something that one only appreciates having, or that one comes to perceive as missing, over time. In its ongoing relationship with a wider political culture, it may well be that a social group reconceives the objects it wants to secure, and finds its sense of mission reconstituted through the very processes of engaging with liberal institutions and laws and the wider culture it may be challenging (1995). Tully also observes the inherently unpredictable character of legislative and institutional changes affecting the standing of groups. These may well serve to benefit or disadvantage these formations in unforeseen ways – splitting them into rival socio-economic sub-groupings – as, for instance, in the case of African-Americans after the demise of the civil rights movement.

Tully's suggestion that the relations of distribution and recognition cannot be plausibly modelled in an ideal form presents a useful corrective to Fraser's model. This emphasis is combined in his writings with his strongly pluralist moral orientation. The politics of identity takes a multitude of social forms and, through the different kinds of collective self-assertion it unleashes, invokes a plethora of moral principles. Tully's multilateralist and dialogic conception of the public domain places great emphasis upon the values that arise from the experience of democratic interaction. From the latter, he suggests, there emerges the possibility of some lasting political agreement covering the reach and workings of the 'ineliminable, agonic democratic games over recognition and distribution' that he foresees (2000a: 473). Given his commitment to the idea that these should not permit the domination of some groups by others, it would appear that Tully must have resort to some reasonably robust, universalizable moral commitments (the benefits of non-domination in particular) that sit somewhat uneasily with his particularist ethical proclivities.

Tully's approach to recognition is effective at highlighting deficiencies in accounts of political legitimacy and democratic debate which rely upon univeralist principles that purport to be non-controversial. It is useful to juxtapose his argument with Fraser's in this regard. Striving to effect a plausible and attractive reconciliation of norms that are widely held to be in tension, Fraser offers a theoretical synthesis that is pitched at a high level of political and moral abstraction. The dualistic categories she invokes appear under some strain when they are brought to bear in concrete social settings. Students of the predominant contours of socialist and Marxist thought, moreover, will detect in Fraser's model the echoes of an older, now discredited, distinction: between the purported inadequacies of social reform and the totalizing necessity of social transformation. One problem with such a model is that it misses those strategies that conform to neither broad designation and tends to downgrade programmes associated with reform and affirmation, underestimating their capacity to set in motion wider, unforeseen changes of culture and outlook among both subordinate and dominant groups. The idea that her theoretical synthesis removes the friction between the imperatives of recognition and redistribution is misplaced. Many kinds of humiliation and forms of moral injury do not tally with the moral logic of inequalities generated by social class or the economy.

Recognition and the social bases of self-respect

Three different understandings of recognition have been introduced here, and each connected with a particular account of its moral character. The first of these understandings relies, in Taylor's work, upon a commitment to the intersubjective character of persons and a holistic conception of culture. The second, considered in relation to Fraser, suggests that we view recognition as one dimension of a broader struggle for justice. And the third, introduced via Tully, regards recognition as an ongoing process, one that is integral to the development of the relations of political inclusiveness needed for a democratic and pluralist polity. While Taylor's project is problematic in its slide between ontology and advocacy, Fraser provides glimpses of a more effective liberal approach to recognition. This takes some of the values pertinent to democratic citizenship – self-respect and civility – as the values against which the merits of recognition claims are to be evaluated. The public recognition of a minority group's festivals would be deemed important, for instance, in so far as this is judged to promote the self-esteem of its members. As Rawls argues, we require self-respect in order to view our own goals as ones that are worthy of pursuit (this position is discussed in greater detail in chapter 2; Rosenblum, 1998b: 92–7). Self-respect arises from the relationships we develop in various social arenas, and is given ethical substance in the rights and duties that we possess as citizens.

In some recent writings, the notion of the social bases of self-respect has been presented as intimately tied up with an attempt to reclaim recognition as a specifically liberal concern, one consonant with the values of neutrality and tolerance that many pluralists currently reject. Elizabeth Galeotti offers an important version of such an argument (2002). She highlights a potent paradox facing liberal democratic states. These are founded upon the assumption that, through the establishment of the just allocation of rights and liberties, they have abolished the principal conflicts that make toleration necessary. In practice, however, as issues such as the Salman Rushdie affair and gays in the military indicate, the question of what toleration means has become more, not less, contentious (2002: 3–4). But toleration need not be abandoned in the face of reasonable disagreement and the divisions that arise from group differentiation. Galeotti suggests that we reconsider toleration so that it comes to mean equality of public standing between minority cultures and majority preferences (2002: 5). A liberal state should effect gestures of inclusion towards, and make accommodations for, the symbols, practices and festivals of a host of non-liberal cultures (2002: 12). Toleration implies that no single culture is favoured over any other. The liberal state should actively seek to give various forms of recognition to, and make accommodation for, 'reasonable' group cultures on the grounds that these will protect the self-esteem and moral agency of the individual members of such groups.

In this argument, emphasis is rightly placed upon the idea that there is a strong public interest in offsetting the harmful and alienating effects of the culturally based processes of normalization and stigmatization (Kymlicka, 2002: 329–31). It is the feelings of 'shame, humiliation and self-hatred' developed by some members of 'deviant' groupings that determine when measures of public recognition might be attempted, not the perceived authenticity or justice of the claims that groups make on their behalf (Galeotti, 2002: 9). Multicultural education and such measures as dual language provision for aggrieved nationalist minorities are justifiable, on this view, if they promote the confidence of individuals and enhance the sense of belonging that groups feel in the wider political community (2002: 10). The democratic state needs to engage sensitively with 'the aspects of dignity, respect and worth which allegedly accompany citizenship – i.e. those very elements which confer the "status" of citizenship' (2002: 96). Such a stance, Galeotti suggests, means that the state must pay some heed to processes that produce among some groups of citizens an internalized sense of shame and self-hatred of the kinds observed by Taylor.

This argument relies upon a reconfiguration of the familiar pattern of liberal ideas on these questions, especially through the presentation of toleration and recognition as allies, not opposites (see also Deveaux, 2000b: 43). It offers a very promising illustration of the potential for a liberal engagement with recognition. It also signals the likely development of other similar attempts to move onto the fertile terrain between multiculturalist assertion and liberal cultural abstinence. Some important practical ideas flow from Galeotti's attempted theoretical reconciliation of recognition and tolerance, not least the idea that a liberal state should go out of its way to present the 'reasonable' heritages, religions and moralities of its citizens as 'normal'. Against those Anglo-American liberal philosophers who argue that contentious and divisive topics should be kept out of the public square, she maintains that liberals might very well encourage the proliferation of public cultural expressions and argue for the state recognition of a variety of minority cultural practices. Less convincingly, her argument reflects a considerable confidence in the causal relationship between the sense of inclusion and self-esteem individuals feel and grand symbolic gestures towards minority cultures.

Conclusions

Galeotti does demonstrate, however, that the concept of recognition is by no means alien to the family of liberal thought, despite the hostility to it of many liberal theorists. They worry, above all, that political demands made under the rubric of recognition are structured in such a way that they are beyond reproach or interrogation by those who do not share a particular cultural background. As Jeremy Waldron observes, the political rhetoric of injured identity is not readily amenable to democratic interchange: 'I can give up many things for the social good, but I will not give up my identity. I should not be required to sacrifice who I am for the sake of the benefit to others' (2000: 158). In this form, the non-compromising rhetoric of recognition is liable to deepen divisions and diminish further the prospects for civic unity and solidarity across cleavages of nation, class and ethnicity. A related concern for liberals is that pluralists are insufficiently clear, or simply wrong, about how we distinguish between legitimate and illegitimate demands for public recognition. As we have seen, the criterion of authenticity that Taylor proposes is morally dubious and practically unwise.

And yet, the idea that recognition is simply alien to liberalism is a misguided one. Galeotti offers one potentially fertile reconfiguration of the relationship between this and other liberal values. A further reason why liberals might do well to reconsider their exclusionary stance towards recognition emerges from the ideas of some deliberative democrats. Both Benhabib and Fraser ask whether the divisive, group-ist and anti-democratic rhetoric that identity politics sometimes generates can be displaced by a more deliberative, self-critical and relaxed public talk about identity and social need (Benhabib, 2002; Fraser, 1997: 69–98). The implication of this view is that democrats should consider more carefully the political, institutional and cultural conditions that make possible the kinds of bivalent identity talk observed by Lichterman, as opposed to the deepening *ressentiment* with which identity politics is often associated. It is important that liberals pay more heed to fostering a common culture and consider what equality of capability means in deeply divided societies (Sen, 1992; 1999; Nussbaum, 1999; 2000b). Moreover, it is paramount to establish a public sphere in which individuals can speak critically and playfully about their own and others' identities; be free to explore and amend the identities imposed upon them; and be treated with a presumption of respect when they do relate to, and draw upon, group cultures and experiences. Developing such a public culture requires arguments, and draws upon principles, that have a bearing on the interests and identities of all citizens, not just those in minority groups. Many contemporary liberals argue for an enhanced sensitivity to cultural difference among public servants and agencies, a position that conflicts with the rival liberal view that the norm of non-discrimination requires, for instance, a police force that is indifferent to the racial backgrounds of its citizens, rather than one that is compelled to be race-sensitive (Green, 2001). Liberals can maintain this first position without recourse to particularist ethics or multicultural claims about cultural authenticity. They would be better advised to deploy the principles and values pertinent to democratic citizenship – stability, self-worth, equal respect and capability – to justify racial sensitivity among public officials.

I suggested at the beginning of this chapter that a valuable distinction could be made between recognition as it relates to whole cultures and its role in relation to injustices affecting individuals. This distinction has been at the heart of this discussion, represented in particular by the contrasting arguments of Taylor and Fraser. In discussing their, and others', ideas I have sought to demonstrate that recognition is a value that is not, as is currently suggested, alien to the liberal tradition, even if liberals are right to be concerned about Taylor's understanding of it. It is possible to take the problems of recognition seriously from within liberalism without the wholesale reconstruction of the foundations of this political tradition.

9

Conclusions

If the tigers of wrath triumph, then we must conclude that really we stand
for nothing defensible, and we stand alone. If the horses of instruction
triumph, then we must conclude that we do stand for something – we stand
for our own values, but again we stand alone. Either way we seem isolated and unable to communicate effectively with others. But in a modern
multicultural society, isolation and separatism are our problems, so they
can hardly be our solutions. (Mendus, 1993: 195)[1]

Throughout the previous chapters, I have suggested that the political and
moral character of identity claims and the drive to bring matters and
relationships often deemed private to public attention have been rather
precipitously and ungenerously theorized by some liberal philosophers.
I join other critics in questioning the merits of the polarized quality of
the normative arguments that have come to the fore between Kantian-
influenced liberals, on the one hand, and proponents of multiculturalism
and 'difference', on the other.[2] Anglophone political theory has become
the site of a dichotomous encounter between liberals, who believe that
truth, progress and reason are on their side, and the new 'tigers of wrath'
– advocates of the integrity and value of local traditions of moral reasoning (Katznelson, 1996: 102–4). Mendus's delineation of this duality
resonates with the contrasting responses of universalist proponents of
liberal values, on the one hand, and multiculturalists and difference theorists, on the other, to the dilemmas posed by identity politics. One result
of the polarized debates triggered by these contending arguments is a
tendency to diminish or marginalize positions and traditions that lie in
the 'no man's land' between, or beyond, them.[3] Mendus hints at the tendency for such contending orthodoxies to feed off the existence of the
other and to function like magnetic poles, rendering it almost impossible to hold the ground between the two.

While philosophers operate at a much higher level of abstraction and
conceptual refinement than the political actors of liberal democracy,

there is a good case for seeing echoes of these philosophical disagreements in debates within the public spheres of both the United States and Britain.[4] The notion that democratic order may well be submerged beneath the rising tide of self-assertion of various forms of ethnic, cultural and religious identity is a claim that spans these different discursive arenas. But a debate about the moral and political nature of the relationship between democracy and social identity that revolves around this polarity is an impoverishing one. Since the particular political episode that Mendus discusses, this bifurcation has, if anything, become more entrenched, as the reactions to the events of 11 September 2001 and subsequent debates about 'the West versus the Rest' attest.

In relation to identity politics specifically, I have sought to illuminate some of the limitations of multiculturalist arguments that seek to press the case for the validity and worth of minority cultures on the grounds of cultural authenticity and integrity. Engagement with the political and moral challenges posed by these social forms tends to undermine, rather than sustain, the notion that this is a tenable position for liberals. The latter should remain sceptical of essentialist and reified understandings of the cultures that purportedly belong to groups, and accept the inherent dynamism and hybridity of cultural formations and collective identities in modern contexts. Any culture necessarily contains conflicting elements and is likely to represent only one of the sources of meaning and value for its adherents. Citizens in a liberal democracy experience, and learn to balance, the simultaneous pull of different loyalties in their lives. Attempts to designate any particular communal inheritance, other than that represented by one's membership of a political community, as intrinsically morally important are likely to hinder, rather than advance, democratic responses to social pluralization. The sociological conditions in which identities are forged mean that balancing different affiliations and constructing meaningful personal identity from various cultural resources are inescapable life-conditions for modern citizens.

The idea that individuals may hold a variety of different loyalties and ties should not be regarded as a situation unique to contemporary, multicultural society. The impact of the ties of community, family and nation has been a staple theme in Western political thought. The relationship between individuals, cultures and social groupings is, in moral and social terms, far more open-ended and multifaceted than contemporary multiculturalists suggest. These are issues that liberals can most usefully grasp if they re-engage facets of their heritage that have been obscured by the mirror-image positions represented by Kantian universalists and difference-focused particularists. Social identities, even if they are imposed and arbitrary, can gain and lose salience in the lives of individuals, depending upon social and political contingencies and the choices that individuals make as constrained social agents. For some participants in such groups, a number of important 'goods' arise from identification with and involvement in them. While Kantian liberals have tended to promote the ideal of the individual who learns the value of scepticism towards affective loyalties and deep commitments, a rather different character-type might well be recovered in liberal thinking. This is the less heroic, but perhaps more familiar, figure who strives to overcome the disadvantages associated with the self-identity given by an imposed identity. Through their tendency to conflate the politics of identity with irrationalist argument and traditionalist claims, some liberal philosophers have neglected to address those redemptive narratives forged by individuals who look within their own complex, cultural inheritance in order to forge a different kind of self and social trajectory.

Identity politics, more generally, should be seen in less essentialist terms by liberals (Young, 2000: 87–92). Particular group identities inform, and are invoked in, various ways by associational ventures and social groups, and are the source of different kinds of political claim. The latter include both the demand to have a group's traditions and values respected and the desire to have alternative ways of inhabiting a settled identity acknowledged. Groups such as the Southall Black Sisters in Britain or Queer Nation in the US derive their purpose from challenging and unsettling established, authoritative accounts of what it means to be an Asian woman or a gay man. Identity politics can lead both to the contestation of the leading version of a group's identity and to a more conservative approach to a community's values and traditions.

The multiculturalist tendency to present the ethical character of group relationships in terms of the imperative of cultural authenticity, however, means that the novelty and character of contemporary pluralism has been mis-specified in much Anglophone political theory. Groupings sometimes deploy identity politics as a behavioural and rhetorical mode within a broader repertoire that includes more familiar forms of collective action, among them interest-group activity, conventional lobbying and public campaigning. Multiculturalism downplays these facets of group behaviour and encourages analysts to overstate the degree to which the logic of recognition diverges from the kinds of bargaining and negotiation that groups undertake in contemporary democratic society. There are good reasons, therefore, to doubt the wisdom and applicability of some of the projects advanced by political theorists who seek to remake liberalism in a more multicultural image. At the same time, liberals can acknowledge the important critical insights these projects offer into the cultural bias and implications of liberal ideas and institutions, and the significance of groups for individual moral development (Bader, 1997).

The responses of Anglophone liberal philosophy to identity politics have emerged from several set-piece debates structured around the 'hard cases' that are supposedly generated for established liberal principles – over group rights, or whether individuals should be held responsible for their group's cultural practices. For all the analytical skill apparent in these encounters, they inevitably draw attention to certain kinds of grouping and moral dilemma, and can sustain a rather narrow-angled focus upon the different socio-political phenomena connected with identity politics (Freeden, 2001; Newey, 2000).

In recent years, some American liberal theorists have sought to contrast identity politics with the logic of democracy for a different reason – because of its supposed incompatibility with a healthy civil society. I have argued, however, that these liberals provide an inadequate framework for comprehending the democratic significance, as well as dangers, of social mobilizations that invoke identity. A more reflexive and self-critical approach to the language through which liberal political theory makes sense of collective action and co-existence is overdue. So too is greater attention to the differential 'public sphere effects' that communities, groups and social movements can exercise (Warren, 2001). Consideration of the political and ethical implications of the 'weak publics' (in Nancy Fraser's (1999) phrase) that subaltern mobilizations develop, however, remains a minority preoccupation among political theorists. Such a focus is squeezed between the prevailing interest of liberal theorists in establishing universal moral principles of right prior to political contestation and their rivals' celebration of the validity of local moral traditions and values. Both perspectives neglect the conditions that shape the kinds of public talk and engagement that groups, and participants in them, tend to develop. These can vary between multivalent and negotiative approaches towards identity that may deepen other citizens' awareness of the plight and needs of particular groups, on the one hand, and insular and defensive projections of a tight-knit communalism, on the other (Lichterman, 1999). The latter is much more likely to alienate fellow citizens and tends to diminish recognition of the importance of advancing identity claims in the form of public reasons. Considered in relation to the public spheres of democratic states, and in terms of struggles to establish communicative norms and participative rights, current forms of identity politics are part of a lineage that stretches back, at least, to the labour and nationalist movements of the nineteenth century. When conducted as a politics of resentment and self-confirming anger, however, this (anti-)communicative politics tends to disrupt and impoverish deliberative interchange. This is especially so when its proponents seek to claim as a trump over other considerations the 'right' for their culture to be protected and exempted from the burdens of democratic life. This is a form of politics that spells considerable danger for the prospects of a progessivist, reformist liberalism, and may well damage democratic society as a whole.

Intellectuals ought to be wary of fanning the flames of such resentment, as opposed to engaging social identity with a politics of emancipation and hope in mind. Critics are, then, right to detect in calls for a politics of recognition the potential for the exacerbation of group rivalry and envy. At the same time, the increased willingness of political theorists to consider culture and identity in relation to the self reflects a growing understanding of the importance of psychological and interpersonal harms that can arise from the systemic marginalization and disrespecting of social collectivities in modern contexts. Liberal theorists remain divided, however, over what are the best ways of overcoming these processes. Debate has focused primarily upon such measures as the allocation of rights to cultural groups or the supply of a veto to minorities in legislative debates (Bickford, 1999: 86–7; Young, 1990). Both of these suggestions, I have argued, carry undue political risks, and neither is likely to be especially effective at improving the self-confidence and self-respect of individual members of ascriptive groups. Finding a set of measures that will provide support and restitution to individuals who are the particular bearers of complex and variable patterns of group humiliation, irrespective of political contingencies, is an impossible task. But it is certainly legitimate for liberals to aspire to a policy framework premised upon the state's responsibilities in relation to the capabilities of its citizens to participate in the common life of the political community. If such capacities are damaged or under-developed because of the arbitrary distribution of unchosen identities, then the norms of democratic citizenship are jeopardized (Nussbaum, 1999). In cases where individuals who share a particular identity experience discrimination, unfairness or humiliation, of the kinds that impinge on their rights and capacities as citizens, measures aimed at the position of groups are justifiable and sensible on liberal grounds. But the claim that justice is best served in culturally diverse societies when the state switches its attention from individuals to group cultures is one, I have argued, that liberals should resist.

This position suggests a particular test that the polity may use to distinguish between identity claims that are, broadly, politically legitimate and those that are not, other than by considering whether these conform to such values as individuality and autonomy. Claims premised upon the infringement of citizens' rights and basic capabilities, or that seek to maintain a collectivity's independence from the kinds of deliberation through which democratic legitimacy is generated and maintained, are unlikely to amount to good public reasons in a liberal democratic polity. But the implications of these broadly drawn principles depend crucially upon the political deliberations and decisions reached in a particular democracy.

In contrast to the pluralist assertion that liberalism should be reconstructed root and branch, I have joined other authors in emphasizing the richness and diversity of the liberal tradition, and in particular the many insights and ideas that remain pertinent for current problems. Among these somewhat forgotten strands are the various ideas associated with the social liberalism that emerged in both Britain and the United States during the early part of the twentieth century, as well as some proximate social democratic arguments. The politics of identity might, for instance, be fruitfully addressed through reapplying the social democratic concern to make liberalism acknowledge the importance of 'second-order inequalities' that limit the effects of allocating equal political and civil rights. Indeed, while they have often been regarded as rivals, it may well be that the contemporary politics of identity is a cousin of the once powerful, but latterly quiescent, paradigm of class politics propounded by thinkers from the socialist and social democratic traditions. While some socialists held to the idea that class distinctions overrode all other social differences, others appreciated that this overarching, ascriptive category contained within it a particular set of gradations and differences – including such groups as skilled workers, the unemployed, and women who work in the home (Wright, 1985). Developing a political language and associated programme in which the common interests and particular needs of these various sub-groups could be aired and balanced was central to the political outlook of numerous labour and socialist activists. The contemporary focus upon the harms and injustices that are arbitrarily perpetuated on members of unchosen groups, many of whose experiences are also shaped by their vulnerable socio-economic position, might well be seen as a continuation of aspects of the social democratic ambition to make liberalism deliver on its promises of real equality for all. Engagement with the harms and injustices perpetuated in terms of identity might then be seen as an augmentation, rather than a displacement, of the concern of social democrats and liberals with overcoming obstacles to the realization of social justice (Rajan, 1998). Identity-based harms matter, these paradigms suggest, when they deprive individuals of status, voice and opportunity. It is on the liberal ground that each person deserves to be treated as an equal (as opposed to merely being treated equally) that some of the humiliations and exclusions about which identity politics protests can be addressed.[5]

Such an argument is also pertinent to recent attempts to restate liberal ideas with an accent upon the importance of political legitimation and co-operation. I have observed the merits and importance of the older John Rawls's consideration of the problems arising from moral disagreement and social difference for a democratic polity, for two reasons. First, Rawls's writings offer a sustained and perceptive consideration of the implications of democratic citizenship in diverse identity-conscious societies. And, second, his arguments provide a rich illustration of the kinds of interweaving of universalist and particularist argument that is likely to sustain a sensitive liberal disposition towards phenomena such as identity politics. Central to his argument was the suggestion that

> One task of liberalism as a political doctrine is to answer the question: how is social unity to be understood, given that there can be no public agreement on the one rational good, and a plurality of opposing and incommensurable conceptions must be taken as given? And granted that social unity is conceivable in some definite way, under what conditions is it actually possible? (1985: 249)

Rawls's well-known solution to this problem involved the formulation of a conception of a democratic community as a 'system of cooperation between free and equal persons' (1985: 249). The allegiance of citizens to the institutions and laws of a democracy, he maintained, cannot be founded on any overarching conception of the good or particular cultural system, 'but on their publicly accepting a political conception of justice to regulate the basic structure of society' (1985: 249).

Pluralist critics tend towards scepticism about the worth of Rawls's idea of a distinct, demarcated political sphere. Some see this as a typical liberal attempt to recuperate those parts of the agendas of various groups that conform to the liberal project, while failing to engage with, and indeed marginalizing, those that do not (Connolly, 1991; Butler, 1990). This criticism, I have suggested, is misplaced. It derives from an interpretative framework that wrongly presents liberal principles as incompatible with social particularity. If we attend to the political ethics that underpin the disparate political claims made by groups and intellectuals in relation to social identity, it is apparent that various universalizable norms, such as equality of respect, are routinely *and necessarily* invoked by these actors.[6] Above all, if we consider the interests that these groups and their members have in establishing a political society in which co-operation and peaceful co-existence are possible, and in which such values as equality of respect and the capacities of citizens to engage in public deliberation are integral, a liberal democracy understood along the lines that Rawls suggests is not as inappropriate a political model as his critics suggest.[7] Both his discussion of the character and importance of self-worth and his sense of the vitality and importance of moral disagreement in a democracy have much to offer contemporary pluralists who are also democrats. Strong forms of philosophical particularism divert analysts from the ambivalence that many groups and movements demonstrate towards the moral principles that sustain liberal democracy. Many of these forces have laid claim to liberal norms, or sought to reinterpret them, rather than oppose them wholesale.

Political liberalism is of interest in part because it cuts across the battle lines drawn by the main intellectual antagonists in debates about cultural diversity. It rightly challenges proponents of value pluralism to consider the necessity of achieving some harmony of political values to sustain the social co-operation that a democratic society requires. Equally, political liberalism is among those liberal theories that doubt the wisdom of remaking democratic societies in the image of individualistic and autonomous characters, and of reiterating the superiority of Western values over others (Laden, 2001; Tomasi, 2001). It suggests an ethos of sensitivity and restraint towards the different identities and cultures that exist in pluralist societies. As such, it offers a generally promising basis for a liberal politics that is able to accept that the politics of identity may in some regards be conducive, and in others damaging, for a democratic order. Such a position suggests a further, as yet unexamined possibility: that liberals may be able to learn from some aspects of identity politics. Various 'goods' arise for individuals from associations, communities and movements that relate to social identities – including a sense of security, belonging and meaning – that are lacking in different liberal cultures (Ignatieff, 1994).

The generally hostile reception that liberal philosophers have afforded to the politics of identity is therefore due for reconsideration.[8] Though some of the worries that these critics register are indeed legitimate, the broad-brush characterizations of these different groups as enemies of democracy, and as parties responsible for the demise of civil society, are overdrawn. Such accusations may result in the marginalization and mis-understanding of forms of collective action and belonging that might, in the long run, be conducive to liberal democracy. Two different currents in Anglo-American political philosophy have, in particular, promoted this rather dismissive approach to the politics of identity. Among Kantian-influenced philosophers, firstly, the desire to establish non-contentious juridical principles in relation to the claims arising from identity groups has resulted in a neglect of the various moral goods that different social groups can generate. This kind of theorizing reveals a noticeable lack of curiosity about the origins and significance of these formations. By framing the politics of identity as irrational and tradition-bound, it negates the possibility that identity claims may tell us something important about the 'processes of cultural communica-tion, contestation, and resignification occurring within civil society' (Benhabib, 2002: 81). Equally, in its philosophical incarnation, Anglophone liberalism is strikingly incurious about the reasons for the emergence of different kinds of identity politics, as well as their poten-tial societal significance.

Second, among liberal theorists who see the decline of trust and civic virtue as the primary problem facing liberal democracies, identity poli-tics appears as a cause of, and indeed a scapegoat for, current difficul-ties. This kind of interpretation neglects the democratic potentiality of some identity-based groups by drawing too rigid a boundary between forms of associational activity deemed conducive to the democratic good and those that would jeopardize it. The reliance of these thinkers upon a neo-Tocquevillian story about the democratizing effects of association negates engagement with the complex and ambiguous motivations and meanings bound up in individuals' identification with particular social groups. In the case of identity-based groupings and movements, these range from self-defeating expressions of impotent rage to attempts to gain some control over the meaning and direction of one's life. Involve-ment and identification with them may well amount to surrogate strug-gles for power and resources in political cultures in which the discussion of social disadvantage and moral fragmentation has moved to the margins of the political agenda. These explosions of righteous, and some-times wrongful, anger constitute essential parts of the public conversation that democratic societies permit. As such, these groups can provide lessons, as well as warnings, for all reasonable citizens. They can make meaningful the liberal idea that we should display a degree of humility towards our own and others' identities, and suggest the importance of vigilance to the possibility of unjust prejudice towards particular social groups.[9]

Understanding these phenomena requires considering identity politics as, in part, a practice that forms an element within the complex repertoire of group behaviour in democratic society, and as integrally bound up with the social processes that link political claims to particular cultures and social identities. Considerations of the kinds of incentive structure that would encourage identity groupings to present their identities and political demands in more multivalent and communicative forms should be a question that is of interest to theorists of liberal democracy and public policy-makers alike. The politics of identity merits a more finely grained moral response from liberals than blanket condemnation. Such an argument carries various political and policy-related implications. It suggests, for example, a more cautious and restrained engagement with the associational ecology of civil society than that envisaged by contemporary liberal-republicans (for instance, Macedo, 1996). It implies too the cultivation, among public institutions, law-makers and policy-makers, of a much greater willingness to listen to, though not necessarily act upon, the different complaints and needs voiced by movements and groups. The capabilities of individual citizens, and the complex character of socio-economic *and* culturally mediated harms, ought to be important concerns when its agents consider the merits of regulating and shaping group activities. So too should the generic problem of establishing terms of social concord for political communities that are increasingly aware of their own heterogeneity. These different norms are both compatible with, and increasingly require, moral and practical consideration of the complex effects of imposed identity upon the lives of individual citizens.

This approach also suggests a rather different policy trajectory to that associated with the currently fashionable Putnamesque concern to re-establish a particular model of civil society (1993). Rather than encouraging only those groups that uphold the norms of the liberal republic, a liberal state would be wise to consider the direct and indirect mechanisms that it can use to promote a diverse, cross-cutting associational culture. This may mean providing public resources for some groups that do not conform to liberal values. These collectivities should be judged in terms of their capacity to promote a variety of moral and social goods, including the enhancement of the confidence and sense of integration of minorities; airing the legitimate grievances of the disadvantaged; and promoting public understanding of the unfair treatment experienced by minorities. Despite its counter-intuitive appearance, it may well be prudential, as well as morally appropriate, for a liberal order to promote unfamiliar and critical voices, as well as those that conform to its own precepts. Such an idea has some bearing upon current debates in Britain about which groupings count as deserved recipients of income generated from the state's lottery. Groups that campaign against the purported injustices of government policy, then, should be awarded grants under this scheme as long as it is shown that they do generate some of the values considered above. Equally, the acceptance by groups of public aid implies responsibilities that the state should be prepared to enforce. It is legitimate, in a liberal democracy, to expect that the identities, values and practices of minority groupings be the objects, as well as sources, of communicative interchange. This may well in practice mean effecting a balance between liberal values, such as freedom of speech and the toleration of offensive opinions, and the desire of some faith communities, for example, to restrict liberty of expression.

According value to social identities within the political life of a democracy does generate challenges and, indeed, costs that pluralists should be prepared to acknowledge in their moral arguments. In particular, when conflicts arise because a group declares that a practice is integral to its identity and another perceives this as harmful to its own being, peaceful and principled resolution is difficult, but not necessarily impossible. I raised earlier the controversy generated by the support of the American Civil Liberties Union for the recent campaign by members of the Ku Klux Klan to be allowed to burn crosses. This practice is indeed integral to this group's self-identity, and is also offensive to many citizens – African-Americans and others – in localities where this organization persists. In weighing the merits of these conflicting arguments, it is not sufficient to favour the claims of those advocating restriction merely because an ascriptive grouping – black Americans – is involved, whereas the KKK represents a voluntary association. As I suggested in chapter 1, the distinction between voluntary and ascriptive groups is a much shakier one than political theorists often admit. Equally, the notion that the right to freedom of speech 'trumps' any other moral claim in this instance – the position adopted by the ACLU – does not consider the valid public reasons that opponents of this practice offer. These may involve arguments that appeal to such principles as civility and the self-worth of minority groups. Despite the difficulty and complexity of this and other related cases – the expression of racist sentiments in football stadiums in Britain, for example – the balancing of conflicting values is the task and duty of a liberal polity. This evaluation is best undertaken, I have suggested, using the norms of democratic citizenship. In this particular instance, this suggests that some considerable weight be given to the likelihood that cross-burning will damage social relationships, diminish civility, and make members of minority groups feel vulnerable and alienated.

Though some stipulations about moral principle can be usefully undertaken at this level of generality, it is a mistake to seek to evade the burdens of context and tradition when considering the relationship between liberal political thought and developments in civil society. The communitarian idea that moral judgement is shaped by local political and intellectual context chimes with the argument offered in chapter 1 about the importance of ideological change and national political culture in relation to prevailing understandings of the challenges posed by the politicization of group identity. In both the US and Britain, the ideological and political difficulties experienced by liberal and left-wing intellectuals since the 1960s have helped shape many of the hopes and fears surrounding these new kinds of mobilization. Moreover, various political traditions are pertinent to a proper historical understanding of the ways in which the politics of identity has been politically constructed. As an illustration of this point, I have stressed the particular connection between arguments about the nature and legacy of New Left politics and subsequent ideas about the threat that social particularity supposedly raises for democratic politics. The fall-out of these earlier debates is still present, I would suggest, in prevailing assumptions among political theorists about the role of gender, faith and ethnicity in political life. Clearly, the New Left is by no means the only intellectual context pertinent to current ideas. But it is an important and neglected one. Current normative understandings of what a politics of identity signifies have their roots in earlier periods and debates. And these in turn need to be understood in relation to the history and cultures of particular states. A sense of the importance of national tradition and political experience helps us understand, in particular, the character of some contemporary American thinkers' nostalgia for the civil society of the nineteenth century, and the conviction of some British egalitarians that multiculturalism has helped undermine the validity of the welfare state.

Somewhat paradoxically, however, the debates considered in this book also possess an intrinsically transnational character. Arguments about such issues as the nature of cultural inheritance, the idea of group rights, the importance of social identity and belonging for individuals, and the shallow roots of democratic citizenship have sustained intellectual developments that are not simply national in character. This is particularly due to the establishment, in the last twenty years, of an English-speaking discourse on political questions that transcends, as well as reflects, national political traditions. To a degree, this situation arises because of the decline of strong notions of American exceptionalism and the fateful sense in Britain, and other European states, that American trends are increasingly pertinent and perhaps inescapable. But it also reflects the diminishing hold of single national traditions upon intellectual enquiry more generally, a development that has various causes. In the context of the multiple economic, cultural and intellectual transformations associated with the globalization of economic and cultural life, the idea of establishing a more appropriate balance between the universalist and particularist aspects of moral and political thought has re-emerged as a vital intellectual task (Linklater, 1998: 5). The hold upon the liberal imagination of one-dimensional forms of moral universalism and particularism threatens to hamper, rather than enable, the development of robust and nuanced responses to the challenges posed by the politics of identity.

Notes

Preface

1 An indication of the polarized character of the debate unleashed among liberals by 11 September 2001 and the subsequent war in Afghanistan can be found in Bunting (2001). See especially her discussion of the terminology of 'hard' versus 'soft' liberalism.
2 On the relationship between contemporary liberal philosophy and the liberal political traditions, see the contrasting positions outlined in Kloppenberg (1998: 3–20), Freeden (1996: 226–75) and Gaus (2000).
3 In this sense, I side with those who argue that it is legitimate to approach philosophical as well as political versions of liberalism as estranged members of the same ideological family (Freeden, 1996).
4 This diversity extends beyond some of the familiar dichotomies that figure in contemporary philosophical treatments of liberalism – between its 'Enlightenment' and 'Reformation' strands, or its articulation of 'autonomy' as opposed to 'tolerance' (Galston, 1995; Gray, 2000a).
5 This idea is given extensive consideration in Gutmann (2003).
6 There are a number of important exceptions to my characterization of Anglophone theorists, especially David Miller's valuable discussion of group rights in relation to citizenship and human-rights arguments (2002a) and Amy Gutmann's thoughtful evaluation of liberal critiques of identity politics (2003).
7 The case for the importance of moral psychology to political philosophy is powerfully made in Rosenblum (1998a).

Chapter 1   The Character and Origins of the Politics of Identity

1 Other commentators have questioned the validity and effects of this particular intellectual rivalry; for instance Kiss (1999) and Katznelson (1996).
2 On the New Left genealogy of identity politics theory in the US, see Farred (2000).

3   These terms, usually offered as interchangeable in this literature, are generally invoked in two contrasting ways. For some commentators the politics of identity represents a particular kind of normative argument, and comes in either 'strong' (and hence unacceptable) or 'weak' (and hence 'reasonable') forms (Cairns, 1999). For others, it is a descriptive category used 'to describe a wide range of political struggles which occur with increasing frequency' (Tully, 1995: 7). Neither usage encourages consideration of other possibilities, such as the idea that identity politics is a socio-political practice rather than a label for particular groups (Young, 2000).

4   Amy Gutmann reminds us that some identity-orientated groupings do conform more readily to the ideal of voluntary association (2003: 86–116).

5   Important discussions of the moral implications of the relationship between unchosen and intentional identities are provided by Tamir (1998), Emcke (2000) and Galeotti (2002).

6   However, a central feature of recent normative debates about nationalism is whether co-members of national communities should be regarded as having entered a contract governing the terms of their nationhood, or whether they are its passive inheritors (Miller, 1995b).

7   On the character and inescapability of traditions, see the contrasting arguments of MacIntyre (1981) and Bevir (1999: 221–64).

8   This is by no means an exhaustive list of macro-social and political interpretations of these phenomena. Offe considers several others in his stimulating discussion of the political ethics of identity politics, in particular the idea that this paradigm may signal the failure of projects of economic and political modernization (1998).

9   The tendency of sociologists to focus upon social movements with which they sympathize is raised in both Jasper (1997) and Diani (1993).

10 The relationship between church and state was also central in British political thinking in the late nineteenth and early twentieth centuries.

11 The only major participant in the Anglo-American philosophical debates engendered by multiculturalism to discuss the significance of the New Left is Brian Barry. He has offered some brief and blunt observations in the context of a discussion of why multiculturalism has emerged as a left-wing concern: 'there is a long line from the New Left through communitarianism to multiculturalism . . . In some ways, multiculturalism is the latest incarnation of the fallacies of the New Left, and I have found that a good predictor of responses to *Culture and Equality* among academics within ten years of my age (either side) is where they stood on the New Left' (2002: 206). The idea that egalitarian liberalism and New Left multiculturalism are irretrievably opposed to one another runs counter to the work of intellectual historians who trace overlaps between, for instance, the American New Left and liberal political thinking (Mattson, 2002).

12 These debates were particularly associated with the journal *Marxism Today*.

13 The report was published as *The Future of Multi-Ethnic Britain: Report of the Commission on the Future of Multi-Ethnic Britain* (London: Profile, 2000).

14 For critical accounts of this historiography, see Lott's assault upon 'boomer liberalism' (1999) and Echols's commentary on characterizations of the 'good' and 'bad' sixties (1992).

Chapter 2 The Politics of Identity in Liberal Political Theory

1 Mason makes the case for distinguishing between an agent's identification with a group, as opposed to her critical detachment from, or engulfment by, it (2000: 58–9).
2 These different conceptions of equality are considered in depth in Phillips (1999) and Levine (1998).
3 These issues are raised in Barry's treatment of some of the 'hard cases' posed by multiculturalist demands for the exemption of cultural and religious groupings from prevailing laws (2001a; especially 19–62). The implications of his arguments are discussed by Miller (2002b) and Caney (2002).
4 Barry makes a clear distinction between the disadvantages associated with physical incapacity and those connected with religion and culture (2001a).
5 For an illuminating discussion of the status of religious groups in relation to identity politics, see Gutmann (2003: 151–91).

Chapter 3 Citizenship, Public Reason and Collective Identity

1 Important challenges to this claim are offered by Williams (2000) and Quong (2002).
2 For insightful discussion of the Rawlsian conception of public reason, see especially Gutmann (1995), Laden (2001), McKinnon (2000), Moon (1993: 98–120) and Macedo (1995).
3 This position, according to one recent commentator, represents 'the first liberal accommodation of communitarianism' (Kymlicka, 2002: 228).
4 Social capital is defined by its leading theorist, Robert Putnam, as 'features of social organization such as networks, norms, and social trust that facilitate coordination and cooperation for mutual benefit' (1995: 67).
5 Similar arguments have been developed by scholars of the social liberalism of the late ninteenth and early twentieth century. See, for instance, Simhony and Weinstein (2001).

Chapter 4 Civil Society and the Morality of Association

1 This question figures centrally in Gutmann (2003).
2 The other main 'seedbed' to figure in recent arguments about civil society is the family. See, for instance, Glendon (1995).
3 Another widely cited Supreme Court judgement arises from the Internal Revenue Service vs. Bob Jones University. The court upheld the right of the IRS to deny this university tax-exempt status as a charitable body on the grounds that it practised forms of racial separation. The moral and constitutional implications of this verdict are discussed in Gutmann (1998b).
4 Whether Rawls's conception of self-respect requires or implies difference-sensitive political institutions and policies has emerged as an important part of the debate over multiculturalism in political philosophy. See, in particular, Barry (2001a: 267–9); Tully (1995: 189–91); and Caney (2002: 94–5).

Chapter 5 The Public Faces of Identity Politics

1 For a useful discussion of primordialist conceptions of social identity in multiculturalist theory, see Tempelman (1999: 19–23).
2 See, in particular, Appiah's critique of such approaches to African-American culture (1996; 1994).
3 Examples might include the elderly or unemployed. Young, it should be said,
   is one of the few theorists of difference to consider such groupings (2000).
4 For a critical evaluation of the applicability of *ressentiment*, see Bickford
   (1997).

Chapter 6 Identities in Motion: the Political Ethics of Social Movements

1 Various contemporary political theorists have considered the character and
   significance of social movements in relation to the politics of identity,
   notably Young (1990), Benhabib (2002), and Cohen and Arato (1992). One
   of the few theorists in this community to engage with sociological theories
   of social movements is Keane (1998b; Keane and Mier, 1989).
2 See the various definitional discussions in, among others, Tarrow (1994),
   Della Porta and Diani (1999), and Diani (1992).
3 For accounts of the development of Touraine's thought, see especially
   Hannigan (1985) and McDonald (2003).
4 Melucci was not alone in interpreting social movements in this way. See also
   Donati's study of the micro-culture of Milanese peace activists (1984).
5 See, in particular, his hyperbolic discussion of the idea of the 'democratization of everyday life' (1989: 165–79).
6 A concern with biology and genetics in fact runs throughout his work. See,
   for instance, Melucci (1989: 45–6).
7 Also, see Warren's observation that identity-based groups with little power
   and few resources tend to place emphasis upon the exercise of 'voice', often
   projecting their demands in a particularly shrill, non-compromising fashion
   (2001: 212).
8 This was, broadly, the case mounted against similar pluralist arguments
   by John Dewey, in his influential *The Public and its Problems* ([1927]
   1990).
9 In this regard, the argument offered by W. G. Runciman in his *Social Science
   and Political Theory* (1963) retains a striking contemporary resonance.

Chapter 7 Liberalism and the Politics of Difference

1 Important critical accounts of her conceptions of oppression and the
   oppressed are offered in Spinner-Halev (2000) and Macedo (1995).
2 For an insightful account of the dilemmas and difficulties facing advocates
   of group representation, see Phillips (1996).
3 For a thoughtful discussion of the different kinds of pluralist challenge
   facing contemporary liberalism, see Bellamy (1999).

4 In this and other respects, Connolly's arguments overlap with those developed by the American theorist Bonnie Honig (1993).

Chapter 8 Liberalism and the Politics of Recognition

1 See the helpful discussion of various influences on Taylor's work in Smith (2002).
2 For a sharp commentary on Taylor's intellectual journey from the New Left to multiculturalism, see Barry (2002: 206).

Chapter 9 Conclusions

1 Mendus here adapts the striking terminology used by William Blake, in his *Proverbs from Hell*, to characterize the friends and enemies of Reason.
2 Similar arguments can be located in Bader (1997); Baumeister's (2000) delineation of 'thin' as opposed to 'thick' forms of multiculturalism; and Benhabib (2002).
3 One example in terms of normative theory is Mendus's own conception of the ethos of neighbourliness, an idea discussed in the context of cultural difference by Katznelson (1996: 173–4).
4 Here, I part company with Gerald Gaus's attempt to defend a clear distinction between liberal political theory, on the one hand, and liberal ideology, on the other (2000).
5 This philosophical distinction is central to Dworkin's account of the role of equality within liberal thought. Treating people equally 'supposes that political decisions must be, so far as is possible, independent of any particular conception of the good life, or of what gives value to life.' Treating people as equals, he argues, means 'that the content of equal treatment cannot be independent of some theory about the good for man or the good of life, because treating a person as an equal means treating him the way the good or truly wise person would wish to be treated' (1978: 127).
6 This point is integral to Habermas's argument that social movements are both the carriers of universalist moral principles and emissaries on behalf of particular lifeworlds and social interests (1981; 1971).
7 See especially Laden's fascinating juxtaposition of Rawlsian reasonableness and various identity-orientated political arguments (2001).
8 Amy Gutmann provides a clear philosophical justification for doing exactly this (2003).
9 For a similar argument, see Kiss (1999: 195) and Bader (1997: 792).

References and Bibliography

Ackerman, B. 1980: *Social Justice in the Liberal State*. New Haven, CT, and London: Yale University Press.

——1983: What is Neutral about Neutrality? *Ethics*, 93, 372–90.

Alibhai-Brown, Y. 1999: *True Colours: Attitudes to Multiculturalism and the Role of Government*. London: IPPR.

Almond, G., and S. Verba 1963: *The Civic Culture: Political Attitudes and Democracy in Five Nations*. Princeton, NJ: Princeton University Press.

Altman, A. 1993: Liberalism and Campus Hate Speech: A Philosophical Examination. *Ethics*, 103, 302–17.

Appiah, K. A. 1994: Identity, Authenticity, Survival: Multicultural Societies and Social Reproduction. In A. Gutmann (ed.), *Multiculturalism: Examining the Politics of Recognition*. Princeton, NJ: Princeton University Press, 149–63.

——1996: Race, Culture, Identity: Misunderstood Connections. In K. A. Appiah and A. Gutmann, *Color Conscious: The Political Morality of Race*. Princeton, NJ: Princeton University Press.

Avineri, S. 1972: *Hegel's Theory of the Modern State*. London: Cambridge University Press.

Avineri, S., and A. De-Shalit (eds) *Communitarianism and Individualism*. Oxford: Oxford University Press.

Bader, V. 1997: The Cultural Conditions of Transnational Citizenship: On the Interpenetration of Political and Ethnic Cultures. *Political Theory*, 25, 771–813.

Banaszak, A., K. Beckwith and D. Rucht (eds) 2003: *Women's Movements Facing the Reconfigured State*. Cambridge: Cambridge University Press.

Banfield, E. C. (ed.) 1992a: *Civility and Citizenship in Liberal Democratic Societies*. New York: Paragon House.

——1992b: Introductory Note. In E. C. Banfield (ed.), *Civility and Citizenship in Liberal Democratic Societies*. New York: Paragon House, ix–xii.

Barber, B. 1998: *A Place for Us: How to Make Civil Society and Democracy Strong*. New York: Hill & Wang.

Barnard, F. M. 2003: *Herder on Nationality, Humanity and History*. Montreal: McGill-Queen's University Press.

Barry, B. 1999: Politics as a Vocation. In J. Hayward, B. Barry and A. Brown (eds), *The British Study of Politics in the Twentieth Century*. Oxford: Oxford University Press, 425–68.

——2001a: *Culture and Equality: An Egalitarian Critique of Multiculturalism*. Cambridge: Polity.

——2001b: The Muddles of Multiculturalism. *New Left Review*, 8, 49–71.

——2002: Second Thoughts – and Some First Thoughts Revived. In P. Kelly (ed.), *Multiculturalism Reconsidered: Culture and Equality and its Critics*. Cambridge: Polity, 204–38.

Bauböck, R. 2000: Social and Cultural Integration in Civil Society. In C. McKinnon and I. Hampsher-Monk (eds), *The Demands of Citizenship*. London and New York: Continuum, 91–119.

Bauman, Z. 2001: *Community*. Cambridge: Polity.

Baumeister, A. 2000: *Liberalism and the 'Politics of Difference'*. Edinburgh: Edinburgh University Press.

Beck, U. 1992: *Risk Society: Towards a New Modernity*. London: Sage.

——1999: *The Reinvention of Politics: Rethinking Modernity in the Global Social Order*. Cambridge: Polity.

Beiner, R. 1995: Introduction: Why Citizenship Constitutes a Theoretical Problem in the Last Decade of the Twentieth Century. In R. Beiner (ed.), *Theorizing Citizenship*. Albany, NY: State University of New York Press, 1–28.

Bell, D. 1998: Civil Society versus Civic Virtue. In A. Gutmann (ed.), *Freedom of Association*. Princeton, NJ: Princeton University Press, 239–72.

Bellah, R. 1996: *Habits of the Heart: Individualism and Commitment in American Life*. Berkeley: University of California Press.

Bellamy, R. 1999: *Liberalism and Pluralism: Towards a Politics of Compromise*. London: Routledge.

——2000: *Rethinking Liberalism*. London: Continuum.

Benhabib, S. 1992: *Situating the Self: Gender, Community and Postmodernism in Contemporary Ethics*. Cambridge: Polity.

——2002: *The Claims of Culture: Equality and Diversity in the Global Era*. Princeton, NJ: Princeton University Press.

Benjamin, J. 1998: *Like Subjects, Love Objects: Essays on Recognition and Sexual Difference*. New Haven, CT, and London: Yale University Press.

Bennett, F. 1999: The Face of the State. *Political Studies*, 47, 677–90.

Bennett, W. L. 1998: The UnCivic Culture: Communication, Identity, and the Rise of Lifestyle Politics. *PS: Political Science and Politics*, 31, 741–61.

Berlin, I. 1999: *The Roots of Romanticism: The A. W. Mellon Lectures in the Fine Arts, 1965, The National Gallery of Art, Washington, DC*. London: Chatto & Windus.

Berman, P. (ed.) 1995: *Debating PC: The Controversy over Political Correctness on College Campuses*. New York: Laurel-leaf.

——1996: The Gay Awakening. In P. Berman, *A Tale of Two Utopias: The Political Journey of the Generation of 1968*. New York and London: W.W. Norton, 123–94.

Bevir, M. 1999: *The Logic of the History of Ideas*. Cambridge: Cambridge University Press.

Bhabha, H. 1994: *The Location of Culture*. London: Routledge.

Bickford, S. 1997: Anti-Anti-Identity Politics: Feminism, Democracy, and the Complexities of Citizenship. *Hypatia*, 12, 111–31.

——1999: Identity and Institutions in the Inegalitarian Polity. *American Journal of Political Science*, 43, 86–108.

Blankenhorn, D. 1995: Conclusions: The Possibility of Civil Society. In M. A. Glendon and D. Blankenhorn (eds), *Seedbeds of Virtue: Sources of Competence, Character, and Citizenship*. Lanham, MD, and London: Madison Books, 271–82.

Blunkett, D. 2002: *Politics and Progress: Renewing Democracy and Civil Society.* London: Politico's.

Bobbio, N. 1988: Gramsci and the Concept of Civil Society. In J. Keane (ed.), *Civil Society and the State: New European Perspectives*. London: Verso, 73–99.

Bohman, J. 1995: Public Reason and Cultural Pluralism: Political Liberalism and the Problem of Moral Conflict. *Political Theory*, 23, 253–79.

Brennan, T. 1991: Black Theorists and Left Antagonists. *Minnesota Review*, 37, 89–113.

Brown, W. 1995a: *States of Injury: Power and Freedom in Late Modernity.* Princeton, NJ: Princeton University Press.

——1995b: Wounded Attachments: Late Modern Oppositional Political Formations. In J. Rajchman (ed.), *The Identity in Question*. London and New York: Routledge, 199–227.

Buechler, S. M. 1995: New Social Movement Theories. *Sociological Quarterly*, 36, 441–64.

Bunting, M. 2001: Intolerant Liberalism. *The Guardian*, 8 October.

Butler, J. 1990: *Gender Trouble: Feminism and the Subversion of Identity.* London: Routledge.

——1998: Merely Cultural. *New Left Review*, 227, 33–44.

Byrne, P. 1997: *Social Movements in Britain.* London: Routledge.

Cairns, A. C. 1999: Introduction. In A. C. Cairns, J. C. Courtney, P. MacKinnon, H. J. Michelmann and D. E. Smith (eds), *Citizenship, Diversity, and Pluralism: Canadian and Comparative Perspectives*. Montreal: McGill-Queen's University Press, 1–22.

Calhoun, C. 1994: Social Theory and the Politics of Identity. In C. Calhoun (ed.), *Social Theory and the Politics of Identity*. Oxford: Blackwell, 9–36.

——1995: New Social Movements of the Nineteenth Century. In M. Traugott (ed.), *Repertoires and Cycles of Collective Action*. Durham, NC: Duke University Press.

Callan, E. 1997: *Creating Citizens: Political Education and Liberal Democracy.* Oxford: Clarendon Press.

Canavan, F. 1995: *The Pluralist Game: Pluralism, Liberalism and the Moral Conscience.* Lanham, MD: Rowman & Littlefield.

Canel, E. 1992: New Social Movement Theory and Resource Mobilization: The Need for Integration. In W. K. Carroll (ed.), *Organizing Dissent: Contemporary Social Movements in Theory and Practice*. Toronto: Garamond Press, 22–51.

Caney, S. 2001: International Distributive Justice. *Political Studies*, 49, 974–97.

——2002: Equal Treatment, Exceptions and Cultural Diversity. In P. Kelly (ed.), *Multiculturalism Reconsidered: Culture and Equality and its Critics*. Cambridge: Polity, 81–101.

Carens, J. 2000: *Culture, Citizenship and Community: A Contextual Exploration of Justice as Evenhandedness.* Oxford: Oxford University Press.

Carens, J., and M. S. Williams 1996: Muslim Minorities in Liberal Democracies: The Politics of Misrecognition. In R. Bauböck, A. Heller and A. R. Zolberg (eds), *The Challenge of Diversity: Integration and Pluralism in Societies of Immigration*. Aldershot: Avebury.

Carver, T. 2001: Marx, Marxism, Post-Marxism. In M. Freeden (ed.), *Reassessing Political Ideologies: The Durability of Dissent*. London and New York: Routledge, 35–48.

Castells, M. 1997a: *The Information Age*, Volume I: *The Rise of the Network Society*. Oxford, and Malden, MA: Blackwell.

—— 1997b: *The Information Age*, Volume II: *The Power of Identity*. Oxford, and Malden, MA: Blackwell.

—— 1997c: *The Information Age*, Volume III: *End of Millennium*. Oxford, and Malden, MA: Blackwell.

Charter '88. 1991: *Make a Date with Democracy: Charter '88: Constitutional Conventional Proceedings*. London: Charter '88.

Chowcat, I. 2000: Moral Pluralism, Political Justification and Deliberative Democracy. *Political Studies*, 48, 745–58.

Cohen, G. 1999: Equality of What? On Welfare, Goods, and Capabilities. In M. Nussbaum and A. Sen (eds), *The Quality of Life*. Oxford: Clarendon Press, 9–29.

Cohen, J. L. 1985: Strategy or Identity: New Theoretical Paradigms and Contemporary Social Movements. *Social Research*, 52, 663–716.

Cohen, J. L., and A. Arato 1992: *Civil Society and Political Theory*. Cambridge, MA: MIT Press.

Cohen, J., and J. Rogers 1995: *Associations and Democracy*. London: Verso.

Connolly, W. 1991: *Identity/Difference: Democratic Negotiations of Political Paradox*. Minneapolis and London: University of Minnesota Press.

—— 1995: *The Ethos of Pluralization*. Minneapolis and London: University of Minnesota Press.

Cooke, M. 1997: Authenticity and Autonomy: Taylor, Habermas and the Politics of Recognition. *Political Theory*, 25, 258–88.

Coole, D. 2001: Threads and Plaits of an Unfinished Project? Feminism(s) through the Twentieth Century. In M. Freeden (ed.), *Reassessing Political Ideologies: The Durability of Dissent*. London and New York: Routledge.

Crick, B. 2000: *Essays on Citizenship*. London and New York: Continuum.

Crittenden, J. 1992: *Beyond Individualism: Reconstituting the Liberal Self*. New York: Oxford University Press.

Crowder, G. 2001: *Liberalism and Value Pluralism*. London and New York: Continuum.

Cummings, M. S. 2001: *Beyond Political Correctness: Social Transformations in the United States*. Boulder, CO: Lynne Rienner.

Dagger, R. 1997: *Civic Virtues*. Oxford and New York: Oxford University Press.

D'Agostino, M. 1996: *Free Public Reason: Making it up as We Go*. New York: Oxford University Press.

Dahl, R. 1963: *Who Governs? Democracy and Pluralism in an American City*. New Haven, CT, and London: Yale University Press.

—— 1967: *Pluralist Democracy in the United States: Conflict and Consent*. Chicago: Rand McNally.

Dallmayr, F. 1996: Democracy and Multiculturalism. In S. Benhabib (ed.), *Democracy and Difference: Contesting the Boundaries of the Political*. Princeton, NJ: Princeton University Press, 278–94.

Dalton, R. J. 1994: *The Green Rainbow: Environmental Groups in Western Europe*. New Haven, CT, and London: Yale University Press.

Dalton, R. J., M. Kuechler and W. Bürklin 1990: The Challenge of New Movements. In R. J. Dalton and M. Kuechler (eds), *Challenging the Political Order: New Social and Political Movements in Western Democracies*. Cambridge: Polity, 3–20.

D'Anieri, P., C. Ernst and E. Kier 1990: New Social Movements in Historical Perspective. *Comparative Politics*, 23, 445–58.

Della Porta, D., and M. Diani 1999: *Social Movements: An Introduction*. Oxford: Blackwell.

Deveaux, M. 2000a: Conflicting Equalities? Cultural Group Rights and Sex Equality. *Political Studies*, 48, 522–39.

——2000b: *Cultural Pluralism and Dilemmas of Justice*. Ithaca, NY, and London: Cornell University Press.

Dewey, J. [1927] 1990: *The Public and its Problems*. Athens, OH: Swallow Press.

Diani, M. 1992: The Concept of Social Movement. *Sociological Review*, 40, 1–25.

——1993: Themes of Modernity in New Religious Movements and New Social Movements. *Social Science Information*, 32, 111–31.

Digesner, P. 1995: *Our Politics, Our Selves? Liberalism, Identity, and Harm*. Princeton, NJ: Princeton University Press.

Donati, R. P. 1984: Organization between Movement and Institution. *Social Science Information*, 23, 837–59.

Dryzek, J. S. 1996: Political Inclusion and the Dynamics of Democratization. *American Political Science Review*, 90, 475–87.

Dunant, S. (ed.) 1994: *The War of the Words: the Political Correctness Debate*. London: Virago.

Dworkin, R. 1978: Liberalism. In S. Hampshire (ed.), *Public and Private Morality*. Cambridge: Cambridge University Press, 113–43.

Echols, A. 1992: 'We Gotta Get Out of this Place': Notes toward a Remapping of the Sixties. *Socialist Review*, 2, 9–34.

Edsall, T. B., and M. D. Edsall 1991: *Chain Reaction: The Impact of Race, Rights, and Taxes in American Politics*. New York and London: W.W. Norton.

Eisenstadt, S. N., and B. Giesen 1995: The Construction of Collective Identity. *Archives Européenes de Sociologie*, 36, 72–102.

Elshtain, J. B. 1995: *Democracy On Trial*. New York: Basic Books.

Emcke, C. 2000: Between Choice and Coercion: Identities, Injuries, and Different Forms of Recognition. *Constellations*, 7, 483–95.

Epstein, B. 1991: 'Political Correctness' and Collective Powerlessness. *Socialist Review*, 21 (3/4), 14–35.

Fanon, F. 1965: *The Wretched of the Earth*. London: MacGibbon & Kee.

Farred, G. 2000: Endgame Identity? Mapping the New Left Roots of Identity Politics. *New Literary History*, 31, 627–48.

Farrelly, C. 1999: Public Reason, Neutrality and Civic Virtues. *Ratio Juris*, 12 (1), 11–25.

Ferree, M. M., W. A. Gamson, J. Gerhards and D. Rucht 2002: *Shaping Abortion Discourse: Democracy and the Public Sphere in Germany and the United States*. Cambridge: Cambridge University Press.

Fine, R. 1997: Civil Society Theory, Enlightenment and Critique. *Democratization*, 4 (1), 7–28.

Fishkin, J. S. 1991: *Democracy and Deliberation: New Directions for Democratic Reform*. New Haven, CT, and London: Yale University Press.

Fraser, N. 1995a: From Redistribution to Recognition? Dilemmas of Justice in a Post-Socialist Age. *New Left Review*, 212, 68–93.

——1995b: Recognition or Redistribution: A Critical Reading of Iris Young's Justice and the Politics of Difference. *Journal of Political Philosophy*, 3, 166–80.

——1997: *Justice Interruptus: Critical Reflections on the 'Postsocialist' Condition*. London and New York: Routledge.

——1998: Heterosexism, Misrecognition, and Capitalism: A Response to Judith Butler. *New Left Review*, 228, 140–9.

——1999: Rethinking the Public Sphere: A Contribution to the Critique of Actually Existing Democracy. In C. Calhoun (ed.), *Habermas and the Public Sphere*. Cambridge, MA, and London: MIT Press, 109–42.

——1999–2000: Social Justice and Identity Politics. *CSD Bulletin*, 7 (1), 3–5.

Freeden, M. 1978: *The New Liberalism: An Ideology of Social Reform*. Oxford: Clarendon Press.

——1996: *Ideologies and Political Theory: A Conceptual Approach*. Oxford: Clarendon Press.

——2001: Conclusion: Ideology – Balances and Projections. In M. Freeden (ed.), *Reassessing Political Ideologies: The Durability of Dissent*. London and New York: Routledge, 193–208.

Freedland, J. 1999: *Bringing Home the Revolution*. London: Fourth Estate.

Freedman, M. H., and E. M. Freedman (eds) 1995: *Group Defamation and Freedom of Speech: The Relationship between Language and Violence*. Westport, CT: Greenwood Press.

Galeotti, A. E. 2002: *Toleration as Recognition*. Cambridge: Cambridge University Press.

Galipeau, C. 1994: *Isaiah Berlin's Liberalism*. Oxford: Clarendon Press.

Galston, W. 1991: *Liberal Purposes: Goods, Virtues, and Diversity in the Liberal State*. Cambridge: Cambridge University Press.

——1995: Two Concepts of Liberalism. *Ethics*, 105, 516–34.

——1999a: Expressive Liberty, Moral Pluralism, Political Pluralism: Three Sources of Liberal Theory. *William and Mary Law Review*, 40, 869–907.

——1999b: Value Pluralism and Liberal Political Theory. *American Political Science Review*, 93, 769–81.

Gamble, A. 2000: *Politics and Fate*. Cambridge, and Malden, MA: Cambridge University Press.

Gamson, W. A. 1988: Political Discourse and Collective Action. *International Social Movement Research*, 1, 219–44.

Gaus, G. 1999: Reasonable Pluralism and the Domain of the Political: How the Weaknesses of John Rawls's Political Liberalism can be Overcome by a Justificatory Liberalism. *Inquiry*, 42, 259–84.

——2000: Liberalism at the End of the Century. *Journal of Political Ideologies*, 5, 179–99.

Geuss, R. 2002: Liberalism and its Discontents. *Political Theory*, 30, 320–38.

Gianni, M. 1998: Taking Multiculturalism Seriously: Political Claims for a Differentiated Citizenship. In K. Slawner and M. E. Denham (eds), *Citizenship after Liberalism*. New York: Peter Lang, 33–55.

Giddens, A. 1994: *Beyond Left and Right: The Future of Radical Politics*. Cambridge: Polity.

Gill, E. R. 1986: Goods, Virtues, and the Constitution of the Self. In A. J. Damico (ed.), *Liberals on Liberalism*. Lanham, MD: Rowman & Littlefield, 111–28.

Gilroy, P. 1987: *'There ain't no Black in the Union Jack': The Cultural Politics of Race and Nation*. London: Hutchinson.

——2001: *Between Camps: Race, Nation and the Alliances of Race*. Harmondsworth: Penguin.

Gitlin, T. [1987] 1993: *The Sixties: Years of Hope, Days of Rage*. New York and Toronto: Bantam.

——1995: *The Twilight of Common Dreams: Why America is Wracked by Culture Wars*. New York: Henry Holt.

Glendon, M. A. 1995: Forgotten Questions. In M. A. Glendon and D. Blankenhorn (eds), *Seedbeds of Virtue: Sources of Competence, Character and Citizenship in American Society*. Lanham, MD, and London: Madison Books, 1–15.

Glendon, M. A., and D. Blankenhorn (eds) 1995: *Seedbeds of Virtue: Sources of Competence, Character, and Citizenship*. Lanham, MD, and London: Madison Books.

Goodin, R. 1996: Inclusion and Exclusion. *Archives Européenes de Sociologie*, 37, 343–71.

Gray, J. 1995a: *Enlightenment's Wake: Politics and Culture at the Close of the Modern Age*. London: Routledge.

——1995b: *Berlin*. London: Fontana Press.

——1998: *False Dawn: The Delusions of Global Capitalism*. London: Granta.

——2000a: *Two Faces of Liberalism*. Cambridge: Polity.

——2000b: Pluralism and Toleration in Contemporary Political Philosophy. *Political Studies*, 48, 323–33.

Green, D. G. 2001: Liberal Anti-Racism. *Prospect*, October, 34–7.

Gutmann, A. 1993: The Challenge of Multiculturalism in Political Ethics. *Philosophy and Public Affairs*, 22 (3), 171–206.

——1995: Civic Education and Social Diversity. *Ethics*, 105, 557–79.

——(ed.) 1998a: *Freedom of Association*. Princeton, NJ: Princeton University Press.

——1998b: Freedom of Association: An Introductory Essay. In A. Gutmann (ed.), *Freedom of Association*. Princeton, NJ: Princeton University Press, 3–32.

——2003: *Identity in Democracy*. Princeton, NJ: Princeton University Press.

Habermas, J. 1971: *Towards a Rational Society: Student Protest, Science, and Politics*. London: Heinemann.

——1981: New Social Movements. *Telos*, 49, 33–7.

——1993: Struggles for Recognition in Constitutional States. *European Journal of Philosophy*, 1 (2), 128–55.

Hall, S. 1987: Gramsci and Us. *Marxism Today*, June, 16–21.

——1988: *The Hard Road to Renewal: Thatcherism and the Crisis of the Left*. London: Verso.

——1989: The 'First' New Left: Life and Times. In R. Archer et al. (eds), *Out of Apathy: Voices of the New Left Thirty Years On*. London: Verso, 13–38.

——1991: Brave New World. *Socialist Review*, 21 (1), 57–64.

Hampsher-Monk, I. 1999: Toleration, the Moral Will and the Justification of Liberalism. In J. Horton and S. Mendus (eds), *Toleration, Identity and Difference*. Basingstoke: Macmillan, 17–37.

Hannigan, J. A. 1985: Alain Touraine, Manuel Castells and Social Movement Theory: A Critical Appraisal. *Sociological Quarterly*, 26, 435–54.

Hegel, G. W. F. 1967: *The Philosophy of Right*. Oxford: Oxford University Press.

Held, D. 1995: *Democracy in the Global Order*. Cambridge: Polity.

Held, D., A. McGrew, D. Goldblatt and J. Perraton 1999: *Global Transformations: Politics, Economics and Culture*. Cambridge: Polity.

Hirst, P. 1994: *Associative Democracy: New Forms of Economic and Social Governance*. Cambridge: Polity.

Hitchens, C. 1993: The New Complainers. *Dissent*, 560–64.

Hobsbawm, E. 1996: The Cult of Identity Politics. *New Left Review*, 217, 38–47.

Honig, B. 1993: *Political Theory and the Displacement of Politics*. Ithaca, NY, and London: Cornell University Press.

Honneth, A. 1995: *The Struggle for Recognition: The Moral Grammar of Social Conflicts*. Cambridge, MA: MIT Press.

——1997: Recognition and Moral Obligation. *Social Research*, 64 (1), 16–35.

Hoover, J. 2001: Do the Politics of Difference Need to be Freed of Liberalism? *Constellations*, 8, 201–18.

Horton, J. 1993: Liberalism, Multiculturalism and Toleration. In J. Horton (ed.), *Liberalism, Multiculturalism and Toleration*. Basingstoke, Macmillan, 1–17.

——1998: Charles Taylor: Selfhood, Community and Democracy. In A. Carter and G. Stokes (eds), *Liberal Democracy and its Critics*. Cambridge: Polity, 155–74.

Hunter, J. 1991: *Culture Wars: The Struggle to Define America: Making Sense of the Battles over the Family, Art, Education, Law and Politics*. New York: Basic Books.

Hutchings, K. 1999: The Idea of International Citizenship. In K. Hutchings and R. Dannreuther (eds), *Cosmopolitan Citizenship*. Basingstoke: Macmillan.

Hutchings, K., and R. Dannreuther (eds) 1999: *Cosmopolitan Citizenship*. Basingstoke: Macmillan.

Hutton, W. 2001: Other People, 1. *Prospect*, January, 4.

Ignatieff, M. 1994: *The Needs of Strangers*. London: Vintage.

Inglehart, R. 1977: *The Silent Revolution: Changing Values and Political Styles among Western Publics*. Princeton, NJ: Princeton University Press.

——1979: Value Priorities and Socioeconmic Change. In S. H. Barnes, M. Kaase et al., *Political Action: Mass Participation in Five Western Democracies*. London: Sage, 305–42.

——1997: *Modernization and Postmodernization: Culture, Economic and Political Change in 43 Countries*. Princeton, NJ, and Oxford: Princeton University Press.

——1999: *Culture Shift in Advanced Industrial Society*. Princeton, NJ, and Oxford: Princeton University Press.

Inglehart, R., and H. D. Klingemann 1979: Ideological Conceptualization and Value Priorities. In S. H. Barnes, M. Kaase et al., *Political Action: Mass Participation in Five Western Democracies*. London: Sage, 203–12.

Ivison, D. 1997: The Secret History of Public Reason: Hobbes to Rawls. *History of Political Thought*, 18, 125–47.

——2000: Modus vivendi Citizenship. In C. McKinnon and I. Hampsher-Monk (eds), *The Demands of Citizenship*. London and New York: Continuum, 123–43.

——2002: *Postcolonial Liberalism*. Cambridge: Cambridge University Press.

Jaggar, A. 1999: Multicultural Democracy. *Journal of Political Philosophy*, 7, 308–29.

James, S. 1992: The Good-Enough Citizen: Female Citizenship and Independence. In G. Bock and S. James (eds), *Beyond Equality and Difference: Citizenship, Feminist Politics and Female Subjectivity*. London and New York: Routledge, 48–68.

Jasper, J. M. 1997: *The Art of Moral Protest: Culture, Biography, and Creativity in Social Movements*. Chicago and London: University of Chicago Press.

Kahane, D. 1998: Liberal Virtues and Citizen Education. In K. Slawner and M. E. Denham (eds), *Citizenship after Liberalism*. New York: Peter Lang, 103–25.

Kateb, G. 1992: *The Inner Ocean: Individualism and Democratic Character*. Ithaca, NY: Cornell University Press.

——1998: The Value of Association. In A. Gutmann (ed.), *Freedom of Association*. Princeton, NJ: Princeton University Press, 35–63.

Katznelson, I. 1996: *Liberalism's Crooked Circle: Letters to Adam Michnik*. Princeton, NJ: Princeton University Press.

Keane, J. (ed.) 1988a: *Civil Society and the State: New European Perspectives*. London: Verso.

——(ed.) 1998b: *Democracy and Civil Society: On the Predicaments of European Socialism, the Prospects for Democracy and the Problem of Controlling Social and Political Power*. London: University of Westminster Press.

——1998c: *Civil Society: Old Images, New Visions*. Cambridge: Polity.

Keane, J., and P. Mier 1989: Editors' Preface. In A. Melucci, *Nomads of the Present: Social Movements and Individual Needs in Contemporary Society*. Philadelphia: Temple University Press, 1–9.

Kekes, J. 2001: *The Morality of Pluralism*. Princeton, NJ: Princeton University Press.

Kelly, P. (ed.) 2002: *Multiculturalism Reconsidered: Culture and Equality and its Critics*. Cambridge: Polity.

Kenny, M. 1995: *The First New Left: British Intellectuals after Stalin*. London: Lawrence & Wishart.

——1999: Reputations: Edward Palmer Thompson. *Political Quarterly*, 70 (30), 319–29.

Kingwell, M. A. 1995: *A Civil Tongue: Justice, Dialogue and the Politics of Pluralism*. University Park: Pennsylvania State University Press.

Kiss, E. 1999: Democracy and the Politics of Recognition. In I. Shapiro and C. Hacker-Cordón (eds), *Democracy's Edges*. Cambridge: Cambridge University Press, 193–209.

Klandermans, B., and S. Tarrow 1988: Mobilization into Social Movements: Synthesizing European and American Approaches. In B. Klandermans, H. Kriesi and S. Tarrow (eds), *International Social Movement Research*, Vol. 1: *From Structure to Action: Comparing Social Movement Research Across Cultures*. Greenwich, CT, and London: JAI Press, 1–38.

Kloppenberg, J. T. 1998: *The Virtues of Liberalism*. Oxford and New York: Oxford University Press.

Kohler, T. C. 1995: Civic Virtue at Work: The Unions as Seedbeds of the Civic Virtues. In M. A. Glendon and D. Blankenhorn (eds), *Seedbeds of Virtue: Sources of Competence, Character, and Citizenship*. Lanham, MD, and London: Madison Books, 131–62.

Kohn, M. 2002: Panacea or Privilege? New Approaches to Democracy and Association. *Political Theory*, 30, 289–98.

Kriesi, H. 1988: The Interdependence of Structure and Action: Some Reflections on the State of the Art. *International Social Movement Research*, 1, 349–68.

Kriesi, H., R. Koopmans, J. W. Duyvendak and M. G. Guigi 1995: *New Social Movements in Western Europe: A Comparative Analysis*. London: UCL Press.

Kukathas, C. 1992: Are There Any Cultural Rights? *Political Theory*, 20, 105–39.

——1998: Liberalism and Multiculturalism: The Politics of Indifference. *Political Theory*, 26, 686–99.

Kymlicka, W. 1989: *Liberalism, Community and Culture*. Oxford: Oxford University Press.

——1995: *Multicultural Citizenship*. Oxford: Oxford University Press.

——1998: Ethnic Associations and Democratic Citizenship. In A. Gutmann (ed.), *Freedom of Association*. Princeton, NJ: Princeton University Press, 177–213.

——2002: *Contemporary Political Philosophy: An Introduction*. Oxford: Oxford University Press.

Kymlicka, W., and W. Norman 2000: Citizenship in Culturally Diverse Societies: Issues, Contexts, Concepts. In W. Kymlicka and W. Norman (eds), *Citizenship in Diverse Societies*. Oxford: Oxford University Press, 1–41.

Kymlicka, W., and M. Opalski (eds) 2001: *Can Liberal Pluralism be Exported? Western Political Theory and Ethnic Relations in Eastern Europe*. Oxford: Oxford University Press.

Laclau, E., and C. Mouffe 1985: *Hegemony and Socialist Strategy: Towards a Radical Democratic Politics*. London: Verso.

Laden, A. 2001: *Reasonably Radical: Deliberative Liberalism and the Politics of Identity*. Ithaca, NY, and London: Cornell University Press.

Laforest, G. 1993: Introduction. In C. Taylor, *Reconciling the Solitudes: Essays on Canadian Federalism and Nationalism*. Montreal: McGill-Queen's University Press.

Lamey, A. 1999: Francophonia for Ever: The Contradictions in Charles Taylor's 'The Politics of Recognition'. *Times Literary Supplement*, 23 July, 12–15.

Larmore, C. 1987: *Patterns of Moral Complexity*. Cambridge: Cambridge University Press.

——1990: Political Liberalism. *Political Theory*, 18, 339–60.

Lasch, C. 1979: *The Culture of Narcissism: American Life in An Age of Diminishing Expectations*. New York and London: W.W. Norton.

Lehning, P. B. 1998: Towards a Multicultural Civil Society: The Role of Social Capital and Democratic Citizenship. *Government and Opposition*. 33, 221–42.

Levine, A. 1998: *Rethinking Liberal Equality*. Ithaca, NY, and London: Cornell University Press.

Levinson, M. 1999: *The Demands of Liberal Education*. Oxford: Oxford University Press.

Levy, J. 2000: *The Multiculturalism of Fear*. Oxford: Oxford University Press.

Lichterman, P. 1999: Talking Identity in the Public Sphere: Broad Visions and Small Spaces in Sexual Identity Politics. *Theory and Society*, 28, 101–41.

Lind, M. 1996: *The Next American Nation: The New Nationalism and the Fourth American Revolution*. Carmichael, CA: Touchstone Books.

Linklater, A. 1998: *The Transformation of Political Community: Ethical Foundations of the Post-Westphalian Era*. Cambridge: Polity.

Lipset, S. M. 1996: *American Exceptionalism: A Double-Edged Sword*. New York and London: W.W. Norton.

Littleton, C. 1980: Towards a Feminist Jurisprudence. *Indiana Law Journal*, 56, 375–444.

Lott, E. 1999: Boomer Liberalism. *Transition*, 78, 24–44.

——2000: After Identity, Politics: The Return of Universalism. *New Literary History*, 31, 665–80.

Lovenduski, J., and J. Outshoorn (eds) 1986: *The New Politics of Abortion*. London: Sage.

Lovenduski, J., and V. Randall 1993: *Contemporary Feminist Politics*. Oxford: Oxford University Press.

Lukes, S. 1997: Humiliation and the Politics of Identity. *Social Research*, 64 (1), 36–51.

Lustiger-Thaler, H., and L. Maheu 1995: Social Movements and the Challenge of Urban Politics. In L. Maheu (ed.), *Social Movements and Social Classes: The Future of Collective Action*. London: Sage, 151–68.

McAdam, D., J. D. McCarthy and M. N. Zald 1988: Social Movements. In N. J. Smelser (ed.), *Handbook of Sociology*. London: Sage, 695–737.

McCarthy, T. 1978: *The Critical Theory of Jürgen Habermas*. London: Hutchinson.

——1994: Kantian Constructivism and Reconstructivism: Rawls and Habermas in Dialogue. *Ethics*, 105, 44–63.

McDonald, K. 2003: Alain Touraine. In A. Elliott and L. Ray (eds), *Key Contemporary Social Theorists*. Oxford: Blackwell, 246–51.

Macedo, S. 1990: *Liberal Virtues: Citizenship, Virtue, and Community in Liberal Constitutionalism*. Oxford: Clarendon Press.

——1995: Liberal Civic Education and Religious Fundamentalism: The Case of God v. John Rawls?, *Ethics*, 105, 468–96.

——1996: Community, Diversity, and Civic Education: Toward a Liberal Political Science of Group Life. *Social Philosophy and Policy*, 13 (1).

MacIntyre, A. 1981: *After Virtue: A Study in Moral Theory*. London: Duckworth.

McKay, G. 1996: *Senseless Acts of Beauty: Cultures of Resistance since the Sixties*. London: Verso.

——(ed.) 1998: *DiY Culture: Party and Protest in Nineties Britain*. London: Verso.

McKenzie, E. 1994: *Privatopia: Homeowner Associations and the Rise of Residential Private Government*. New Haven, CT: Yale University Press.

McKinnon, C. 2000: Civil Citizens. In C. McKinnon and I. Hampsher-Monk (eds), *The Demands of Citizenship*. London and New York: Continuum, 144–64.

Mansbridge, J. 1996: Using Power/Fighting Power: The Polity. In S. Benhabib (ed.), *Democracy and Difference: Contesting the Boundaries of the Political*. Princeton, NJ: Princeton University Press, 46–66.

Margalit, A. 1996: *The Decent Society*. Cambridge, MA: Harvard University Press.

Marneffe, P. de 1998: Rights, Reasons, and Freedom of Association. In A. Gutmann (ed.), *Freedom of Association*. Princeton, NJ: Princeton University Press, 145–73.

Mason, A. 2000: *Community, Solidarity and Belonging: Levels of Community and their Normative Significance*. Cambridge: Cambridge University Press.

Mattson, K. 2002: *Intellectuals in Action: The Origins of the New Left and Radical Liberalism, 1945–1970.* University Park: Pennsylvania State University Press.

Mehta, U. S. 1998: *Liberalism and Empire: A Study in Nineteenth-Century British Liberal Argument.* Chicago: University of Chicago Press.

Melucci, A. 1984: An End to Social Movements? *Social Science Information*, 23, 819–35.

——1985: The Symbolic Challenge of Contemporary Movements. *Social Research*, 52, 789–816.

——1988: Social Movements and the Democratization of Everyday Life. In J. Keane (ed.), *Civil Society and the State: New European Perspectives.* London: Verso, 245–60.

——1989: *Nomads of the Present: Social Movements and Individual Needs in Contemporary Society.* Philadelphia: Temple University Press.

——1995: The New Social Movements Revisited: Reflections on a Sociological Misunderstanding. In L. Maheu (ed.), *Social Movements and Social Classes: The Future of Collective Action.* London: Sage, 107–22.

——1996a: *Challenging Codes: Collective Action in the Information Age.* Cambridge and New York: Cambridge University Press.

——1996b: *The Playing Self: Person and Meaning in a Planetary Society.* Cambridge: Cambridge University Press.

Mendus, S. 1993: The Tigers of Wrath and the Horses of Instruction. In J. Horton (ed.), *Liberalism, Multiculturalism and Toleration.* Basingstoke: Macmillan, 193–206.

——2002: Choice, Chance and Multiculturalism. In P. Kelly (ed.), *Multiculturalism Reconsidered: Culture and Equality and its Critics.* Cambridge: Polity, 31–44.

Meyer, J. 1998: The Politics of Differentiated Citizenship. In K. Slawner and M. E. Denham (eds), *Citizenship after Liberalism.* New York: Peter Lang, 57–79.

Miller, D. 1995a: Citizenship and Pluralism. *Political Studies*, 43, 432–50.

——1995b: *On Nationhood.* Oxford: Clarendon Press.

——2002a: Group Rights, Human Rights and Citizenship. *European Journal of Philosophy*, 10, 178–95.

——2002b: Liberalism, Equal Opportunities and Cultural Commitments. In P. Kelly (ed.), *Multiculturalism Reconsidered: Culture and Equality and its Critics.* Cambridge: Polity, 45–61.

Modood, T. 1998: Anti-essentialism, Multiculturalism and the 'Recognition' of Religious Groups. *Journal of Political Philosophy*, 6, 378–99.

——2001: Their Liberalism and our Multiculturalism? *British Journal of Politics and International Relations*, 3, 245–57.

Moon, J. D. 1993: *Constructing Community: Moral Pluralism and Tragic Conflicts.* Princeton, NJ: Princeton University Press.

Moore, M. 1995: Political Liberalism and Cultural Diversity. *Canadian Journal of Law and Jurisprudence*, 8, 297–310.

Mouffe, C. 1995: Democratic Politics and the Question of Identity. In J. Rajchman (ed.), *The Identity in Question.* London and New York: Routledge, 33–46.

Mulgan, G. 1994: *Politics in an Antipolitical Age.* Cambridge: Polity.

Nagel, T. 1987: Moral Conflict and Political Legitimacy. *Philosophy and Public Affairs*, 16, 215–40.

Nedelmann, B. 1984: New Political Movements and Changes in Processes of Intermediation. *Social Science Information*, 23, 1029–48.

Newey, 1998: Value-Pluralism in Contemporary Liberalism. *Dialogue*, 37, 493–522.

——2000: *After Politics: The Rejection of Politics in Contemporary Liberal Philosophy*. Basingstoke: Palgrave.

——2001: How Do You Like your Liberalism: Fat or Thin? *London Review of Books*, 7 June, 3–6.

Nicholson, L. 1996: To Be or Not to Be: Charles Taylor and the Politics of Recognition. *Constellations*, 3 (1), 1–16.

Nussbaum, M. 1996: The Sleep of Reason. *Times Higher Education Supplement*, 2 February, 17–18.

——1999: A Plea for Difficulty. In S. M. Okin, *Is Multiculturalism Bad for Women?*, ed. J. Cohen, M. Howard and M. C. Nussbaum. Princeton, NJ: Princeton University Press, 105–14.

——2000a: Religion and Women's Equality: The Case of India. In N. L. Rosenblum (ed.), *Obligations of Citizenship and Demands of Faith: Religious Accommodation in Pluralist Democracies*. Princeton, NJ: Princeton University Press, 335–402.

——2000b: *Women and Human Development: The Capabilities Approach*. Cambridge: Cambridge University Press.

Offe, C. 1985: New Social Movements: Challenging the Boundaries of Institutional Politics. *Social Research*, 52, 817–68.

——1998: 'Homogeneity' and Constitutional Democracy: Coping with Identity Conflicts through Group Rights. *Journal of Political Philosophy*, 6, 113–41.

Okin, S. M. 1999: Is Multiculturalism Bad for Women? In S. M. Okin, *Is Multiculturalism Bad for Women?*, ed. J. Cohen, M. Howard and M. C. Nussbaum. Princeton, NJ: Princeton University Press, 9–24.

Oliver, J. E. 2001: *Democracy in Suburbia*. Princeton, NJ, and Oxford: Princeton University Press.

O'Neill, J. 1997: Hegel against Fukuyama: Associations, Markets and Recognition. *Politics*, 17, 191–6.

O'Neill, S. 2000: Liberty, Equality and the Rights of Cultures: The Marching Controversy at Drumcree. *British Journal of Politics and International Relations*, 2 (1), 26–45.

Parekh, B. 2000: *Rethinking Multiculturalism: Cultural Diversity and Political Theory*. Basingstoke: Macmillan.

Patten, A. 2000: Equality of Recognition and the Liberal Theory of Citizenship. In C. McKinnon and I. Hampsher-Monk (eds), *The Demands of Citizenship*. London and New York: Continuum, 193–211.

Petit, P. 1999: *Republicanism: A Theory of Freedom and Government*. Oxford: Oxford University Press.

Phillips, A. 1993: *Democracy and Difference*. Cambridge: Polity.

——1996: Dealing with Difference: A Politics of Ideas, or a Politics of Presence? In S. Benhabib (ed.), *Democracy and Difference: Contesting the Boundaries of the Political*. Princeton, NJ: Princeton University Press, 139–52.

——1997: *Feminism and Equality*. Oxford: Blackwell.

——1999: *Which Equalities Matter?* Cambridge: Polity.

Philp, M. 2000: Motivating Liberal Citizenship. In C. McKinnon and I. Hampsher-Monk (eds), *The Demands of Citizenship*. London and New York: Continuum, 165–89.

Plotke, D. 1996: Norms: Social and Legal. *Good Society*, 6 (1), 10–12.

Pocock, J. G. A. 1975: *The Machiavellian Moment: Florentine Political Thought and the Atlantic Tradition*. Princeton, NJ, and London: Princeton University Press.

Pogge, T. 2002: *World Poverty and Human Rights: Cosmopolitan Responsibilities and Reforms*. Cambridge: Polity.

Poole, R. 2000: Justice or Appropriation? Indigenous Claims and Liberal Theory. *Radical Philosophy*, 101, 5–17.

Purvis, T., and A. Hunt 1999: Identity versus Citizenship: Transformations in the Discourses and Practices of Citizenship. *Social and Legal Studies*, 8, 457–82.

Putnam, R. 1993: *Making Democracy Work: Civic Traditions in Modern Italy*. Princeton, NJ: Princeton University Press.

—— 1995: Bowling Alone: America's Declining Social Capital. *Journal of Democracy*, 6 (1), 65–78.

Quong, J. 2002: Are Identity Claims Bad for Deliberative Democracy? *Contemporary Political Theory*, 1, 307–27.

Rajan, N. 1998: Multiculturalism, Group Rights and Identity Politics. *Economic and Political Weekly*, 4 July, 1699–1701.

Rajchman, J. (ed.) 1995: *The Identity in Question*. London and New York: Routledge.

Rawls, J. 1971: *A Theory of Justice*. Cambridge, MA: Harvard University Press.

—— 1985: Justice as Fairness: Political not Metaphysical. *Philosophy and Public Affairs*, 14, 223–52.

—— 1993: *Political Liberalism*. New York: Columbia University Press.

—— 2000: *Lectures on the History of Moral Philosophy*, ed. Barbara Herman. Cambridge, MA, and London: Harvard University Press.

—— 2001: *Justice as Fairness: A Restatement*, ed. E. Kelly. Cambridge, MA: Harvard University Press.

Raz, J. 1986: *The Morality of Freedom*. Oxford: Clarendon Press.

Rorty, A. O. 1994: The Hidden Politics of Cultural Identification. *Political Theory*, 22, 152–66.

Rorty, R. 1991: On Ethnocentrism: A Reply to Clifford Geertz. In R. Rorty, *Objectivity, Relativism, and Truth: Philosophical Papers, Vol. 1*. Cambridge and New York: Cambridge University Press, 203–10.

—— 1998: *Achieving our Country: Leftist Thought in Twentieth-Century America*. Cambridge, MA: Harvard University Press.

—— 1999: Love and Money. In R. Rorty, *Philosophy and Social Hope*. Harmondsworth: Penguin, 229–39.

Rosenblum, N. L. 1994a: Democratic Character and Community: The Logic of Congruence? *Journal of Political Philosophy*, 2 (1), 67–97.

—— 1994b: Civil Societies: Liberalism and the Moral Uses of Pluralism. *Social Research*, 61, 539–62.

—— 1998a: *Membership and Morals: The Personal Uses of Pluralism in America*. Princeton, NJ: Princeton University Press.

—— 1998b: Compelled Association: Public Standing, Self-Respect, and the Dynamic of Exclusion. In A. Gutmann (ed.), *Freedom of Association*. Princeton, NJ: Princeton University Press, 75–108.

Rowbotham, S., L. Segal and H. Wainwright 1980: *Beyond the Fragments: Feminism and the Making of Socialism*. London: Merlin.

Rucht, D. 1991: Sociological Theory as a Theory of Social Movements? A Critique of Alain Touraine. In D. Rucht (ed.), *Research on Social Movements: The State of the Art in Western Europe and the USA*. Boulder, CO: Westview Press; Frankfurt: Campus Verlag, 355–85.

Runciman, W. G. 1963: *Social Science and Political Theory*. Cambridge: Cambridge University Press.

Rustin, M. 1985: *For a Pluralist Socialism*. London: Verso.

Saggar, S. 2000: *Race and Representation: Electoral Politics and Ethnic Pluralism in Britain*. Manchester: Manchester University Press.

Sandel, M. 1984: The Procedural Republic and the Unencumbered Self. *Political Theory*, 12, 81–96.

Sassoon, J. 1984: Ideologies, Symbolic Action and Actuality in Social Movements: The Effects on Organizational Forms. *Social Science Information*, 23, 861–73.

Schlesinger, A. M., Jr. 1998: *The Disuniting of America: Reflections on a Multicultural Society*. New York and London: W.W. Norton.

Scott, A. 1990: *Ideology and the New Social Movements*. London: Unwin Hyman.

Scruton, R. 2002: *The West and the Rest: Globalization and the Terrorist Threat*. London: Continuum.

Seglow, J. 1998: Universals and Particulars: The Case of Liberal Cultural Nationalism. *Political Studies*, 46, 963–77.

Seligman, A. 1995: *The Idea of Civil Society*. Princeton, NJ: Princeton University Press.

Sen, A. 1992: *Inequality Re-examined*. New York: Russell Sage Foundation; Oxford: Clarendon Press.

——1999: *Reason Before Identity*. New York: Oxford University Press.

Shapiro, I. 2001: *Democratic Justice*. New Haven, CT: Yale University Press.

Shklar, J. 1985: *Ordinary Vices*. Cambridge, MA: Harvard University Press.

——1995: *American Citizenship: The Quest for Inclusion*. Cambridge, MA: Harvard University Press.

Simhony, A., and D. Weinstein 2001: Introduction: The New Liberalism and the Liberal–Communitarian Debate. In A. Simhony and D. Weinstein (eds), *The New Liberalism: Reconciling Liberty and Community*. Cambridge: Cambridge University Press, 1–25.

Skinner, Q. 1998: *Liberty Before Liberalism*. Cambridge: Cambridge University Press.

Slawner, K. 1998: Uncivil Society: Liberalism, Hermeneutics, and 'Good Citizenship'. In K. Slawner and M. E. Denham (eds), *Citizenship after Liberalism*. New York: Peter Lang, 81–101.

Slawner, K., and M. E. Denham (eds) 1998: *Citizenship after Liberalism*. New York: Peter Lang.

Smith, A. M. 1991: The End of the Rainbow. *Marxism Today*, February, 24–5.

Smith, N. 2002: *Charles Taylor: Meaning, Morals and Modernity*. Cambridge: Polity.

Smith, R. 1997: *Civic Ideals: Conflicting Visions of Citizenship in US History*. New Haven, CT, and London: Yale University Press.

Smits, K. 2000: *Identity Politics and the Reconstruction of Liberal Pluralism*. DPhil. dissertation, Cornell University.

Somers, M. 1994: The Narrative Constitution of Identity: A Relational and Network Approach. *Theory and Society*, 23, 605–49.

Spång, M. 2002: Recognition, Misrecognition and Capitalism. ⟨http:www. theglobalsite.ac.uk/press/112spang.htm⟩.

Spinner-Halev, J. 2000: Land, Culture and Justice: A Framework for Group Rights and Recognition. *Journal of Political Philosophy*, 8, 319–42.

Spragens, T. A. 1999: *Civic Liberalism: Reflections on our Democratic Ideals*. Lanham, MD: Rowman & Littlefield.

Stevens, D. 2001: *Education, Fraternity and Social Cohesion: A Liberal Argument about Civic Virtue*. PhD dissertation, University of Nottingham.

Stevenson, N. 2003: Manuel Castells. In A. Elliott and L. Ray (eds), *Key Contemporary Social Theorists*. Oxford: Blackwell, 91–6.

Stocker, M. 1990: *Plural and Conflicting Values*. Oxford: Clarendon Press.

Strong, T. 1990: *The Idea of Political Theory: Reflections on the Self in Political Time and Space*. Notre Dame, IN: University of Notre Dame Press.

Sunstein, C. 1995: Incompletely Theorized Agreements. *Harvard Law Review*, 108, 1733–9.

—— 1998: Beyond the Republican Revival. *Yale Law Review*, 97, 1539–90.

Tamir, Y. 1991: Whose History? What Ideas? In E. Margalit and A. Margalit (eds), *Isaiah Berlin: A Celebration*. London: Hogarth Press, 146–59.

—— 1993: *Liberal Nationalism*. Princeton, NJ: Princeton University Press.

—— 1998: Revisiting the Civic Sphere. In A. Gutmann (ed.), *Freedom of Association*. Princeton, NJ: Princeton University Press, 214–38.

Tarrow, S. 1991: Comparing Social Movement Participation in Western Europe and the United States: Problems, Uses, and a Proposal for a Synthesis. In D. Rucht (ed.), *Research on Social Movements: The State of the Art in Western Europe and the USA*. Boulder, CO: Westview Press; Frankfurt: Campus Verlag, 392–420.

—— 1994: *Power in Movement: Social Movements, Collective Action and Politics*. Cambridge: Cambridge University Press.

Taylor, C. 1957: Socialism and the Intellectuals. *Universities and Left Review*, 2, 18–19.

—— 1958: Alienation and Community. *Universities and Left Review*, 5, 11–18.

—— 1985: *Human Agency and Language: Philosophical Papers 1*. Cambridge: Cambridge University Press.

—— 1989: *Sources of the Self: The Making of the Modern Identity*. Cambridge, MA: Harvard University Press.

—— 1991a: The Importance of Herder. In E. Margalit and A. Margalit (eds), *Isaiah Berlin: A Celebration*. London: Hogarth Press, 40–63.

—— 1991b: *The Ethics of Authenticity*. Cambridge, MA: Harvard University Press.

—— 1994: The Politics of Recognition. In A. Gutmann (ed.), *Multiculturalism: Examining the Politics of Recognition*. Princeton, NJ: Princeton University Press, 25–73.

—— 1995a: Invoking Civil Society. In C. Taylor, *Philosophical Arguments*. Cambridge, MA, and London: Harvard University Press, 204–24.

—— 1995b: Liberal Politics and the Public Sphere. In C. Taylor, *Philosophical Arguments*. Cambridge, MA, and London: Harvard University Press, 257–87.

—— 1999: Democratic Exclusion (and its Remedies?): The John Ambrose Stack Memorial Lecture. In A. C. Cairns, J. C. Courtney, P. MacKinnon, H. J. Michelmann and D. E. Smith (eds), *Citizenship, Diversity, and Pluralism: Canadian and Comparative Perspectives*. Montreal: McGill-Queen's University Press, 265–87.

Tebble, A. J. 2002: What is the Politics of Difference? *Political Theory*, 30, 259–81.

Tempelman, S. 1999: Constructions of Cultural Identity: Multiculturalism and Exclusion. *Political Studies*, 47 (1), 17–31.

Thompson, E. P. 1961: *The Making of the English Working Class*. Harmondsworth: Penguin.

Thurlow, R. 2000: *Fascism in Modern Britain*. Stroud: Sutton.

Tilly, C. 1985: Models and Realities of Popular Collective Action. *Social Research*, 52, 717–47.

——1994: Social Movements as Historically Specific Clusters of Political Performances. *Berkeley Journal of Sociology*, 39, 1–30.

Tocqueville, A. de [1835] 1969: *Democracy in America*. New York: Harper & Row.

Tomasi, J. 2001: *Liberalism beyond Justice: Citizens, Society, and the Boundaries of Political Theory*. Princeton, NJ, and Oxford: Princeton University Press.

Touraine, A. 1981: *The Voice and the Eye: An Analysis of Social Movements*. Cambridge: Cambridge University Press.

——1985: An Introduction to the Study of Social Movements. *Social Research*, 52, 749–87.

——2000: *Can We Live Together? Equality and Difference*. Cambridge: Polity.

Touraine, A., M. Wieviorka and F. Dubet 1984: *Le Mouvement ouvrier*. Paris: Fayard.

Tucker, K. 1991: How New are the New Social Movements? *Theory, Culture and Society*, 8, 75–98.

Tully, J. 1995: *Strange Multiplicity: Constitutionalism in an Age of Diversity*. Cambridge: Cambridge University Press.

——2000a: Struggles over Recognition and Distribution. *Constellations*, 7, 469–95.

——2000b: The Challenge of Reimagining Citizenship and Belonging in Multicultural and Multinational Societies. In C. McKinnon and I. Hampsher-Monk (eds), *The Demands of Citizenship*. London and New York: Continuum, 212–34.

Vincent, A. 1989: Can Groups be Persons? *Review of Metaphysics*, 42, 687–715.

——2002: *Nationalism and Particularity*. Cambridge: Cambridge University Press.

Vogel, L. 1993: Critical Notices: 'The Ethics of Authenticity' and 'Multiculturalism and the Politics of Recognition' by Charles Taylor. *International Journal of Philosophical Studies*, 6, 325–35.

Wainwright, H. 1994: *Arguments for a New Left: Answering the Free-Market Right*. Oxford: Blackwell.

Waldron, J. 1992: Minority Cultures and the Cosmopolitan Alternative. *University of Michigan Journal of Law Reform*, 25, 751–93.

——1993: *Liberal Rights: Collected Papers 1981–1991*. Cambridge and New York: Cambridge University Press.

——2000: Cultural Identity and Civic Responsibility. In W. Kymlicka and W. Norman (eds), *Citizenship in Diverse Societies*. Oxford: Oxford University Press, 155–74.

Walker, R. B. J. 1994: Social Movements/World Politics. *Millennium*, 23, 669–700.

Wallman, S. 1983: Identity Options. In C. Fried (ed.), *Minorities: Community and Identity: Report of the Dahlem Workshop on Minorities: Community and Identity. Berlin 1982. Nov. 28–Dec. 3*. Berlin: Springer-Verlag.

Walzer, M. 1993: Exclusion, Injustice and the Democratic State. *Dissent*, 55–64.

——1995: The Civil Society Argument. In R. Beiner (ed.), *Theorizing Citizenship*. Albany, NY: State University of New York Press.

——1998: On Involuntary Association. In A. Gutmann (ed.), *Freedom of Association*. Princeton, NJ: Princeton University Press, 64–74.

Warren, M. 2001: *Democracy and Association*. Princeton, NJ: Princeton University Press.

West, C. 1994: *Race Matters*. New York: Vintage.

Whitebrook, M. 2001: *Identity, Narrative and Politics*. London and New York: Routledge.

Williams, M. S. 1998: *Voice, Trust and Memory: Marginalized Groups and the Failings of Liberal Republicanism*. Princeton, NJ: Princeton University Press.

——2000: The Uneasy Alliance of Group Representation and Deliberative Democracy. In W. Kymlicka and W. Norman (eds), *Citizenship in Diverse Societies*. Oxford: Oxford University Press, 124–52.

Wingrove, E. 1998: Educating for Citizenship: Reflections on Pedagogy as Conservation and Critique. In K. Slawner and M. E. Denham (eds), *Citizenship after Liberalism*. New York: Peter Lang, 127–46.

Wolfe, A. 1991: *Whose Keeper? Social Science and Moral Obligation*. Berkeley: University of California Press.

Wolfe, A., and Y. Klausen 1992: Identity Politics and the Welfare State. *Social Philosophy and Policy*, 14, 231–55.

——2000: Other People. *Prospect*, December, 28–33.

Wolff, J. 1998: John Rawls: Liberal Democracy Restated. In A. Carter and G. Stokes (eds), *Liberal Democracy and its Critics: Perspectives in Contemporary Political Thought*. Cambridge: Polity, 118–34.

Wolin, S. 1993: Democracy, Difference, and Re-cognition. *Political Theory*, 21, 464–83.

Worpole, K. 2001: Other People, 2. *Prospect*, January, 4.

Wright, E. O. 1985: *Classes*. London: Verso.

Young, I. M. 1986: Difference and Policy: Some Reflections in the Context of New Social Movements. *Cincinnati Law Review*, 56, 535–50.

——1989: Polity and Group Difference: A Critique of the Ideal of Universal Citizenship. *Ethics*, 99, 250–74.

——1990: *Justice and the Politics of Difference*. Princeton, NJ: Princeton University Press.

——2000: *Inclusion and Democracy*. Cambridge: Cambridge University Press.

——2001: Equality of Whom? Social Groups and Judgements of Injustice. *Journal of Political Philosophy*, 9 (1), 1–18.

Young, N. 1977: *An Infantile Disorder? The Crisis and Decline of the New Left*. London: Routledge & Kegan Paul.

Young, T. 2002: 'A Project to be Realized': Global Liberalism and a New World Order. In E. Hovden and E. Keene (eds), *The Globalization of Liberalism*. Basingstoke: Palgrave, 173–9.

Index

Almond, Gabriel 79
American Civil Liberties Union 35, 178
American exceptionalism 2, 11–20, 179
American Revolution 1
Anglo-American political philosophy vii, xi, xii, 29, 31, 44, 47, 59, 65, 66, 77, 100, 129, 140, 148, 160, 166, 176, 182 n.11
Anglophone political theory vii, xi, xiii, 2, 10, 29, 31, 44, 61, 89, 100, 103, 116, 117, 121, 126, 129, 169, 171, 176, 181 n.6
anti-colonial struggles 154
anti-globalization 162
anti-politics xi, 11, 68
anti-racist movement 13, 111, 124
anti-war movements 15, 18, 113
Appiah, Kwame Anthony 41, 108, 184 n.2
Arato, Andrew 71, 114
Arendt, Hannah 112, 123
Aristotle 45, 97
ascriptive group membership 34, 99, 102, 155, 157, 173, 174, 178
ascriptive identity 4, 24, 27, 29, 30, 35, 36–8, 39, 40, 41, 51, 74, 84, 89, 99

Australia xi, 3
authenticity xiii, 19, 38, 152, 153, 155, 157, 158–60, 166, 170, 171
autonomy ix, 23, 24, 25, 26, 29, 30, 31, 42, 52, 53, 60, 78, 80, 91, 95, 96, 108, 115, 141, 159, 173, 175, 181 n.4

Bader, Veit 185 nn.2, 9
Barry, Brian 31–2, 48, 182 n.11, 183 nn.3, 4, 185 n.2
Baumeister, Andrea 185 n.2
Bell, Daniel 95, 100
Bellamy, Richard 184 n.3
Benhabib, Seyla 25, 162, 167, 184 n.1, 185 n.2
Benjamin, Jessica 151
Bennett, W. L. 68–9
Berlin, Isaiah 6, 23, 97, 112
Berman, Paul 19
Bevir, Mark 182 n.7
Bickford, Susan 184 n.4
Black Panthers 18
Black Power 124
Blake, William 185 n.1
Bohman, James 51
Brown, Wendy 104–7
Bunting, Madelaine 181 n.1
Butler, Judith 141
Byrne, Paul 123

Canada xi, 3, 26, 149
  Canadian Charter of Rights 155
  Francophone culture 155
Caney, Simon 183 nn.3, 4
capitalism 68, 72, 93, 105, 107, 124, 125, 161
Christian Right 142
citizenship ix, xiii, 9, 10, 14, 22, 24, 43–63, 65, 66, 67, 68, 70, 76, 81, 82, 83, 86, 87, 88, 91, 125, 132, 133, 134, 146, 166, 181 n.6
  citizenship education 65
  democratic citizenship vii, xiii, 9, 24, 43, 47, 58, 60, 64, 65, 70, 77, 79, 80, 86, 87, 95, 137, 160, 165, 167, 173, 174, 178, 179
  egalitarian citizenship 9, 39, 72, 77, 100
  liberal citizenship 10, 46, 47, 50, 128, 130, 131, 141
  national citizenship 114
  social citizenship 60
civic culture xi, xiii, 63, 64, 67, 68, 69
civic decline xi, 44–5, 45, 46, 47, 67–80
civic education 64–5
civic virtue 44–7, 63, 64, 65, 67, 79, 81–2, 88, 95
civility x, 84–6, 165
civil rights 113, 124, 125, 163, 174
civil society vii, ix, xi, xii, 4, 8, 12, 14, 23, 30, 44, 45, 46, 61, 63–88, 99, 111, 114, 117, 119, 126, 127, 159, 172, 176, 177, 179, 183 n.2
  democratic civil society 7, 8, 85, 87
  in Britain 13, 14, 15, 72
  in United States 11, 12, 67, 68, 69
class 4, 11, 14, 20, 35, 73, 81, 92, 98, 118, 121, 125, 129, 131, 140, 161, 162, 164, 167, 174
Cohen, Jean 71, 114, 122, 184 n.1

Cohen, Joshua 96
Cole, G. D. H. 15
communism 4
communitarianism 24, 28, 29, 31, 44, 65–6, 72, 73, 92, 93, 100–1, 102, 104, 107, 129, 136, 142, 151, 182 n.11, 183 n.3
Connolly, William 128, 140–6, 185 n.4
conservatism 5, 6, 7, 17, 23, 34, 64, 74, 98, 113
constructivism 102, 104
contractarianism 92
Cooke, Maeve 159
cosmopolitanism 114, 115
  cosmopolitan liberals 59
counter-culture 15, 18, 19, 103, 113, 117
Crittenden, John 31
cultural rights 26, 120
cultural theory 27, 140, 146
culture 8, 12, 13, 14, 16, 17, 18, 19, 21, 23, 24, 25, 26, 27–8, 31–6, 38, 39, 56, 63, 89, 94, 98, 102, 103, 106, 107, 112, 136, 138, 141, 149, 154–8, 161, 162, 183 n.4
  cultural politics 6, 9, 106, 128
  'culture wars' 16–17, 43, 84
  diversity xii, xiii, 20, 23, 25, 26, 51, 56, 61, 94, 97, 103, 109, 128–9, 154, 160, 161, 175
  mass culture 116
  non-liberal culture 18, 28, 100, 165
  United States 17, 19

Dahl, Robert 91
Della Porta, Donna 184 n.2
democracy xi, xiii, 1, 24, 35, 42, 48, 58, 67, 71, 74, 76, 78, 87, 90–1, 96, 98, 112, 114, 119, 121–4, 129, 133–4, 139, 145, 149, 151, 153, 155, 159, 162, 163, 164, 166, 167, 170, 171, 172, 175, 177

democracy (cont'd)
　associational democracy 8, 12,
　　46, 62, 63, 82, 86, 99
　constitutional democracy 77
　deliberative democracy 47, 48,
　　49, 51, 56, 116, 123–33, 137,
　　150, 167, 173
　democratic renewal 45, 63
　liberal democracy vii, ix, 2, 6,
　　23, 25–6, 40, 41, 43, 45, 49,
　　61, 64, 69, 70, 76, 77, 79, 84,
　　87, 90, 94, 95, 97, 116, 120,
　　132, 134, 143, 144, 145, 146,
　　165, 169, 170, 173, 175, 176,
　　177, 178
　multicultural democracy 26
　pluralist democracy 47, 55, 71,
　　150, 165
　radical democracy 61, 97, 111,
　　122, 124, 133, 145
　representative democracy 145,
　　146
　social democracy 2, 15, 16, 18,
　　20, 45, 71, 134, 160, 174

democratization 144, 163–4, 184
　n.5
de Tocqueville, Alexis 12, 76, 77,
　95–7, 98, 100, 176
Dewey, John 184 n.8
Diani, Mario 110, 182 n.9, 184
　n.2
difference vii, viii, ix, xiii, 1, 3, 8,
　9, 19, 20, 24, 25, 28, 29, 31,
　32, 33, 52, 57, 60, 61, 77, 85,
　97, 102, 106, 112, 114, 116,
　120, 128–47, 148, 153, 155,
　156, 159, 161, 169, 170, 184
　n.3
Donati, Robert 184 n.4
Dryzek, John 96–7
Dworkin, Ronald 129, 141, 185
　n.5

Echols, A. 182 n.14
ecology 14
education 10, 26, 76, 78, 85, 86,
　89, 133

associations as classrooms for
　civic virtue 66, 83, 91, 95, 96,
　99
civic education 64–5
moral learning 87, 89, 90
multicultural education 80, 153,
　166
and religion 10, 11, 16, 17
schools 10, 11, 16, 17
students 15, 18, 107
universities 10, 18, 106
egalitarianism: see equality
Elshtain, Jean 74
emancipation xi, 4, 19, 20, 71, 72,
　107, 114, 119, 118, 122, 130,
　155, 172
Emcke, Carolin 104, 182 n.5
emotion 43, 112
Enlightenment x, 20, 22, 23, 139,
　142, 181 n.4
　counter-Enlightenment 23
environmentalism 59, 111, 117,
　120, 122
　sustainability 120
Epstein, Barbara 106
equality viii, xiii, 4, 5, 10, 12, 20,
　24, 27, 31–6, 38, 40, 47, 72,
　78, 84, 97, 103, 105, 108,
　130, 144, 146, 148, 149, 152,
　153, 158, 159, 161, 162, 163,
　164, 165, 167, 174, 175, 179,
　183 n.2, 185 n.5
　egalitarian citizenship 9, 39, 72,
　　77, 100
　feminism 33, 162
　liberal egalitarianism xiii, 16,
　　31–4, 36, 39, 41, 161, 182
　　n.11
ethnicity xii, 1, 2, 3, 5, 7, 9, 10,
　12, 13, 14, 27, 28, 34, 36, 37,
　41, 42, 46, 59, 63, 67, 90, 91,
　94, 97, 99, 101, 107, 114,
　124, 129, 134, 152, 167, 170,
　179
Europe viii, ix, 3, 12–13, 16, 17,
　25, 60, 95, 110, 111, 116,
　117, 118, 120, 143, 179
exceptionalism 2, 11–20, 179

faith schools 11, 78
family 36, 39, 61, 64, 66, 72, 90, 92, 93, 136, 140, 170
Fanon, Frantz 154–5
Farred, Grant 124–5, 181 n.2
fascism 4
federalism 155
feminism: see women's liberation
Foucault, Michel 140
Fraser, Nancy 123, 149, 150, 160–3, 164, 165, 167, 168
Freeden, Michael 181 n.2
French Revolution 1

Galeotti, Elizabeth 34, 165–6, 167, 182 n.5
Galston, William 46, 54, 64, 79, 82
Gamble, Andrew 113
Gaus, Gerald 181 n.2, 185 n.4
gender x, 1, 4, 9, 23, 33, 34, 41, 46, 52, 63, 73, 90, 101, 113, 129, 131, 179
  maternity and paternity rights 6, 33
  and race 171
Geuss, Raymond xiii
Gianni, M. 102, 141
Gitlin, Todd 18, 112–13
Glendon, Mary Ann 183 n.2
globalization 68, 117, 179
  anti-globalization 162
Gramsci, Antonio 70
Gray, John 127
Green, Thomas Hill 82
groups vii, x, xii, 7, 8, 9, 22–3, 24, 25, 27, 42, 46, 47, 48, 58, 69, 75, 78, 102, 103, 107, 114, 121, 129–39, 148, 155, 157–8, 161, 162, 163, 167, 177, 179, 183 n.1
  anti-democratic 6, 7, 20, 42, 46, 48, 87, 92, 176
  cultivation of democratic dispositions 83, 95, 96
  group pluralism 2, 4, 23, 49, 108, 111, 133, 139

group rights xii, 9, 39, 113, 120, 179
  non-liberal 5, 6, 28, 77–80, 91, 94, 95, 97, 177
  representation 137, 184 n.2
Gutmann, Amy 181 nn.5, 6, 182 n.4, 183 nn.1, 2, 5, 185 n.8

Habermas, Jürgen 71, 114, 115, 122, 124, 185 n.6
Hall, Stuart 20, 71
Hannigan, John 184 n.3
Hegel, Georg Wilhelm Friedrich 60–1, 72, 90, 159
Heidegger, Martin 102
Herder, Johann Gottfried 23, 25
hermeneutics 30, 110, 111, 112, 113
heterosexism 158
Hitchens, Christopher 73
Hobbes, Thomas 73
Hobsbawm, Eric 12
homosexuality xi, xiii, 3, 4, 8, 10, 11, 13, 14, 15, 18, 19, 23, 26, 27, 34, 40, 41, 43, 73, 85, 90, 91, 101, 103, 105, 111, 113, 125, 132, 141, 157, 162
  gays in the military 6, 10, 17
  homophobia 34, 39, 125
  and race 171
  Stonewall 19, 124
Honig, Bonnie 185 n.4
Honneth, Axel 150, 159
Hoover, Jeffrey 130
Horton, John 38
human rights 9
Hume, David 84
Hunter, James 16–17
Hutton, Will 16

ideology vii, x, xi, 1, 3, 4, 5, 7, 11, 18, 41, 54, 57, 61, 70, 75, 81, 84, 97, 116, 117, 120, 125, 138, 142, 157, 161, 179, 181 n.3
immigration xi, 3, 5, 12, 28, 29, 101, 142, 143, 144
  anti-immigrant populism 143

immigration (cont'd)
  Britain 13, 143, 163
  Europe 143
  United States 17
incommensurability of values vii,
  55, 62, 97, 145, 153, 174
incongruity 77, 81
indigenous peoples xi, 1, 151,
  155
inequality: see equality
Inglehart, Ronald 69
Islam in Britain 14, 72, 80, 140
Israel 96

Jasper, James 182 n.9
justice viii, 4, 9, 12, 20, 47, 52, 54,
  103, 139, 144, 146, 149, 153,
  154, 160, 161, 162, 163, 165,
  167, 173, 174, 177, 178

Kahane, David 47
Kantianism xiii, 29, 46, 47, 79, 80,
  84, 97, 112, 115, 170, 176
  Kantian liberals 97, 153, 169,
  170
Kateb, George 97
Katznelson, Ira 181 n.1, 185 n.3
Keane, John 119, 184 n.1
Kiss, Elizabeth 181 n.1, 185 n.9
Klausen, Ytte 16, 17, 60
Kloppenberg, James 181 n.1
Kohler, Thomas 76
Kukathas, Chandran 93, 94
Ku Klux Klan 35, 178
Kymlicka, Will 26–9, 97

labour movement 13, 15, 21, 172
Labour Party 15–16
Laden, Anthony 51, 53, 183 n.2,
  185 n.7
Lasch, Christopher 75
Laski, Harold 15
Levine, Andrew 183 n.2
Levinson, Meira 30
liberal democracy vii, ix, x, 2, 6,
  23, 25–6, 40, 41, 43, 45, 49,
  61, 64, 69, 70, 76, 77, 79, 84,
  87, 90, 94, 95, 97, 111, 114,
  132, 138, 142, 147, 165, 169,
  170, 173, 175, 176, 177, 178
liberal nationalism 58–9
liberal pluralism 59, 95, 140, 143,
  155
liberal republicanism xiii, 44, 48,
  77, 95, 97, 177
libertarianism 5, 15, 65, 111, 136
liberty viii, 30, 44, 72, 105, 108,
  129, 152, 160, 178
Lichterman, Paul 125–6, 167
Lott, Eric 182 n.14
Lukes, Steven 39

McDonald, Kevin 184 n.3
Macedo, Stephen 45, 96, 183 n.2,
  184 n.1
MacIntyre, Alisdair 182 n.7
McKinnon, Catriona 56, 183 n.2
Madison, James 96
Mansbridge, Jane 123
Margalit, Avishai 38–9
market 45, 66, 67, 71, 75, 81,
  111, 124
Marshall, Alfred 60
Marx, Karl 72, 155
Marxism 15, 161
Mason, Andrew 183 n.1
Melucci, Alberto 110–11, 113,
  117–21, 184 nn.4, 6
Mendus, Susan 169, 170, 185
  nn.1, 3
Mier, Paul 184 n.1
Mill, John Stuart 40, 82, 127
Miller, David 9, 35, 39, 181 n.6,
  183 n.3
Mills, Charles Wright 15
modernity 5, 21, 23, 27, 81, 82,
  92, 103, 105, 107, 112, 113,
  115, 116, 118, 121, 129, 144,
  151, 152, 156, 158, 170, 182
  n.8
Montesquieu, Charles-Louis de
  Secondat 84
Moon, Donald 183 n.2
moral pluralism 2, 93, 114
multiculturalism viii, ix, x, 6, 8,
  11, 13, 15, 16, 23, 24, 25,

26–9, 30, 32, 33–4, 42, 44, 48, 49, 55, 71, 72, 80, 100, 102, 108, 114, 123, 131, 140, 141, 146, 150, 151, 153, 154, 156, 162, 166, 167, 169, 170, 171, 179, 182 n.11, 183 nn.3, 4, 184 n.1, 185 n.2
liberal multiculturalism 24–6, 154
multicultural states 114

nation xi, 28, 29, 43, 59–60, 81, 92, 118, 148, 155, 167, 170
ethno-national community 27, 28, 42, 155
multinational states 26, 58
nationality 1, 37, 58, 155, 158, 179
nationhood 26, 58, 59, 81, 154
nation-state 12, 44, 59, 90, 93, 115
National Association for the Advancement of Colored People (NAACP) 36
nationalism 4, 25, 44, 59–60, 73, 81, 114, 127, 130, 154, 166, 172, 182 n.6
neo-Conservatism 74, 75, 142
networks vii, xiii, 5, 13, 71, 81, 111, 115, 118, 119, 136, 183 n.4
neutrality 148, 149
New Left 2, 14, 15, 18–20, 70, 74, 75, 154, 155, 179, 181 n.2, 182 n.11, 185 n.2
American New Left 2, 14, 18–20, 182 n.11
British New Left 2, 14, 15, 154
and difference 19
new model pluralism 8–10
New Zealand xi
Nicholson, Linda 155–6
Nietzsche, Friedrich 104, 140, 144
non-liberal groups 80
non-liberal practices 29, 160
arranged marriage 14, 16, 32
female circumcision 14
homophobia 34, 39

minority cultural practices 14, 87
and the New Left 18
polygamy 32
racism 13, 34, 39, 178
Northern Ireland 153
Nussbaum, Martha 37, 40, 79, 84

Offe, Claus 182 n.8
Okin, Susan Moller 8
Oliver, J. Eric 69
Oxford University 154

Parekh, Bikhu 16
patriarchalism 158
peace movement 13, 111, 117, 118, 184 n.4
Phillips, Anne 183 n.2, 184 n.2
pluralism vii, viii, ix, x, xiii, 4, 6, 7, 8, 9, 24, 31, 32, 37, 45, 48–50, 51–8, 62, 63, 65, 70, 71, 73, 74, 77, 81, 89, 91, 95, 98–9, 103, 105, 117, 123, 126, 129, 130, 131, 133, 143, 145, 146, 156, 164, 165, 167, 171, 173, 175, 178, 184 n.2
group pluralism 2, 4, 23, 49, 108, 111, 133, 139
liberal pluralism 59, 95, 140, 143, 155
new model pluralism 10
pluralist democracy 7, 47, 55, 71, 150, 165
socialist pluralism 15
social pluralism vii, 20, 30, 128, 140, 144, 170
political correctness 73, 105, 106
post-materialism 69
postmodernism 141, 144
post-structuralism 128, 140, 141, 142
power 72, 104, 105, 107, 118, 121, 131, 134, 139, 141, 149, 158, 161, 176
psychoanalysis 141
psychology 31, 52, 83, 121, 150, 151, 155, 160, 161, 173, 181 n.7

Putnam, Robert 67–70, 100, 177, 183 n.4

Queer Nation 171
Quong, Jonathan 49, 183 n.1

race x, 1, 14, 23, 35, 41, 69, 73, 101, 131, 167, 183 n.3
African-American 27, 35, 39, 41, 69, 101, 103, 139, 163, 178, 184 n.2
Bangladeshi 163
black 4, 19, 40, 85, 101, 103, 132, 141
and class 14, 20
and gender 171
Hispanic 157, 163
in Britain 12, 13, 101, 163, 178
in United States 12, 69, 163
Latino 4
native American 132
racism 13, 34, 39, 125
and sexuality 171
white 14, 20
racism 13, 34, 39, 178
radical democracy 61, 97, 111, 122, 124, 133, 145
rainbow coalition 15, 19, 105
Rawls, John ix, xiii, 47, 48, 49–58, 79, 83–5, 86, 87, 129, 165, 174–5, 183 nn.2, 4
Raz, Joseph 82
recognition x, xiii, 8, 9, 148–68, 155–60
redistribution 162, 163
religion 1, 2, 3, 4, 5, 7, 9, 12, 17, 26, 37–8, 43, 46, 49, 51, 53, 56, 67, 73, 79, 94, 101, 105, 107, 118, 142, 146, 158, 170, 179, 183 nn.4, 5
and abortion 6
activists 8
Amish 3, 4, 94
Christianity xiii
fundamentalism 17
Islam xiii, 14, 29, 39, 49, 80
and moral liberalization 17
and the state 3, 12, 182 n.10

representation 132, 134, 137, 139, 140, 142, 145, 146, 184 n.2
republicanism 34, 44, 77, 81, 82, 87, 123, 129, 130, 132, 133, 137
liberal republicanism xiii, 44, 77, 95, 97, 177
Residential Community Associations (RCAs) 100
ressentiment 104–7, 125, 167, 184 n.4
rights vii, xi, 36, 42, 44, 51, 60, 61, 84, 86, 113, 129, 130, 132, 152, 153, 159, 162, 165, 172, 173
civil rights 174
cultural rights 26, 93, 120, 173
gay rights 113
group rights xii, 9, 39, 113, 120, 149, 173, 179
human rights 16, 78, 181 n.6
land rights 3
minority rights 50
representative rights 140
Rogers, Joel 96
romanticism 2, 23, 24, 38, 158
Rorty, Richard 18–19, 20, 32, 41, 142, 160–1
Rosenblum, Nancy 8, 45, 76, 77–9, 80, 81, 84, 87, 98, 99, 181 n.7
Rousseau, Jean-Jacques 47
Runciman, W. G. 184 n.9
Rushdie, Salman 11, 29, 49, 165

Schmitt, Carl 142
self vii, x, 11, 17, 18, 20, 24–31, 34–6, 39–40, 52, 68, 79, 82–4, 85, 87, 90, 95, 98, 99, 104, 118, 120, 128, 129, 130, 132, 133, 138, 140–3, 149, 150, 151, 152, 156, 157, 159, 160, 164, 166, 167, 170, 171, 172, 173, 175, 177, 178, 183 n.4
self-development 31, 26, 40, 116, 135
Sen, Amartya 39

September 11, 2001 viii, 29, 170, 181 n.1
Shklar, Judith 112
Simhony, Avitai 183 n.5
Smith, Adam 44, 66, 72, 84, 90, 98, 127
Smith, Nicholas 185 n.1
social capital 45, 58, 62, 67, 100, 126, 145, 183 n.4
social individuation 5, 9–10, 14, 120–1
socialism 4, 15, 18, 20, 44, 70, 81, 99, 117, 130, 134, 160, 164, 174
  Marxism 15, 161
  social democratic thought 2, 15–16, 18, 20, 45, 71, 134, 160, 173, 174
  socialist feminism 8
  socialist pluralism 15
social liberalism 160, 173, 183 n.5
social movements xii, 5, 13, 15, 21, 26, 60, 70, 71, 72, 85, 97, 109–27, 140, 172, 182 n.9, 184 n.1, 185 n.6
  British social movements 13, 14, 15, 72, 73, 89, 108
social theory 109, 114, 116, 126, 140, 146
sociology 27, 28, 68, 111, 114, 170, 182 n.9
Southall Black Sisters 171
Spinner-Halev, Jeff 184 n.1
Spragens, Thomas 138
state 3, 8, 9, 12, 25, 26, 35, 36, 39, 40, 45, 50, 52, 54, 56, 58, 60, 61, 66, 75, 76–80, 81, 82, 85, 92, 94, 95, 96, 97, 107, 111, 112, 121, 122, 124, 126, 134, 142, 143, 148, 153, 173, 178
Stonewall 19, 124
structuralism 131, 136, 161
student movements 15, 18, 124
suffragette campaign 21, 127

Tamir, Yael 96, 182 n.5
Tarrow, Sidney 184 n.2

Tawney, Richard Henry 60
Taylor, Charles xi, 20, 66, 123, 148, 149, 150–60, 164–8, 185 nn.1, 2
Templeman, Sonja 184 n.1
Thatcherism 15
Third World 154
Thompson, Edward 139
Tilly, Charles 110
Tomasi, John 56
Touraine, Alain 114–17, 120, 121, 184 n.3
trade unions 36–7, 67
  trade union movement in Britain 15
tradition 5, 6, 13, 27, 29, 30, 31, 35, 45, 48, 56, 59, 66, 68, 69, 74, 76, 79, 85, 93, 97, 104, 115, 136, 141, 142, 169, 171, 172, 176, 179, 182 n.7
tragedy of the commons 45
Tully, James 149, 150, 163–4, 165, 183 n.4

United States viii, ix, xi, 1, 7, 8, 10, 29, 35, 64, 65, 67, 68, 69, 72, 74, 75, 76, 96, 97, 110, 112, 127, 140, 170, 173, 179, 185 n.4
utilitarianism 95

Verba, Sidney 79
Vietnam War 15, 18
voluntary association 23, 26, 36–8, 65, 66, 68, 69, 70, 76, 78, 89, 91–5, 99, 178, 182 n.4
  non-voluntary association 23, 66, 81, 92, 93, 99, 100, 102, 129

Waldron, Jeremy 91, 166
Walzer, Michael 20, 61–2, 72, 81–2, 92–3, 95, 102
Warren, Mark 77–8, 81, 87, 98, 184 n.7
Weathermen 18
Weber, Max 40, 161
Weinstein, David 183 n.5

welfare state 16, 45, 58, 60, 124,
 162, 179
West, Cornel 20
Williams, Melissa 103, 183 n.1
Wolfe, Alan 16, 17, 60, 73
Wolin, Sheldon 8, 9, 10, 75
women's liberation xi, 3, 5, 7, 8,
 13, 14, 15, 18, 19, 23, 26, 29,
 32, 34, 39, 44, 52, 59, 69, 74,
78, 79, 84–5, 91, 99, 106,
 107, 111, 113, 117, 120, 122,
 124, 125, 129, 132, 134, 139,
 140, 141, 162, 163, 174
egalitarian feminism 33
socialist feminism 8

Young, Iris 102, 122, 128, 129–40,
 146, 158, 184 n.1